The Turn of the
MILLENNIUM

The Turn of the
MILLENNIUM

An Agenda for

Christian Religion

in an Age of Science

JEFFREY G. SOBOSAN

The Pilgrim Press
Cleveland, Ohio

The Pilgrim Press, Cleveland, Ohio 44115
© 1996 by Jeffrey G. Sobosan

Biblical quotations are from the New Revised Standard Version of the Bible, © 1989 by the Division of Christian Education of the National Council of the Churches of Christ in the U.S.A., and are used by permission

Printed in the United States of America on acid-free paper
01 00 99 98 97 96   5 4 3 2 1

Library of Congress Cataloging-in-Publication Data

Sobosan, Jeffrey G., 1946–
    The turn of the millennium : an agenda for Christian religion in an age of science / Jeffrey G. Sobosan.
        p. cm
    Includes bibliographical references and index.
    ISBN 0-8298-1083-8 (alk. paper)
      1. Religion and science.   2. Christianity—Forecasting.
    I. Title.
BL240. 2. S65   1996   95-50971
261.5'5—dc20   CIP

A single cry comes down the millennia
telling of our want of love,
the gain of its humor
the favor of its mercy
the splendor of its peace.
Sometimes the cry is heard
and great beauty is born.
This book is for Tom,
my friend of thirty years,
whom I love.

Contents

Foreword

John B. Cobb Jr.

THERE IS A pensive mood among many of us Christians today. An earlier confidence that as Christians we were automatically on the side of truth has long been shattered. On the contrary, we know that the church has taught many things about the world that science, over the years, has shown to be in error. The several ways in which Christians have adjusted to the authority of modern science are all questionable. And now we find ourselves ill-prepared to face a whole new set of changes introduced by a postmodern science. Will they destroy the delicate compromises with which we have lived, forcing us finally to choose between Christ and science? Or will they enable us to find a new synthesis in which our faith is less compromised?

Even more serious, perhaps, is the loss of conviction that we are on the side of righteousness. Wave after wave of justifiable criticism has swept over us. We know now that we, historically and collectively, bear heavy responsibility for the Holocaust, for the decay of the natural environment, for the oppression of women and minorities, for our individual and collective alienation from the body, for our society's callousness toward the suffering of other animals. Somehow Jesus' message of love has been so distorted that in his name Christians have heaped violent abuse on themselves, on one another, and on the rest of the world.

As we have heard the truth about our sins, we have repented, again and again. We have watched, with ready sympathy, as many of our friends have separated themselves from the church. Sometimes they have sought fuller truth and righteousness elsewhere. Sometimes they have thought it more honest to recognize the hopelessness of such a quest and simply to settle down in the world as it is. We wonder at times whether they have chosen the better part.

But, for ourselves, we cannot leave the church. We know that we are Christians and that the church is our home. Does this mean that we are less aware of, or pained by, the errors, the sins, and the absurd pretensions of the church? Are we blind to the wisdom and goodness that are to be found in other communities? Are we lacking in the courage to act that our friends exhibit? Are we naively hoping that repentance will bring the church to a fullness of truth and righteousness it has never had in the past? What is the strange hold that Christ has over us? Does it block us from full participation in the creativity of our time? Or does it provide a compass that can direct that creativity?

Our pensiveness is heightened as we approach the end of the millennium. It is a time for looking back at what has been. Some reviews discern great progress. The millennium, it is thought, began in darkness and ends in light. It began with a world of isolated and superstitious cultures, ignorant of nature, in the context of which they lived. It ends with a world that has been united by science, technology, and economics, and, despite all continuing problems, now ruled by reason. It began with miserable poverty for almost all. It ends with affluence for many and confidence that prosperity can be extended to all.

Those who hold that view of the millennium are not likely to be pensive. Our pensiveness begins with the recognition that there is some truth in this celebration of progress, but that the price we are paying for the new world order is vast. Having repented as Christians the errors, the sins, and the pretensions of our churches, we cannot simply celebrate the Enlightenment and its legacy in the global market. It, too, is replete with errors and sins, and its pretensions are preposterous. Today these are far more dangerous to humanity as a whole than are the errors, sins, and pretensions of the church.

The end of the millennium is a time to look forward as well as backward. What are our planetary prospects? Will the global market-driven society bring us unity, peace, and prosperity? Are the values to which we cling as Christians no longer needed? Are they even obstacles to the realization of the new world order to which economic forces lead? Or is the new, globalized economy rushing us over a precipice to inevitable self-destruction? Are our traditional Christian concerns for communities and our new Christian concerns for the other creatures with whom we share the planet critically needed in order to halt, or at least to slow, this rush to catastrophe?

Even if we decide that there is a role for us to play as Christians, and even if we decide that our failure to play that role will seal the doom of our civilizations, we remain pensive. Can the church in its present confusion affirm its central teachings convincingly? Can it act upon them in such a way as to make a difference in history? Or should we reconcile ourselves to the inevitability of global catastrophe? Is our only realistic task to find a way to live here and now regardless of the larger course of history? Should we find our mission in ministering to the victims?

There are many thoughtful Christians who muse about such matters. But few have shared their reflections so openly, so richly, or so beautifully as Jeffrey Sobosan. Like most thoughtful Christians, he thinks out of a much wider history than simply the past reflections of the church. If "theology" is defined as advancing an inner-ecclesiastical conversation that is little influenced by what is occurring elsewhere, then this book is not theology. But if "theology" is understood as Christian reflection about matters of great importance, drawing on wisdom and knowledge wherever they are to be found, then this book is important theology. The topics with which Sobosan deals are ones that concern Christians generally rather than the problems defined as central by professional "theologians."

To his musings on these topics Sobosan brings intelligence of the highest order, sensitivities that are so deeply Christian that they bring the whole Christian community under judgment, and a wide range of information and knowledge. The result is wisdom. Jeffrey Sobosan is a wise man.

One area of his knowledge is especially impressive. That is in the physical sciences. For several hundred years the worldview of thoughtful people, Christians and others, has been shaped most of all by physics and the cosmology it has offered us. We all know that physics has changed in our century, but we are confused about the implication of these changes for our basic understanding of the world. The interpretations we receive from physicists and philosophers in this regard are varied in the extreme. Few of us have sufficient knowledge of the sciences to evaluate these judgments on our own. Theologians generally do their work as if little were changed or as if change with regard to cosmology is unimportant for Christian belief. Sobosan, on the other hand, has educated himself in such a way as to be able to speak with some authority. Among the many contributions of this book, one of the most important is the guidance he gives us as to the meaning of the new science for our understanding of ourselves and our world.

He is a Christian, but, for him, to be a Christian is not to exclude anything human. He reflects on Christianity in a global context. There is nothing parochial or biased about his vision. Christians seeking a defense of Christianity, or an apologetic appeal to others to join the movement, will not find it here. The Christian task is to understand the truth and embody righteousness—not to show what is wrong with others or that only Christians can be saved. Perhaps because Sobosan's reflections are so nondefensive, so open to learning from others, so little concerned to argue for one tradition, they will turn out to be the sort of Christian evangelism that can be effective among truly thoughtful people in the future.

The reader who plans to skim this text to get the gist of the argument will be disappointed. The style is meditative and the writing is beautiful. Readers who allow themselves to be drawn into the meditation will be richly rewarded. They will be enriched not only by thinking Sobosan's thoughts with him, but also by being stimulated in their own meditations. Christian readers may be helped to see that as they muse on these matters of such great importance to them and to all of us, they are helping to shape the community of authentic Christian faith. If the Christianity of the next millennium emerges from such musings, we can have real hope for the future.

I am myself deeply grateful to Sobosan for sharing himself so fully, so openly, and so honestly. Few Christians have more to share. Often those who feel and think as he does believe themselves to be isolated. They do not realize that there are millions of others who feel and think much as they do. Sometimes they leave the church altogether because of their discomfort with what it seems to expect of them.

Too often such Christians identify Christianity with what others affirm, those who are less pensive, less critically reflective, less penitent, more willing to accept ideas on authority. One grave danger today is that our great heritage will be captured by those who substitute set doctrines and fixed moral rules for faithful meditation and sensitive action. Few things could be more important than that we reclaim our Christian heritage for what is most liberating and healing within it. The world does not need parochial dogma. It desperately needs liberation and healing.

Jeffrey Sobosan in sharing himself in this book is doing what can be done to bring liberation and healing. May it find its readers and bless them!

Preface

To CELEBRATE EVENTS is a distinctly human interest, unshared, as far as we know, by other life-forms. We set aside time for celebrations, and toward many of them feel not just an inclination but an obligation: that neglecting them somehow diminishes what we ought to value and cherish in remembrance or anticipation. And while many celebrations are times of festivity, a joyfulness in community with others, or only with our own memories and hopes, this joy is not essential to the notion of celebration as such. For to celebrate means simply to draw something to attention in undistracted and intense ways, to give ourselves over to it as if, for the length of the celebration, it is what truly matters to us—a full-heartedness that honors the importance of what is being celebrated, and so, primarily, something that goes on in the mind. This is why the half-hearted celebrant among us always seems a bit sad or negligent or discourteous, either not sharing or knowing or caring about this importance. In this book I am proposing that the turn of the millennium is a time of such celebration for Christian religion, instigated by the birth of its founder 2,000 years ago and the history he inaugurated. But like all other celebrations, too, the importance of its cause frequently leads us to attendance on other matters as well. The importance of some of these matters is obvious—the past has settled it—but of others it is more oblique, needing to be coaxed from this history as it is now occurring.

For purposes of clarifying the ambience of the book, there are a series of points I would like to make in this preface before the reader begins the text proper. There are eight of these:

1. As the title and first part of the subtitle indicate, the book is proposing an agenda for Christian religion at the end of its second and the beginning of its third millennium. As the composer of the agenda this

means that I have isolated certain topics I have judged worthy of attention at this juncture in Christian history. These assessments, however, are not only mine but can also be found percolating throughout much that has been written by other theologians, particularly in this and the preceding generation. I have congregated these under five headings, with a chapter devoted to each: the universe, the earth, plants and animals, humanity, and God. Needless to say, in working out my reflections in each of these areas I had to make exclusionary decisions and ones of emphasis due to limits of space as well as personal interest and competence. More specifically, then, chapter 1 will be concerned with the issues of the beginning of the universe, the end of the universe, and life elsewhere in the universe. In the traditional description, its context will be *cosmology* and three of the interests that have dominated it. Chapter 2 will center its reflections on the three major components constituting the earth as a habitat suitable to its particular life-forms: the land, the water, and the air. Chapter 3 will then supplement this discussion by concentrating on the nonhuman life-forms, issuing in a sentiment that I will describe as the communion of all life. The concern of both these chapters together will therefore be what we commonly describe as *ecology*. The fourth chapter will be the one most directly involved with us, with humanity. In pruning this down to manageable size, and given the interests particularly of chapters 2 and 3, I decided to do this with an emphasis on ethics. I then chose to allow a thorough influence to operate, drawn from my understanding of the way of life Jesus taught, and isolated three components of this teaching above all: the doctrines on childlikeness; the traits of the messianic servant (obedience, mercy, generosity, poverty, and humility); and most importantly of all, the great doctrine on love. Chapter 4 will thus revolve around considerations of *anthropology*. Chapter 5 will contend with the issue of God. How may I go about describing this, my special love in the book? In the first section I take up claims regarding God's power and justice, as well as a series of conceptual tools that Christians might utilize when attending to the privileged fount of their knowledge of God, the scriptures. In a second section I address this issue of knowledge of God specifically within the context of the concept of revelation. And in a third section I allow much freedom to what imaginative and speculative talents I have in meditating on metaphors and a metaphysics of God. This chapter will consolidate many ideas circulating throughout the previous four, and represents the central task of *theology*.

2. The fact that the book wishes to provide an *agenda* for Christian religion has two major repercussions. First, it is in the nature of an agenda to provide only brief statements for purposes of reflection and/or action. This will be honored in the sixth and final chapter, where the agenda itself is presented. I have put it there rather than at the beginning of the book so that the previous five chapters can provide an initial background or context for appraisal of the issues there listed. The second and related repercussion is that since an agenda either includes or presumes topics for reflection that are intended to affect behavior, and since the first five chapters are devoted precisely to this purpose, the book also functions as an ancient practice in Christian religion—as an examination of conscience.

3. The terms *religion* and *Christian religion* are used throughout the book to indicate, respectively, the general phenomenon of which Christianity is a specific, sometimes singular expression. Thus, if in the course of the reflections I take up something I judge unique to Christian interest (or to that of any other religion or viewpoint on the topic being discussed), I will note it. Otherwise what I say of Christian religion will report observations or suggestions I would offer for every religion. As a result, the text is influenced by radically diverse traditions while seeking an *oikumene* of the mind, a union of common concerns.

4. I will be presuming throughout these pages that the heart of any religion is its understanding of God. While chapter 5 deals specifically with the topic of God and my own particular understanding of deity, this understanding nonetheless permeates the whole book so that reading only chapter 5 would give an abbreviated rendition of it. Two brief additional points also need to be made. The first is that since my concern in the book is with Christian religion, the impetus for my understanding of God will derive from my appropriation of the teachings of Jesus. The second is that this appropriation has led me to conclude that in the final analysis our purpose as Christians is not to serve Christianity but the universe (chap. 1), the earth (chap. 2), its living forms (chaps. 3 and 4)—*all* of creation—and God (chap. 5). This, I think, is something with which Jesus would agree.

5. I will be approaching the distinction between religion and theology in the following ways. Religion I will designate the system of belief, be-

havior, and worship centered on an affirmation of God that characterizes the cohesiveness or communal character among the members of a group. Theology I will designate the continuing reflection on this system that enriches the meaning of its parts and proposes mandates or suggestions for their application. Religion is where theology is lived; theology is where religion is thought.

6. "Millennarianism" tends to be a pejorative term in Christian theology, harking back to the eleventh to fourteenth centuries, when massive social disorientations and biological plagues decimated the lives of many and produced hysterical and extreme images of God's punishing wrath visited on a sinful humanity, along with an obsessive interest in talismanic and incantatory magic. I will have no part of this millennarian sentiment in what follows, at least regarding the image of God it produced and its superstitious practices. But with its assessment of human sin I will be in large accord.

7. Socrates once noted that no forced learning abides in the soul. What he was getting at is the truth that enduring knowledge is the result of a chosen wedding of the deeds and thoughts of other lives with the deeds and thoughts of one's own. What he doesn't note, however, is that before any two partners wed, and ever afterward, there are times of approval and disapproval, agreement and disagreement, until a final certainty is reached that no matter how enduring the knowledge of each other, like the knowledge of all living things, it is always tentative, and in the folds of the future might need to change. There will be agreements and disagreements with this book as the reader comes to know it, and perhaps too many disagreements to permit a partnership. If conveyed—adding new knowledge to my own—these might even be sufficient for me to seek a friendly separation from the book, or at least parts of it. This is always the risk in putting forth ideas; in this risk lies their ultimate tentativeness.

Finally, let me close this preface by noting that the issue of orthodoxy tends to assume great importance in the various Christian churches, and that it is commonly defined as agreement with whatever the current magisterial or official teaching on an issue might be. There is certainly nothing wrong with the members of a particular church wishing to secure a consensus on their creed—so long as they avoid in the process the trap of intellectual tyranny. But this also represents a truncated understanding of orthodoxy, whose full significance derives from a two-parted definition. In the first part the word has its root in the Greek *dokein* and means to possess a positive or right (*ortho-*) reputation because it is deserved, to enjoy the well-earned affirmative opinion of others. Under this meaning it also includes the idea of an informed and competent intellectual opinion on an issue, and thirdly, the official opinion of the leadership or whole population of a given community or organization (and here shows itself as dogma, or orthodoxy's usual connotation). But the second part of the definition emerges from a further meaning of *dokein,* this time as the "glory" exhibited in someone's admirable or praiseworthy behavior. When joined together, then, the two parts exhibit the intent of what I have wanted to accomplish in this book from its beginning, namely, to propose an orthodoxy that gives right judgment to the ways God's glory is manifested to us, and on this account to give right glory to God.

Chapter one

THE UNIVERSE

ANTHROPOLOGISTS TELL US that there are some symbols whose meanings are immediate, like one smile indicating joy, another resignation, or the wave goodbye and the shaking fist of anger. We are told that we are inevitable symbol-makers, that this is a privileged way whereby we establish communion with each other, and that a failure of effective symbols threatens this union, as when a smile of joy is taken as a threat or one of resignation as indifference. Yet the most encompassing symbol available to us is not one that we generate in gestures or art forms; it is not a dance or a flag or a cross, but rather the ambience in which all these become possible. It is that singular vastness of all that is, the universe itself, whose source and continuing gestalt are to some the result of a peculiar but discernible chanciness, to others of a deliberating God, to still others of a brute and ultimately intransigent unknown. We are linked inextricably to this symbol, not just in metaphors and dreams of hugeness, however, but quite literally too. For the elements that compose us, bestowing the molecules shaping our flesh, were all born in exploding stars lost in time past, swimming through emptiness until gathered by the geometries of gravity on this small place to consort with each other and produce life upon life.

The word *symbol* comes from an old Greek verb, *symbolein*, meaning "to unite or bring together." Its antonym is *diabolein*, meaning "to sunder or tear apart." These origins give us a salient insight into how the symbolic and diabolic function in our experiences and provide an initial suggestion that life is perhaps better understood as a verb than a noun, an activity that at any given point can manifest either communion or discord. They also lend sympathy to Tillich's lament over the easy contemporary dismissal of the importance of these terms. His pleading is eloquent and uncompromising that at the core of any hope for religious, political, or personal wholeness lies fidelity to the symbolic and betrayal of the diabolic in our behavior. Symbols themselves, the nouns that "stabilize" the activity they represent, are secondary to this behavior and can only represent but never create it. A failure to appreciate this distinction inevitably encourages that singular flaw in all religions that insist on the generative power of the symbol itself, mindless of the predisposition of the symbol's adherent, much like a talisman is thought to possess preternatural power triggered solely by proper manipulations or incantations. There is still much of this, for example, in my own religious tradition, a Catholic Christianity that requires more of its primary cultic symbol, the Eucharist, than it can possibly bear—asking that it fashion what it can only depict: communion among believers. Side-by-sideness, mere juxtaposition in common liturgies, or any gathering, must always remain a blank symbol, useless and frequently aggravating, until it captures a symbolic *activity* outside itself that infiltrates the whole of life and motivates the desire to share. I am therefore in agreement with Paul Ricouer's judgment that "the symbol gives rise to thought," insofar as it is never the symbol itself but the thinking it encourages that produces the behavior defining our lives. It is this behavior, when it conduces toward unity, that the symbol then designates or celebrates.

In this chapter I am proposing the universe as the widest-ranging symbol that lends itself to thinking of ourselves as communal beings—that is, as the symbol indicating our linkage with the whole of creation. Religions throughout the world have always been particularly susceptible to this symbol to the extent that it involves the originating and sustaining effects of divine activity and can also be construed according to comforting indices of order, stateliness, and reliability in its movements and transformations to the observing eye. But since the Enlightenment, and certainly in the last several decades of this century, the symbol has lost much of its attractive force due to the discovery of immensities of time and space in the universe as well as the intricacies of its various component parts, especially in the early phases after its initiating event (some commentators speak of an explosion rather than an event; I tend to prefer the latter term, since what happened was surely nothing like any explosion we can now experience). In size and age and physical details the universe has become for many, perhaps most, an alien and violent place producing more a spirit of xenophobia than at-homeness. In fact, it has become diabolic, a theater of massive detonations and collisions where order, stateliness, and reliability are reduced to chronic discord. In this modern scenario, particularly in the preaching and practice of devotional piety, Christian religion has remained largely dumbstruck, responding much as it did when confronting the bothersome fact of the extinction of species in the last century and trying to adjust this to God's providential care in creation.

In some fashion Christian religion in the new millennium will have to overcome this embarrassment and be robust in its affirmations both of the scientific data, which cannot be denied, and the presence of God's providence, which cannot be relinquished. On the other hand, deism will always be an option, the viewpoint that while God may have initiated the universe—the question of the absolute beginning being ceaseless yet inherently nonbreachable by scientific fact, though obviously not by scientific theory—and perhaps intrudes here and there to guarantee its predictable maneuvering, at least on the grand scale of things, God otherwise remains quite removed from events. For many, of course, the weakness of deism is precisely in this removal and the seeming inconsequence it imposes on such common religious themes as revelatory experiences in history and prayer. Deism seduces the scientist because it requires little contention over the idea of God; it repels more demanding believers because there lurks in it the suspicion that God's reality functions as little more than an explanatory convenience to plug up gaps in our knowledge. The profound religious piety we find in the works of men like Newton and Einstein, deists both, allays little of this suspicion, since such finely chiseled minds delight in the stark and simple elegance of things in a way that rarely overcomes the more common religious need for an effusive and immediate presence of God in the course of events. At several points throughout this book I will be addressing this situation.

One of the most sensitive and eloquent scientific minds to have graced this century, Loren Eiseley was caught up in the above ambiguity, and it pestered his thoughts repeatedly. In his later years he came to image the whirl of events in the universe as a game in which these events constitute one of the players and God the Other Player, the one who is never quite seen, whose moves are unpredictably but intentionally made, and whose motive appears to be benevolent victory. Since I first read of this image I have found it a source of both enchantment and consolation. The enchantment lies in the beauty of its simplicity and the consolation in its familiarity of persons at play. The outcome of the game is assured as a symbolic act by the description of benevolent victory, and the excitement making it a game derives from awaiting the moves that bring this victory about. Eiseley is right in then saying that this excitement—the fascination of discovery—should be the core of the spiritual life, just as the very same term, "excitement," can be used to describe the activity at the core of the universe in its play between atomic and subatomic particles. We are also not far here from the idea of God's hiddenness that ripples throughout many religions, emphasized in Christian theology especially by Luther and later confessed with great simplicity when Schleiermacher remarked that the older he got, the more he became aware that we cannot know nearly as much about God as we think we can. The same idea courses through the Hindu mythology of Shiva's secret dance, the veiled workings of the Buddhist Nirvana, and the camouflage of God's presence in history sometimes taught by the Hebrew prophets.

But the game never ends. And the turn of a millennium can only be a small recess for thought to take account of where it has been and how it wishes to proceed; a recess, in other words, requiring both judgment and decision. When this is religious thought, and it is centered on our current concern with cosmology, my own suggestion is that the game of discovery should pursue three specific directions, much like what happens in the child's game of hide-and-seek when three children go separate ways in searching for a fourth one who is hiding. To each of these directions I will devote specific remarks in the following three sections. None of them recommends brand new paths for religion to follow—since all three have occupied us to varying degrees since religious reflection began—but rather offers a refreshed intensity in examining their outlines and perhaps provides new turns to these very old but monotonously traveled paths. The three directions pertain to: the beginning the universe, its end, and the existence of life elsewhere than on earth. The only definite point of confidence I would care to assert for the moment about each of them is that at the end of the coming thousand years, should we continue to progress in scientific and technical skills without employing any of them to our own regression or demise, we will know an immeasurably greater amount about each of these issues than we do now.

In all these considerations it is clear that theology, as the self-reflective discipline in any religion, will have to link itself closely with the findings of science. For the past thousand years this has occurred either not at all or only grudgingly, save in the works of individual visionaries. For much of this time the relationship has instead been one of opposition, even outright hostility, with either party gaining predominance largely because of the vagaries of political patronage; the treatment of Copernicus and Galileo is at once recalled. And this is true both in Western and Eastern cultures, in Christianity as well as Buddhism, in Judaism as well as Islam. Yet slowly, like the haltering moves of a newborn, *facts* began to assert themselves—facts of science whose denial made those who denied, even when these were teaching authorities within the religion, ridiculous. Coupled with the facts there also emerged more consistent theories resolving anomalies in previous ones and eliciting the allegiance of increasing numbers of the learned. In an embarrassment of examples religion was denigrated in many minds by its intransigence or, in a final move to save face, its indifference toward scientific fact and theory. With but a few examples in contemporary Christianity, and even less from other religious matrices, this indifference still characterizes theology. A lagging therefore occurs, in which religion now proclaims not its antagonism but the tentativeness of too many critical scientific finds and the inadvisability of incorporating them into theology. Unfortunately, this inadvisability too often cloaks intellectual irresponsibility, and the educated begin to see religion more and more as a foot-dragging phenomenon to be ridiculed, or at best condescendingly, perhaps even patiently, tolerated, but not respected. The visionaries seeking science and religion as companions are still in short supply, are still often persecuted, no longer by racks but by ridicule, yet still call forth to those in the new millennium to work quickly and effectively to put an end to this ill-will or neglect wherever each exists. In them all can be heard the embarrassed whisper of Einstein's judgment that religion without science is lame, whereas science without religion is blind.

The above comments are not suggesting that religion, or theology, should abandon its more traditional partners, philosophy and psychology. They both have assisted and sustained religion through many centuries as it has attempted to incorporate itself in ever more thorough ways into a culture's life through their own continuing histories of diagnosis and prescription. Subsidiary disciplines such as political, economic, and sociological studies have also assisted this incorporation. Nor do I wish to downplay the original articulation of the religious consciousness in mythic forms or the perennial effectiveness these have in the lives of countless people. In fact, I will be using one of these myths in the following section, and throughout the book I will be adverting several times to still others, especially as their intent is reformulated around contemporary concerns and language. I am not going to so emphasize science that it works to the detriment, let alone exclusion, of these other formats of thought in seeking service to Christian religion (and vice versa). Rather, I will simply be acknowledging a conviction that in the new millennium, at least at its turn and in the reliably foreseeable years afterwards, it is science to which religion will be most productively wed, for both theological and pastoral interests.

A certain intensification of symbols will occur throughout the remaining pages of this book. We will move from the universe as the symbol denoting our emplacement in the whole panorama of space-time we can observe and assess, to the earth as our more immediate domain, to plants and animals as sharers of organic life, to ourselves as the most familiar and exclusionary designation of our communality, and finally to God as both the most intimate and intense symbol seeking to make us one, not just among ourselves, together with the planet and its other life-forms, but with the whole of creation. Science will assist us in all these areas, assist us enormously in contributing to an agenda for Christian religion in the new millennium that in its specifics will draw from knowledge already gained yet reworked in the forge of theological imagination, while at the same time undergoing periodic reformation as it seeks fidelity to those traits that any workable vision of the future, or for that matter of the past and present, must possess—those that Whitehead delineated more succinctly than anyone: internal consistency, relevance to the facts of the world in which we live, and illuminating power as the bestowal of new insight. Finally, the gradual intensification of the above symbols will be accompanied by an intensification of passion and subjectivity in responding to them as they each drive close to the heart of our lives.

The Beginning of the Universe

There is a certain seduction in experiencing the beginning of things. Initially it is the result of aesthetic appeal, the beauty in the creation of something that was not there before, which in its final stage is the beauty of birth. The seduction can be pluriform. It can be peacefully exciting, as in watching exquisite form grow from stone at a sculptor's touch, or frighteningly exciting, as in nature's indulgence in building crescendos of violent weather, or awesomely exciting—that is, both peacefully and frighteningly, in a peculiar blend of experience—as in a slow meditation on the clear night sky and the sudden novelty of sight or thought this can produce. What endures beyond the birth is often of less excitement, the beauty becoming too familiar, a commonplace whose novelty has metamorphosed into the ordinary, something taken for granted and grown tedious because our observations now lack imagination. Yet it is exactly this, imagination as the breeding ground of excitement, that reflection on the beginning of the universe requires: the very beginning, before birth in the formation of galaxies and the settling down of general contours remarkably similar to what we still see, many eons later, whenever we gaze outward.

There is a second and related seduction to experiencing the beginning of things. It is the seduction of knowledge, specifically captured in the premise that to know how something begins is to know what will follow. Most people comfortable with it would probably not apply this premise clear across the board, making it unqualifiedly reliable, but would prefer that it be limited, if only to acknowledge the possibility of the future holding unpredictable novelty. Nonetheless, how something begins would still contain some reliable knowledge regarding what it will become. Psychological analysis, for example, makes use of this premise continually, as do statistics and much of genetic analysis. The statement opening the Bible, "In the beginning God created . . . ," has built into it the conviction that this is the way God will subsequently be known—not the only way, of course, but the irreplaceably defining way: God is the Creator. This is then embellished slightly in the opening to John's gospel, "In the beginning was the word . . . ," where the speaking of the word is understood as the fundamental and enduring generative act of God, as at a later point in Genesis itself, "God said, let there be . . ."

We have noted the truism that the absolute beginning of the universe is unknowable; that the closest we can get is to a state of affairs subsequent to the initiating event. At the very moment of the event science speaks only of a singularity, an utterly unique condition that is impenetrable to experimentation. All that can be done is to theorize as to its composition from the observable effects it later had, while also recognizing that many of these effects, especially within the first few moments after the initiating event, resulted from stochasticity, that is, a state or situation subject to random, indeterminate, and unpredictable changes or fluctuations (a fundamental tenet of quantum mechanics as well as all scientifically workable notions of freedom and novelty in the universe). I myself find much of this theorizing enormously intriguing and am continually amazed at the disciplined imaginations it represents. Some of it I will describe briefly in succeeding paragraphs. But for now I wish only to make the point that the unknowability of its beginning tells us something of the universe as such: that it is permeated with unknowns, and that this permeation is so thorough that a completely satisfied knowledge of the observable universe is beyond feasibility. Or differently: There is built into the universe from the very start a metaphysical "cloture" that precludes a full, inerrant, and conclusive awareness of its behavior. Some scientists speak of this same conclusion as a hallmark of the principle of indeterminacy, though theologians might typically prefer such terms as "mystery" or "transcendence." But both groups are in fundamental agreement that, since we too are made of elements born only in the explosion of stars, and these stars link us back to the originating event, we also have the unknowable built into us metaphysically—in the sense that we can neither be known nor know anything else completely. This sometimes goes against our species self-confidence, producing that peculiar Jekyll-and-Hyde syndrome whereby we assert with one part of our mind what we deny with another. The acknowledgment of unbreakable cognitive or epistemological limits can then be avoided, especially in moments of naive and poorly reflected judgment, as an arbitrary confinement of the ultimate success of the human intellect. Yet whatever our stance might be at any point in the workings of this syndrome, now sympathetic to the one side, then to the other, the final determinant explaining our endless fascination for riddles, conundrums, enigmas, puzzles—any play of the mind—leading us to affirm that there are things we do not know, must be the confession that there are things we cannot know, and that the parent of this awareness is ceaselessly fertile.

After the event initiating the universe, results occurred with almost incalculable rapidity; on this point all scientists agree. A generally accepted rough sketch of these results would look something like the following:

1. What existed before the initiating event cannot be described; the singularity cannot be probed, and speculation will always lack experimental data. Any observable residues are of the event itself, not what preceded it. Many scientists are comfortable with describing the preceding situation as infinity.

2. From the initiating event to 10^{-43} seconds. This is the so-called Planck time (after the renowned physicist Max Planck), during which there was only one force and one particle: to a scientist a situation of utter beauty because of its simplicity—a beauty recognized in the Greek origin of the very word scientists most commonly use as a synonym for the universe, *cosmos,* and which most people might have an inkling of in the word "cosmetic." This is when many theorists suggest that space and time as we know them, or space-time, began. Estimates of the size of the universe at this time are often on the order of a planet to a baseball to a proton, or smaller.

3. From 10^{-43} to 10^{-35} seconds. The strong force becomes distinct from two others, gravity and the electroweak force, allowing for the binding of protons and neutrons.

4. From 10^{-35} to 10^{-10} seconds. This is a particularly critical juncture for the physical contours our universe possesses. The weak and electromagnetic forces become distinct (now we have the four fundamental forces still operative in the universe: these two, plus the strong nuclear force and gravity), allowing for radioactive decay and the attractive/repellent force of electromagnetism. Like gravity, the range of this latter force is designated as limitless, so that a charged particle on one side of the universe is theoretically capable of exerting a force on a charged particle on the other side of the universe, though an infinitesimally small one because of the distances involved (this is one of the bases of the currently popular chaos theory and its assertion of "micro-unpredictability"). Electromagnetism is what binds electrons to atomic nuclei and separate atoms into molecules, which are then bound together into solids.

5. From 10^{-10} seconds to three minutes. Quarks combine to form protons and neutrons.

6. From three minutes to 500,000 years. Atoms form when positively

charged nuclei attract negatively charged free electrons. From 500,000 years until now is commonly called the "present era," where the forces and particles in the universe remain in general outline as we now know them.

In all these various stages the major player is temperature, which diminishes rapidly and thereby readjusts relationships within and between the forces and particles. At 10^{-33} seconds, for example, the temperature of the universe was 10^{28} degrees Kelvin; today it is about 3 degrees Kelvin. (The Kelvin scale is the one commonly used in physics, in which the "zero" is approximately equal to −273.1 degrees Celsius and represents the point of absolute freezing, at which all atomic movement ceases. On the Celsius scale water freezes at 0 degrees and boils at 100 degrees, just as on the Fahrenheit scale it freezes at 32 degrees above the zero point and boils at 212 degrees.) Finally, we might note that the age of the universe—usually given as the time between the initiating event and the present—is roughly fifteen billion years, and the distance to the horizon of the observable universe as it continues to expand is roughly twelve to fourteen billion light-years in any direction from Earth. These figures, though, change regularly as observational technologies develop.

I should repeat here that even the above descriptions, so generally stated, do not enjoy unanimity among theorists. Moreover, as further details are added to delineate a greater precision of theory, this lack of unanimity increasingly becomes a lack of consensus, and finally, at an extreme, a confusing miasma of variant and frequently hostile opinions. This is especially the case as increasing anomalies in either data or logic in a paradigmatic theory (one that has achieved at least consensus, more rarely unanimity) can no longer be assigned as mere appendages to the theory, but must become determinants in thoroughly revising or even discarding it. For a while—sometimes a long while—confusion becomes rampant as these time-weary explanations are dying and new ones are laden with a heavy tentativeness, as with the slow demise of geocentrism in astronomy, mechanistic determinism in physics, and species preservation in biology. In this situation, therefore, I would suggest that what conclusions we can draw with the highest probability (sufficient, that is, to be maintained against all current and currently predictable experimentation) from the above outline of events are relatively sparse and involve at least the following statements: (1) there was a beginning to our known universe, and this beginning did not emerge out of a "pure" nothingness, since such a purity is scientifically unfeasible (there is no such thing as a complete vacuum where even virtual particles and forces, or some perturbations, are entirely absent); (2) temperatures of almost unimaginable intensity were involved during the initiating event, dissipating quickly at first, more gradually over time; (3) atoms and molecules formed to produce solids; (4) since the initiating event, the universe has been expanding at an enormously energetic rate. Each of these four conclusions is a commonplace known to most educated people. But as we link them to the remarks preceding them, what they elicit is the idea that any given paradigm tends increasingly toward reliability the more it can maintain its axiomatic probabilities, or what we might also call its operative certainties, as inclusively general as possible. It must always be kept in mind, however, that these certainties can only be operative, not absolute; the last one on the list, for example, becomes badly described should the idea become observationally or theoretically powerful that our universe is part of something much larger, making the expansion very slow.

In its finest expressions religion has always acknowledged the above description of paradigms. The fundamental ethical maxim of all religions, do good and avoid evil, is a case in point, though how it becomes detailed in specific injunctions can clearly vary among religions. So too is the creation narrative in nearly every religion that possesses one. They all tell of a singularity whose nature is beyond human comprehension; that an expressive act of this singularity originates the universe as we know it; that only tentative statements about the singularity can be made based on an examination of the results of the originating act, presuming that some characteristics of this act are maintained in the results and continue to define the subsequent history in influential ways; and that a small selection of these statements achieve such a high degree of probability that they are operative certainties within the creation paradigm. In the vocabulary of religions what we are describing here is otherwise captured in terms like "God," "God's creative power," "God's providence," and "God's revelation" (polytheists, of course, will pluralize deity, and religions will vary in their metaphors of divine personhood, their anthropomorphism). Since I will be spending time on these topics in chapter 5, I wish only to make one further point here—namely, that a religion's creation narratives, like their counterparts in science, verge toward greater attractiveness, a more compelling beauty, the more they are elegantly simple in the expression of their inclusiveness. In this light, then, and in my judgment by way of example, the narratives in Genesis are extraordinarily worthy ones.

One of the more obvious recommendations I will be making for the tasks of science at the turn of the millennium is that in many, though not all, of its current projects it maintain its interests. This is even the case in so pragmatically obscure an enterprise as tracing out the beginnings of the universe. A proviso is that great care must therefore be exercised to keep these interests as free as possible from political and especially military control, so that never again will scientists looking to unharness the atom to reveal the powers originating the universe be forced as well to unharness the power of nuclear weapons: a familiar warning and example that I simply wish to acknowledge now as my own. For while the technological application of knowledge is often of benefit to the world, and demeaning this in a context of otherwise legitimate criticism is an act of sniping ingratitude, it is the pursuit of knowledge in itself that is the primary value—again, a familiarity that we can trace from the musings of pre-Socratic philosophers to those of many adroit contemporary commentators. It is true that knowledge is power, and Nietzsche is still one of our best analysts for how this power can be put to uses of domination, the excesses of self-will imposed on others, while the uses taught by those like Jesus and Gautama Buddha and St. Francis are too often muted by a dismissal of their unworkability in the arenas of human pride and endless self-aggrandizement. *All* military ideologies deserve not just constant critical control, but every effort to make them intellectually obsolete. For at heart they are diabolical, as I have described this. And sympathizers to the opposing view are never to be trusted in the shaping of our values in the coming ages. Militant religious ideologies are to be treated the same way. I would also recommend two further points. First, while religion as such will not engage the actual science searching for reliable data and logical theory regarding the beginning of the universe, it can celebrate this search in the structures of its preaching and modes of worship—both of which would then encourage this search in ways that a well-meaning but tight concentration on specific human events—even one so wondrous, say, as the life of Jesus—would not. Secondly, religion could suggest a reversion in the next millennium to an attitude that characterized so much of the doing of science in this millennium, namely, that the final intent of science, like the final intent of religion itself, is to give honor to God and the wisdom guiding divine purpose.

There is yet another point I wish to make about the lure embedded in the search for the universe's beginnings that extends it beyond the brute appeal of knowledge for its own sake. It is that this search can provide interstices in the everyday, far more immediate concerns of life and provide a richer, more robust wonder within us that these other concerns might not. Nor need you be a trained physicist for this, since the literature on the topic is large and easily accessible to those with even limited educations. However, this is not wonderment solely as surprise, though it is that too: the feeling subsequent to an experience that allows us to proclaim its enchantment. It is also wonder *during* the experience, or what we usually capture when describing the excitement of discovery. We should nurture all areas of inquiry that encourage this situation, areas whose intellectual reconnaissance is guided by benevolent, that is, good-willed or, in our previous term, symbolic motives and satisfactions. Religion must likewise encourage all such accesses away from the humdrum, the comfort that ordinariness often provides because we know how easily this comfort can become spiritually disastrous, a deadening and boring monotony. In fact, religion must work especially hard at this, in its priests and teachers and storytellers, its theologians and psychologists and magistrates, since observations of religious boredom are so achingly common—and are frequently made in the context of religion's general neglect of science, creating a posturing that quickly becomes mutual, with each side, science and religion, claiming irrelevance toward the other's rendition of the beginning of things.

As one reads through the pertinent literature, four issues above all seem to emerge as major perplexities about the observable universe, effects whose causes most theorists locate in the universe's remote beginnings. While religion is scarcely capable of addressing any of these within the confines of its own competence, it still can have the honorable task of encouraging their study, and thus participate in their unfolding resolution in the years to come. In the following brief descriptions I will be relying on the excellent work, among others, of James F. Trefil in *The Moment of Creation*. I will mention some of the current proposals being

offered to address the first three of these perplexities, with more attention to the fourth in the next section—all the while acknowledging that
each is forbiddingly intricate in the knowledge of mathematics, and especially of geometry, it requires, and none has yet to achieve an enduring
consensus among scientists. This will have to await the hard work of
accumulating observations and tight reasoning in the next millennium.
First, there is the problem of why there is a so little antimatter in the
observable universe. Particles of antimatter have been recorded in laboratory experiments (e.g., the positron as the antimatter equivalent of the
electron, with the same mass but positively charged) and are theoretically required in the very early stages of the universe's beginning. Two
somewhat interrelated proposals have dominated to explain this absence:
(1) since matter and antimatter annihilate each other on contact, there
must have been a slight quantitative edge to matter that allowed enough
of it to survive these collisions to construct the universe as we know it
(a typical proportion is that of one billion antiprotons to one billion and
one protons); and (2) if substantial quantities of antimatter in fact
escaped collisions with their matter equivalents, they are congregated in
discrete parts of the universe not yet convincingly detected. Secondly,
there is the problem of why the microwave radiation of the universe is
isotropic. In physics "isotropism" means that a quantity is the same, or
virtually so, when viewed or measured in any direction (the microwave
radiation is isotropic to an accuracy of better than 0.01 percent). The
problem centers on the fact that we can now observe regions of the universe from which the radiation was emitted 500,000 years after the initiating event (the so-called Big Bang), but that these regions were more
than 500,000 light-years from each other at the time—and so, since nothing travels faster than the speed of light, could not have related to each
other in something like the distribution and equalizing of their temperatures. How could they have the same temperature if they never had
any contact with each other? As Trefil says, this is the sort of situation
that gives physicists gray hairs. Two possibilities are offered to explain it:
(1) the universe was created in thermal equilibrium, though this would
require the dismantling of a number of respected theories regarding other
phenomena in the very early and later universe; and (2) that some process as yet unknown but probably occurring before the particle era at

the beginning of the universe (plus 3 minutes and earlier) accounts for it and would preclude the apparent paradox. Needless to say, a great deal of theoretical work, especially in an area known as inflationary theory, has been devoted to what this process might have been. Thirdly, and for physicists perhaps the most exasperating of the four, is the problem of how the galaxies could have formed in the time that current knowledge allots for the process. The issue centers on the length of time it would have taken atoms to gather together gravitationally to form a galactic mass during a period when the universe was undergoing very rapid expansion. If the collections of atoms do not reach a large enough size quickly enough, the universal expansion will have moved the remaining collections out of reach of each other before anything even remotely the size of a galaxy could have been formed. And physicists have known for decades that the time needed for random atomic motion to produce such large aggregates is very long—much longer than the time between the formation of atoms (if they were formed as listed in the time frame given earlier in the chapter, at approximately 500,000 years after the initiating event) and the appearance of the early galaxies. At present there seem to be only two ways out of the problem: (1) the universe was created with matter already clumped together into aggregations that could gravitationally resist the rapid expansion and form galaxies—though at present this view is not taken seriously; and (2) there is some as yet unknown process that would allow such aggregations before the creation of atoms. Fourthly, there is the problem of whether or not enough mass exists to close the universe, preventing its continuing expansion and causing its eventual gravitational collapse upon itself, implying another initiating event followed by another universe, in perhaps an endless succession.

All four of the above problems intrigue the mind and tantalize imagination. But as promised earlier, the fourth is the one to which I now wish to attend, since it captures in the clearest terms the issue of the end of the universe. Religion will again, as with the universe's beginning, have something to offer us on this issue, whose worth can only be enriched and made more widely appropriate in a partnership with science as both seek the ways of beauty and the hints of truth in a creation given us obscured and often confused by the limits of human interest and intellect.

The End of the Universe

To many of us how something will end evokes greater interest than how it began. I suspect this is so because while much of what something becomes is dictated by how it began, its ending is often open to greater degrees of control. Our individual lives are probably the most persuasive example of this. Even a decision to begin something such as our own child, a work of art, or a deed of illustrious valor often changes its initial meaning, and so its pursuit, as we reflect on its relationship to an encompassing end or goal we have in mind for our lives, such as what will endure of us beyond the end of life itself. If we never died, and if this issue of endurance were our only consideration, children, art, and heroic valor would be pointless and we would have to look elsewhere for the other satisfactions each might also produce. The end of things has a finality to it, a sense of completeness or, sometimes, devastation, that the beginning of things denies—so that much of human thought has been devoted to attempts at blending these two in such a way as to maintain, if not unbroken continuation, at least a repetition of beginnings so that the finality is never absolute. Religions have been particularly adept at these attempts in their various formulations of doctrines of rebirth. So too has common reflection on the rhythms that punctuate so many of our experiences: all of them speaking of a symmetry of birth-death-birth in singular, long-lived, or permanent cycles. It is this rhythm that will be our guiding image in this section, and we will be seeking to discover if what we can say of sunrises and sunsets we can say of the whole universe, or if a metronome, swinging once, can never swing back again without denying its very nature.

The image of rhythms has been the source of great consolation as well as dread in human reflection. To some it is consoling as long as the rhythms are identical to each other: this is the consolation of reliability, of repetitious and comfortable sameness, and is the heart's treasure of every thoroughgoing conservative. To others it is consoling as long as the rhythms hold some degree of novelty, a chance at the new: this is the consolation of hope, the excitement that while the new might bring dissolution, it is also capable of bringing progress, improvement, the satisfactions of pleasures and peace of mind. In biological science, for example, the preference might be to speak of benevolent and malignant mutations held secret in a shifting puzzle of genes. But even to the second group an *encompassing* novelty is a cause for dread, a xenophobic response whenever what succeeds the familiar is the utterly strange, until the strange keeps succeeding itself. This is the dread depicted so accurately in Ursula LeGuin's novella *The Lathe of Heaven,* when the young man discovers upon awakening that whatever dream he had while asleep has altered reality in completely disorienting ways. It is the same theme that controls the dread of Lot's wife when she must leave her home and journey into new lands, new situations of which she has had no experience. LeGuin's young man and Lot's wife are perplexed and terrorized, however, not so much because of the novelty itself awaiting them as by the fact that they themselves have not changed in ways that correspond to this novelty and help establish some degree of mutuality with it. This is precisely the situation that Toffler describes as future shock, the deep anxiety produced whenever the pace of novelty is unrelenting and outstrips even conscientious efforts at adaptation. While it is true that the thoroughgoing conservative is anyone who foolishly tries to deny the essence of the universe, which is change, only the unhealthy or very desperate mind does not want to discover *some* semblance of identifiability, no matter how remote, within it.

Many religions have occupied themselves at some length with the end of the universe, usually in ancient apocalyptic musings that have come down to most of us in their Judeo-Christian dress. It is clear that throughout this literature, given the available astronomy, the universe was understood almost exclusively as the earth and its "immediate" environs in the day and night sky. It also leans heavily toward describing this end as cataclysmic, a congeries of natural disasters such as wind, fire, and earthquake that sunder and tear apart the world as we know it—in other words, events that are diabolic in their results. So, too, this destruction is almost always understood as the result of divine activity, commonly motivated for purposes of wrathful or benevolent judgment to bring about a renewal of the world. This last point is particularly important, especially if we confine ourselves to the biblical tradition. For just as this tradition does not suggest a creation *from* nothingness, but rather the giving of recognizable or at least decipherable shape (from the Hebrew *barah*, "create") to what was previously without it (the Hebrew *tohu wa bohu*, or what a scientist might describe as the primordial singularity), so it nowhere suggests a termination of the world *into* nothingness. Most would have found the concept of absolute nullity, as I myself do, unimaginable and thus intellectually barren, and would have likely maintained this judgment despite later Christian efforts at insisting on it as a prelude to creation that guarantees an appropriate dignity to God's limitless power. We are caught here, then, in a rhythm at the very least of one cycle: creation-destruction-creation (or re-creation). Inevitably in the biblical vision the re-creation is understood as a wondrous advance upon what preceded it, both in the just punishment accorded the wicked and the serenity awarded the good, though in other traditions, such as Hinduism, this is not so, since the cycles can be many and do not necessarily guarantee successive improvement. This explains in part the melancholy we often observe in various strands of Hindu spirituality and others similarly oriented toward a series of cyclical rebirths. It is the sadness of the Buddhist sage and the Greek seer, even of so affirmative a figure as Nietzsche's ever-recurring Dionysius.

How one views the results of these cycles is frequently persuaded by how one views God. In the majority tradition of Christianity, for example, with its view of creation as an act of intemperate divine generosity, and with its single cycle of birth-death-rebirth (resurrection), the image of God is suffused with benevolence (as when Jesus' own theology of God's loving-kindness is maintained) or at least with a fair and inexorable justice (as when its Jewish roots or appropriation of Greek thought comes to the fore). In Hinduism, on the other hand, there is a distinct theme—also found, though less frequently, in Buddhism—that the creation of the world was a mistake, a type of divine bungling or careless play, and that the continuing cycles are geared toward a gradual correction of it (the Hindu term for play, *Lila*, is also used positively, a game of delight, as Islamic spirituality also recognizes when Allah reveals, "I was a hidden treasure, and in order to be found I created the world"). Still different is a recurrent theme of Greek mythology, often honed by philosophic meditation, which inclines toward a view of divine indifference toward the world, or now and then its usefulness in assisting divine playfulness or a need for praise, with the cycles consequently characterized by repetitious sameness. And in Nietzsche's reflections, where there is either no God concept at all or a distorted Christian one he seeks to destroy, the creation of the world is a happenstance having no personal or resolute agency, and the cycles of rebirth (a favorite designation for future possibilities) are a struggle of humanity against itself in an attempt to produce what he calls the Superman: a creature of incomparable joy at being alive, replete with laughter and a will to power seeking to overcome all that weighs us down of politics, religion, self-delusion, and weakness. A liberated science is the privileged avenue to this goal, with investigations of psychosomatic phenomena of special worth, and the satisfactions of discovery its reward.

Religions, however, must encourage an acceptance of novelty not just regarding the term of creation's development, but also of novelty along the way. For even those religions seeking to emphasize in their spiritual vision the consolation of sameness must still recognize the occurrence of unpredictability and find some way of making it their own. Otherwise the vision must remain a fancy, a work of pure imagination like Botticelli's Venus rising from the sea, perhaps enchanting, even desirable, but never able to provide a workable image of reality—that is, reality appraised but never obliterated by imagination. Moreover, the term of development in most of these religious visions is not just an object of hope but of faith as well, in that it not only conspires in history to occur, but to occur in a certain fashion and with certain results. While something new, therefore, the novelty is not a complete unknown, at least within these categories of hope and faith. Yet no such confidence necessarily prevails along the way, in day-to-day living, which is sometimes suffused with the unknown, the surprises and shocks that religions in fact see as the testing ground for one's worthiness as an adherent to the vision of what awaits creation in its final cycle. And so the Christian must live in a universe of novelty to exemplify loving-kindness, the Hindu and Buddhist to demonstrate compassion, the ancient Greek to become courageous, and the Nietzschean to achieve a self-willed autonomy. Not in the end but in the struggle toward it does life take on meaning, or lose it. The end or goal functions only as a seduction; how one lives proves its strength.

The currently prevailing view among most cosmologists tells us that the end of the universe will occur in either one of two basic ways, and that determining which one is premised on a single fact. This is an example of the extraordinary simplicity the universe often exhibits not just in its physical foundations but also in the processes describing its motion. The single fact pertains to the quantity of mass or matter in the universe, and determining this provides the sole basis for assessing the fate of the universe as "closed" or "open." These options are easily enough described. If the universe is closed it means there is sufficient mass to curtail its outward expansion, finally stopping it altogether, then gradually initiating its contraction back to something like the singularity with which it began some 15 billion years ago. A new initiating event would then presumably occur—though on this point some cosmologists demur, largely because of the mathematical physics involved, and whether it might not indicate a continued contraction into infinitude, or nothingness—and the next cycle, like this one, would last roughly 100 billion years from beginning to end. On the other hand, if the universe is open it means there is not enough mass to stop the present expansion, guaranteeing gradual dissipation to a point of near total oblivion, an endless thinning out in limitless space. (A third option, the "flat" universe, is a modification of the second, and roughly means that at some future time a permanent balance between expansion and contraction will occur, a type of gravitational equilibrium, and the universe will "freeze" in that condition forever. A fourth option, today largely dismissed, is that of the "steady-state" universe, one which remains forever the same with new mass continually added—though how this might happen the theory does not say with certainty; perhaps through portals to other universes—to keep the density constant as the universe expands but never contracts.) The search for mass in the universe has therefore become one of the foremost challenges to contemporary astronomy, particularly since its measurable quantity so far amounts to roughly 1 to 10 percent (depending on the interpretations of individual observers) of that needed to close the universe. For many scientists, as for many theologians, any suggestion that this mass will never be found is an intellectually abusive situation, since it denies to the character of the universe's end the remarkably rhythmic pattern we find everywhere else in its macroscopic movements—which in turn may reflect a more basic ambiguity about assigning to anything a limitlessness without renewal. It is the notion of *renewal* that is critical here, and with it, again, the idea of novelty.

Many scientists have become increasingly inclined toward the idea of a closed universe, however, not entirely because of philosophical or theological disposition. There is also considerable data now accruing to justify their viewpoint, most of it centering on the so-called dark matter that increasingly appears to populate the universe: from the "halos" surrounding galaxies (composed predominantly of hydrogen atoms), to the thickness of mass lying at the center of galaxies and galactic clusters prohibiting through gravitational attraction their dissolution, to black holes of varying size scattered randomly, to countless presumed objects like planets and asteroids whose distance and dimensions prohibit current detection, and to any and all forms of mass composed of particles other than ordinary protons and neutrons (this last being required because of theoretical considerations regarding how many of these "ordinary" particles could have been formed shortly after the universe's beginning). The confidence that such sources exist in sufficient abundance to close the universe is very high—either because of "spot" observations of some of them, or because of near compelling statistical or theoretical requirements—though some still argue that prediction should be based *solely* on the observational data we *now* have. This argument is judged by many others, though, as much too confining, overly reliant on the data at hand, and excessively reluctant to draw intelligible conclusions from what data we do possess. But for its proponents it leads ineluctably to the conclusion, at least in one popular scenario, that after a very long period of time (most estimates place it at 10 to several hundred powers, $10^{?00}$ years from now) black holes of increasingly larger sizes will form, evaporate, and leave nothing in their place known to us, or as some would conclude, unobservable to us and so nothing at all. This aching conclusion is also affirmed by some theorists of a closed universe who claim that unless some of the basic laws of physics do not apply everywhere throughout the universe, or alter during the cycles, then eventually the rhythms of an oscillating universe must give way to entropy (disorder due to a flattening out of the cohesive energies holding matter together) so that the whole system would finally have to run down and cease at some point of utter equilibrium, some cycle in which further growth or contraction are stymied.

Of course, no one living on the earth will observe either one of these scenarios play itself out to completion. In fact, no one living on the earth will likely see a universe much different at all from the one we can now observe. For the fate of our immediate solar system, particularly that of our Sun, demands this. We are locked to a star that is classified as a medium/yellow in size, luminosity, and energy release, one roughly 5 billion years old and about halfway through its evolution. In another 5 billion years, through a process of gravitational collapse gradually increasing because of a decrease in the centrifugal forces at its core and surface pushing outward against the gravity force, the Sun will expand into a massive red-giant star whose diameter will likely reach to the orbit of Mars and definitely to that of Earth. At this point our planet will either dissolve completely or be scorched to only a small fraction of its current size, a cinder floating around in space either still attached to some radically altered orbit around the new red Sun or voyaging because of the blast of the detonation until captured by the gravity of some of other object, or perhaps colliding with it to obliterate completely whatever is left of the planet. The only way our descendants, if there are any, could survive this situation would be to develop technologies that for the most part still seem outlandishly improbable: to move off the earth to some other planet with a younger sun similar to our own; to cloak the earth impregnably against the blast and make it self-sustaining while still in its altered solar orbit; to construct machines capable of moving the planet in a directed fashion; and permutations on each of these proposals or the option of others not mentioned. Surely our history has chastened us enough not to prohibit the possibility of science determining workable technologies to secure our escape from the Sun going red, if the time left us is fairly accurate—an estimate that obviously precludes such radical interruptions as new knowledge of the Sun's workings, rogue planetary or stellar bodies producing catastrophic gravitational or collision effects disrupting the central portions of the solar system, or communication with entities capable of providing a successful exodus well in advance of the Sun's explosion. And I say "our" escape advisedly because while it is possible that biological technologies might guarantee something similar to us several billion years from now, it is also possible that by then we will have evolved into or been replaced by some radically different life-form.

The ancient prophetic insight of Joel has some merit, therefore, when he speaks of one sign of the earth's demise as the moon turning to blood. The prophet, of course, was no more naive in this description than any of us are. He knew that the moon would not literally liquify into blood. But what makes the prophecy powerful to us is that we can discover in it a texture of reality that Joel could not. For we know that when the Sun goes red, the Moon's light as reflected back to Earth will also glow red in the several minutes before the moon is destroyed. This same texture is also found in further, remarkably similar descriptions among religions of the terminal events as bringing earthquakes, wind, and fire. All these images until a few decades ago were considered by many as being the bad boy of theology, at least in mainstream Judaism and Christianity, and were embarrassingly kept in the closet, out of sight and speech, out of mind. But the facts of stellar evolution have now given them a degree of respectability, and have illustrated as well the curious way that intuitive awareness—or what many theologians would comfortably call "revelation" as the deliverance of this awareness—sometimes predicts with remarkable accuracy what the future later confirms as reliable knowledge. To this could also be added the destruction by fire, wind, and geologic disruption that we ourselves can now unleash on the earth through the detonation into tiny suns of materials housed in our nuclear warheads. The apocalyptic, as an anticipation of the end of things, is only foolishly ignored, and to silence its language is to betray a fear that the subsequent renewal the language also describes is a facade masking hopelessness. Things will just end, inevitably, violently, and without further possibility.

All religions have as one of their major tasks the consolation of melancholic and fearful minds, just as they must challenge arrogant and indifferent ones. The brute fact of the distant destructions we've been describing can have psychic or spiritual effects now, as in feelings of the final absurdity of things, or a lethargy that seeks little beyond the satisfaction of present wants. When a scientist of the stature of Steven Weinberg can conclude a book with the statement, "The more the universe seems comprehensible, the more it also seems pointless," lesser intellects can take this as a canonical judgment from which there is no reprieve. Or when a flood of philosophies and psychologies announce the inevitability of nihilism in any fair appraisal of life—that nothing finally matters—and joins this to an encouragement to seek what pleasures one can—the "eat, drink, and be merry" ethos of Epicurus—it is small wonder that a vastness of disciples accumulates to them. All religions must respond to both these situations in ways that accentuate other possibilities, alternate visions that dissuade the melancholy of the one and the superficiality of the other, or that break the circle of humanity by giving access to that singular possibility all of them have variously named as God. One way, if the universe does keep contracting and expanding, would be to view God under the metaphor of a parent giving us over continually to new life in ceaseless rhythms of affirmation. And if the universe expands just once, though it is a proposal I have already abandoned, then under the same metaphor God channels the life elsewhere, away from us and our universe, to something else, some other reality we can never know. Only these few remarks are necessary now, since I will be devoting chapter 5 to the issue of God, with the further cautionary note that the suggestion of new possibilities, especially radically new ones, does not automatically preclude a realistic assessment of the world—as scientists, I suspect, are especially aware—and that these suggestions are born from that talent of the mind we call imagination. It is here above all, in the workings of imagination, that I would argue science and theology can become, not twins, but siblings, and ones not alienated by chronic disagreement or indifference in the same household, but by mutual devotion. It surely will not take yet another thousand years to bring this about.

Circulating throughout the previous reflections has been an implicit control that I would now like to set forth clearly. It is obvious that I favor the idea of a closed over an open universe, for reasons already partially given. But the control I am referring to provides the foundational motive for these reasons, and it takes the form of a theological/philosophical bias. The word *bias* is critical here. As used in older days—and in Greece, a country where so much of the soil is compacted and hard on or just beneath the surface—the meaning was drawn principally from the practice of agriculture. The bias was the angle or slant on a hillside delineating the furrows in which you planted seeds, so that when it rained they would neither drown, as with horizontal furrows, or desiccate, as with vertical ones. But the Greeks, being eminently inquisitive people, were also intrigued by seeking knowledge of themselves from knowledge of their ordinary activities, like how they grew their food. As a result the word *bias* eventually came to be applied cognitionally, that is, as an acknowledgment that all of us approach experiences or ideas presented to our reflection from a particular slant or angle, or what we might otherwise call a prejudice or prejudgment, no matter how inarticulate it might be. The Greeks pushed this fact hard enough so that their usual judgment was that a recognition of one's biases was the first step toward wisdom. The notion of bias consequently did not have built into it the generally pejorative meaning it now has for us, but rather a positive one regarding a characteristic of self-awareness. My own bias in the preceding reflections, then, what controlled them and led me to refuse the idea of an annihilation of the universe at some point in the future, now needs articulation; in fact, this need is doubled, since the same bias will also control much of what follows. The bias is this: *Once a possibility becomes an actuality, the actuality from that point on remains a possibility*. I am obviously not talking here of identical repetitions, since such things cannot exist, but of recognizable ones, like the closed universes succeeding, possibly preceding, the one in which we now live. I cannot overemphasize how important it is for the reader to keep this bias in mind whenever pertinent, so that any judgment on what I say, whether beguiled or offended, will at least be premised on an understanding of why I said it. A further application of it controls what we will now take up in the concluding section of this chapter.

Life Elsewhere in the Universe

The above bias, which will function as an axiom throughout these reflections—because axioms at heart are also judgments made prior to a discussion or set of experiences—provides the basis for assessing the issue of intelligent life elsewhere in the universe. This is a fascinating topic, not just in itself but also in the responses it elicits, even when we confine our research to the serious analyses of serious minds. These responses can be cast generally into one of three categories: definite affirmation, definite denial, and indifference, or perhaps agnosticism. The first response will tend to emphasize statistics based on confident data we already possess about the universe, especially its size, and the extreme likelihood of many Sun-Earth combinations therein (just in our own galaxy, for example, there are approximately one hundred billion stars, and in the observable universe as a whole, somewhere around the same number of galaxies). The second response, on the other hand, will tend to emphasize the putative uniqueness of our planet, isolating the very delicate balance of the many chemical and physical components that produced and maintain our life-forms and the enormous unlikelihood of this balance being achieved elsewhere. Proponents of the "hard" version of the so-called Anthropic Principle are especially fond of this view and its attractive ability to reinstate humanity into a privileged position in the universe, a place of special exception which was denied for our home planet by Copernicus, for our organic development by Darwin, for and our mastery of our fate by Freud. Finally, as with indifference wherever we meet it, the third response takes no stance at all, either because the issue has not yet accumulated *enough* confident data for a definite resolution, inevitably meaning a direct encounter, or, far more typically, because it plays no role in the individual's life and therefore becomes, in the strict sense, impertinent.

Two provisos must now be added to the discussion. The first is that most of the analyses are concerned with *intelligent* life elsewhere in the universe, and that this intelligence involves at the very least the following traits: methods of communication, the ability to use tools, an appreciation of the relationship between cause and effect, the capacity to formulate abstractions, the utilization of memory and anticipation in determining present behavior. While it would undoubtedly create much initial excitement, the discovery of extraterrestrial life that did not meet such specifications, like microbes or primitive plants on earth, could probably maintain this excitement only as it became identified as a harbinger of more complex forms, ultimately intelligent ones. This is a predictable stance, since simple life-forms as a terminus of evolution amount to little more in popular imagination than the barest advance on inanimate objects. Even for many professionals, particularly biologists and chemists, interest would likely wane with the completion of structural analyses unless something outrageously unexpected came to light. It is only when life begins to become more complex, showing hints of similarity to our own, that it begins to encourage a curiosity about it that satisfies self- or species-infatuation: a peculiar but extraordinarily powerful motive of human inquiry, though also, understandably enough, of the fear many also feel for these other life-forms should they exist—the fear that perceives our self- or species-infatuation as the core of our wickedness. Nonetheless, it is this very infatuation, sometimes hankering to be something else, something more noble, like kindness or compassion toward our own kind, that we hear so constantly among biologists and animal experimenters as the singular justification of their work: it is an avenue to knowledge about ourselves. Since I will be taking up this issue of our uses of other life at some length in chapter 3, I will do no more than mention it here, provoking at the same time a concern about our values, the ones we assert and the ones we apply, that I will then take up in chapter 4.

Whereas the first proviso pertains to the issue of intellectual talent, the second is centered on aesthetic appeal. If intelligent life is found elsewhere in the universe, or if it finds us, there is nothing that demands of it a humanlike appearance, nor any other one we might find appealing to eye, ear, or touch. All the horrors of frightened imagination can break loose at this point, as they have when infiltrating so much of our popular entertainment, and sometimes our dreams. It is amazing to note as well how frequently these depictions are insectile, though even more commonly reptilian in shape, activity, and composition, with such features as bulging eyes vertically slit, a quickness of killing movement, and, of course, chitinous or scaly skin. Religion may be a major culprit in this, especially Judeo-Christianity along with its predecessor and successor creeds, in the ways it has leeched into the subconscious of many through ancient myths, literalist commentaries on them, and a never ending portraiture of revulsion toward these life-forms, particularly serpents. Or perhaps a Jungian might say that the revulsion is there innately, in that the primitive segment of our brains that is often designated the limbic structure or system is also known as the reptilian cortex, capturing inadvertently in the name the very sorts of frightening visage, stealthy demeanor, and rapid violence in which we ourselves so often successfully engage. At any rate, if intelligent forms of extraterrestrial life exist, only conceit would propose that the intelligence demands a humanlike body, just as only a limited appreciation of organic and inorganic arrangements, with the abundance of forms chemical combinations can take and the whole variety of atmospheres in which they can come alive, would propose our own biological structure as *the* pinnacle of life's development. An intelligent metamorph, after all, a shapeshifter of deliberating mind would prove us well down the ladder of this development: an identical judgment, we might note, though now needing no imagination, in which a very old man or woman in the throes of close death might concur when looking at the parrot who will live 130 years or the tortoise surviving two centuries.

I suspect that had most religions contemplated the possibility of other worlds in the universe when their foundational myths were constructed, they probably would have been comfortable populating them. Yet be-

cause of the particular cosmology controlling them this possibility was
not entertained, except rarely and in the vaguest ways that remained
well off the periphery of mainline views. For the cosmology insisted that
the universe was quite restricted in spatial distance, its limits not too far
in fact from the outreaches of the earth's sky, and its visible objects, like
the sun and moon and stars, more or less the size they appear to be to
the unaided eye, with their distance providing minimal shrinkage in
perception, and all of them too cold or too hot to support any physical
life. Of course, they were always the possible dwelling places of spirits,
gods and goddesses, demons and angels. And while most religions preferred such dwellings to be predominantly ethereal, they were always to
some extent material realms, heavens and hells that were not available
to human senses except in preternatural experiences bestowed by their
inhabitants. Depictions of these locales are quite colorful, aesthetically
pleasing or terrifying, and clearly indicative of the willingness to con-
strue life, albeit in much different forms, as possible elsewhere than on
our planet. With the demolition of this cosmology, however, there occurred almost simultaneously a general negligence among the educated
of the feasibility of any off-world habitations of life, a distaste for it bred
in the embarrassment of past mistakes. The whole notion was consequently assigned by many to the meanderings of fictional tales or to the
ill-informed minds of the superstitious or scientifically naive.

In recent decades, however, this negligence has begun to subside, and
for two major causes we've already touched on. First, there is *statistics*.
As our knowledge of the universe's size together with the objects and
forces composing it has become more secure, there has been a growing
acquiescence to the likelihood of many planet-star relationships like
our own; for many proponents of extraterrestrial life, this planet-star
similarity is a requisite for confident discussion. Secondly, there is *chemistry*. Knowledge of the primitive earth and its chemical makeup, together with the relatively simple structure of amino acids that produce
proteins, has permitted a greater latitude in proposing similar situations
elsewhere. To appreciate this, one needs to understand that a workable
axiom in sciences like chemistry is that the simpler an item is, the more
abundant it tends to be in the universe. Coupled with this is the growing
acceptance of the idea that life need not be possible solely on a protein-
carbon basis—that the bonding intricacies of the known elements, or
perhaps others not yet identified or even present in our galactic neigh-

borhood, could just as possibly produce ambiences in which life could emerge and flourish. In short, it is no longer an overarching cosmological vision that determines possibilities in the universe, but the details of observational data and what fair options of interpretation they offer. In fact, there are some scientists who even suggest that all we need for the possibility of life is the existence of hydrogen, which composes about 75 percent of the matter in the universe; that in the permutations of its growth into other elements, and these into molecules, an abundance of physical conditions can be manufactured, from the stars and planets themselves to the microchemistries on them, to produce life. This is an appealing sentiment to many, including myself, because of the sheer generosity of possibilities it proposes.

Yet religions have usually balked at the above description, since it takes no account of their primary interest, namely, the recommendation of belief in God in the context of human experience. There is an age-old dispute coming to the fore here, centering on the legitimacy of explanatory principles when interpreting sense data, *or* conclusions based on them. We are referring particularly to the uneasiness of scientists in employing a God-concept on an ad hoc basis whenever gaps or anomalies appear that the prevailing interpretation does not or cannot successfully resolve. Isaac Newton is a frequently cited example here, with his predilection for employing God whenever a glitch appeared in his mechanical universe. But this is a criticism that has merit only with the benefit of hindsight—the prevailing theism of most of Newton's contemporaries was amenable to his view—and cannot fairly comment on other contexts in which God, the universe, and the relationship between them are understood, such as, I think, the one I will outline in chapter 5. For now I would only note that the generosity I mentioned in the previous paragraph also has theological repercussions insofar as the existence of life throughout the universe would testify to a divine largess, which confinement of life, especially intelligent life, to the earth does not. It is, I will argue in chapter 5, the life itself, not its particular format, that matters in divine agency, and that this is repeatedly recognized throughout the finest strands of almost all religions, most notably in their willingness to infuse divine presence into *all* that lives while abdicating any idea that this somehow "democratizes" human specialness and, because of its seeming indiscretion, diminishes divine dignity. In this sense creation as an activity of God might be more richly understood, metaphorically, not as an external act but an internal one comparable to gestation.

There is emerging toward the end of this millennium an increasing appreciation of ecology, spearheaded in Euro-American cultures but slowly, very slowly infiltrating most other cultures as well. I want to acknowledge as my own the well-worn idea that at the heart of all ecological awareness is the notion of linkages; that this is implied in the meaning of the word itself: an ecology is a household defined by its relationships as worthy of attentive study; and that the notion of any life-form capable of surviving independently of other life-forms, or more generally of the whole world in which it lives, is not only theoretically infantile but pragmatically catastrophic, or potentially so. In fact, the appraisal that we are now in a vast ecological crisis—a verdict to which even a minimally reflective individual would bow—is in my judgment centered on this very issue of pragmatism and the tremendous ambiguity of its Jekyll-and-Hyde endorsements and applications (as I am using it here, *pragmatism* has the fairly precise meaning of "any viewpoint arguing that the purpose of thinking, and the primary test of its truthfulness, is achieved in the observable actions it produces"). There can be no doubt that the practicality of our industrial technologies and the easing of tasks they provide, such as the availability of textiles and travel that has made for greater security against the sabotages of nature and a facility in personal encounters and adventurousness, have largely gone to human benefit. But the fumes and exhaust, the gouging of the land for its ores and minerals, the toxification of water that have all simultaneously occurred, have in their own turn sabotaged the benefit. Linkages have become abundantly apparent in this situation, as has the reformed pragmatism needed to seek a well-being for the earth that understands the meaning of *networks* and refuses the isolated or individual advancement that might threaten the whole. This reformation will be a major task for the coming millennium, and both religion and science must gear up to engage it in far more conscientious ways than have yet occurred: "religion" and "science," as always in this book, meaning the people who affiliate with them. I will be taking up this issue of mutual linkages on our planet with some thoroughness in the next two chapters, though right now it also presents us with a further context for approaching the possibility of extraterrestrial life.

The primary linkage would be a sharing in the rhythms of the universe, with a special concentration on how it will end so as to acknowledge the common destiny of all. A second linkage is in the stardust. Perhaps a degree of poetic sentiment is required here, along with touches of scientific data. I mentioned earlier in the chapter that the only source we know of for many of the elements constituting our own bodies is located in the products of stellar explosions. Unless we wish to hypothesize that other life could emerge confined to relationships between hydrogen and helium (with just infinitesimal traces of a very few other elements), it is likely that stardust would account for its forms as well. There is also the linkage implied in our definition of life itself. Attempting such a definition can of course involve us in a labyrinth of viewpoints, such that adding one upon another might either forbid a final conclusion acceptable to all, causing the effort to die of exhaustion, or be a source of endless debate, causing the effort to die of confusion, probably accompanied by great rancor. As a result I would like to propose just four constituents to the definition, not in the hope of avoiding the above two difficulties, since such a hope would be naive, but because I think everyone would agree that these four are bedrock characteristics that no extended definition could do without (in chapter 5, when dealing explicitly with God's life, I will suggest not an extension but an intensification of these four into four others, and then examine how they might affect our understanding of these first four—though in this task I know my proposal will not meet the universal acceptance I am presuming for the first four). The characteristics are: metabolism, growth, reproduction, and autonomous abilities of adaptation to immediate environment. In life-forms other than terrestrial, including intelligent ones, it is obvious that the particular functioning of each of these might well be completely unknown to us. Finally, and looping us back to the first linkage, would be the communality shared by an assertion that a single source, a singularity in our previous descriptions, grounds the entirety of what is and effectively pervades it.

Two cautionary notes are now in order. The first pertains to how we would treat this extraterrestrial life should we come into contact with it. The prognosis here is quite dismal and is based on an appraisal of how we treat the nonhuman life we encounter here on earth. In my view the weight of this appraisal is overwhelmingly negative, as will become clear in chapter 3. Save for the occasional Gautama or St. Francis, or simply the unreservedly kind neighbor down the street, what we inevitably meet is an attitude or proprietorship over this life for the purpose of appropriating its use to our own ends; in other words, exploitation. This becomes exceptionally vicious when we move from our treatment of plants to that of animals when our exploitation serves no other purpose than the satisfaction of a grotesque vanity, as with the slaughter of animals so the wealthy can drape themselves in fur for the love of softness and the admiration of others, or the gratification of blood-lust through the maiming and killing of animals for sport, or the pursuit of lost years through the use of animal oils for the advertised effect of smoother, younger-looking skin. If this attitude weren't so disgusting and reprehensible, it would be laughable in its naivete and superficiality. The weight of the evidence indicates that we would proceed in exactly the same fashion with nonterrestrial life, at least if it were intellectually and therefore technologically our inferior. We would exploit it rapaciously for the basest of motives after a short initial period of curious suspicion as to how it might damage us. And if the life-forms were intelligent like ourselves, and we then looked toward how we treat each other for a sense of how we would treat them, the weight of the evidence would again suggest inevitable violence and attempts at exploitation, even should this intelligence, and correspondingly its technology, be clearly—perhaps vastly— superior to our own. We would also tend to attempt a justification of this by portraying the others in nonhuman terms or caricatures: the "gooks" or "krauts" Americans have fought in their various wars, for example, and the innate depravities and savagery attributed to them, are not far distant from the same xenophobic portraits that populate our literature with monstrous and hostile entities from other planets. This would stand a vague chance of being allayed only if the others were consistently benevolent, tolerant of our initial suspicion, generous in benefits we desired, and willing to embrace servitude long before equality would be entertained. These are harsh judgments about which I do not wish to quarrel with the reader. I can speak only for myself and some others, and in this way point out what I think millennia past as well as this present one imply as perhaps the singularly most important goal in the millennium approaching: the refinement of our moral life. This will occupy us again, more intensely in later pages, where religion will play a direct and irreplaceable role in the proposals offered.

The second caution is that while they were not described in religious terms, the four linkages are nonetheless rich ground for religious appropriation. This is a caution, in other words, against dismissing religion too easily from the discussion. Each of the linkages would provide an arena in which the primary category employed in the appropriation, as in all religious discourse, would be God, though not as an explanatory device distinct from the science involved in the linkages—this ancient preference, a concentration on transcendence as the ontological separateness between God and the universe, no longer assists dialogues between science and theology, though it is still the usual inference in prayer and piety—but as an integral and active factor in them: the origin and term of the universe, the source of life and maintenance of its characteristics. If God as such a factor is taken seriously, then we have a fifth linkage, the religious one identifying the same God as immanent to the whole of the universe, including whatever other life it houses. A second part of the caution pertains to the concern of the previous paragraph. It emerges from the disturbing observation that casting a cold eye on the history of human violence toward all forms of life tells of the chronic willingness of most religions—and especially Judaism, Christianity, and Islam—to justify and encourage this violence. Yet since I am allowing criteria to influence my judgment here that I will discuss only later when assessing religious convictions, I will simply suggest at this point that another task for Christian religion in the coming millennium, a basic one, is to highlight the moral refinement I mentioned above by building into its various theologies and pieties a *permanent* spirit of repentance acknowledging past wickedness, as well as a demand to refuse its repetition by labeling it clearly and without recourse evil, or in the more theologically exact designation, sin. For religion always has a properly parenetic function to fulfill, and this includes not only consolation but also accusation. A weakness of resolve in either area, producing in the first an undue harshness and in the second an undue laxity, becomes a weakness in moral persuasiveness that generates not refinement but degradation in the religion.

In the workings of the human mind there is an incomparable tendency to concentrate on concerns that appear to be uniquely human. I am thinking here not just of illustrations like ambition, pride, and hurt feelings, but also of weather forecasting, medical analysis, agricultural planning, and weapons theory. There is poetry, too, music, mathemat-

ics, and myth making. Also, as far as we know, we alone construct theologies. What I have been proposing in this chapter is that in the coming
millennium an attentiveness to the universe, its beginning, end, and likely
generation of other life-forms, encourages us away from a too intense
focus of these talents on ourselves toward a wider compass of interest.
Yet this does not forbid an appropriate self-interest, since we too are a
part of the universe to which we must attend. Nor does it try to deny
that in one sense all our thinking and feeling is centered on ourselves,
since we are the one engaging them in the language and continuous judgment going on in our minds. I am talking, in short, about a double
movement we must learn to engage more gracefully and generously: a
centripetal movement whereby we become willing to gather in all the
richness of experience we can, and then a centrifugal movement whereby,
in the processes of thought and feeling, language and judgment, we give
them out again in action as far as we can reach beyond ourselves: first to
the world and *all* its life, then to the universe and *whatever* it holds,
including the whispers of God. Then the ecology of which I previously
spoke becomes anchored in its only reliable source, an ecology of the
mind, and any agenda set for that most ancient passion taking us beyond ourselves, the passion of religion, becomes inclusive of everything
we can think, feel, articulate, and assess. The rest of the book is an attempt to assist a further delineation of such an agenda.

Chapter two

THE EARTH

PSYCHOLOGISTS TELL US that when people are asked what circumstance has provided them with the most satisfying sense of security and feelings of acceptance in their lives, they typically respond by recounting experiences of mother love. There is something intriguing in this response, both in itself and when it is also linked to the nearly universal imagery of our planet as Mother Earth. This seems to indicate that as individuals and as myth-making societies there is built into us from the very early realms of reflective consciousness the idea that the maternal captures in a privileged way our longing for safety and our desire for contexts in which we can exercise freedom without fear of its being ridiculed or withdrawn. Yet it is also this very safety in freedom that often causes us to act against the maternal in the certainty that no final or lasting punishment will occur but only temporary reproof and eventual forgiveness (those of us fortunate enough to have had good mothers in our family life know what I mean; those of us who have not will have to utilize testimonies from the first group). Religions have always made much of this positive experience of mother love—even ones, as most are, dominantly patriarchal in their foundational teachings and in the doctrines and past or present behavioral patterns based on them. Everywhere it is the woman-mother *in relationship to the child* who is presented as best demonstrating the human capacity for love, with its loyalty, compassion, tenderness, and humor. And any denigration of this idea is tolerated badly in most cultures, not just because the idea assists the power of mother-child bonding but because of its paramount importance in maintaining a continuous witness from one generation to the next of how our finest moral possibilities get expressed. For this reason we rarely incorporate into our mythologies, or even our everyday expectations, the idea of the wicked mother, though not of wicked step-mothers or of women directing their malice toward others different from their children. Also, we have preferred to de-emphasize in the mythologies and expectations similar positive traits of the father, with the possible exception of loyalty, even though we know that a man acting toward his children can demonstrate just as profound a compassion, tenderness, and humor as a woman toward hers. The cause of this discrepancy is a deeply acculturated one, apparently possessing no biological basis. Of herself a woman is neither more virtuous nor more viceful than a man.

Expectations of some similarity to those above also appear to guide much of our current attitude, and to the extent that we still image Earth as mother and allow this to affect our behavior, the image becomes *active*—that is, one eliciting more than just aesthetic appreciation—and begins to disregard overly literalist and dim-witted analyses, dismissing it as a morphological fantasy (the dominant tradition of Judeo-Christianity, on the other hand, has always been uncomfortable with the image, and therefore deprived it of much of its power, because in many mythologies it tends to divinize the earth's importance—typically captured in literate, often beautiful personifications as a goddess—whereas in Judeo-Christianity the planet can never be more than a creature). A certain presumption reigns that the planet will always provide the *security* we need to maintain our own life as a species, and other species their lives, and a *safety* against cosmic interlopers that might threaten it. Regarding this last, the science is inarguable that the earth has survived even mammoth collisions, debilitating to life-forms but never in three billion years annihilating them altogether. Nor have internal catastrophes such as volcanism, earthquakes, and glacial freezings even in massive instances been sufficient to snuff out vitality, and certainly not human vitality as it began to emerge in our ancestors some two to three million years ago. A feeling of safety thus occurs both because of the internal dynamics of the planet and the apparent protection our place in the solar system, and our solar system in the galaxy, provides—all the while recognizing, of course, that at particular locales these dynamics and protection are nonetheless regularly breached in destructive ways. Yet it is not this safety that will occupy us much in this chapter; we've already noted its ultimate failure when discussing the fate of the earth in chapter 1, and more profoundly still—should we develop technologies to escape the explosion of the Sun into red gianthood—the fate of the universe. Rather, our focus here will be on the issue of security, since it is the one far more pertinent to the coming millennium, and how it is we should exercise our freedom in safety. For while the safety seems guaranteed, at least for the planet as a whole and for a future of many millions of years, the security is surely not. My concentration will be on three constituents of the planet that are at the root of this security, that coax from our imaginations the very image of Earth as a life-giving and love-giving mother, and that provide elementary contexts in which we affirm or deny our cherishing of the image. The three constituents are land, water, and air.

A further preliminary point must be made. The presumption of forgiveness in most expectations of maternal behavior toward a child's errant and ungrateful ways, along with provisions of safety and security, is also frequently transferred to the earth. The earth will forgive damage to itself (this defined by an imposition on nonhuman agencies of human aesthetics) through efforts at restoring ecological balances—which here means health—by processes still only vaguely understood: a mixing and remixing of chemical and physical relationships that restore a marauded environment. To some extent this viewpoint has merit. Volcanoes can explode with exterminating effects and within a year many of the same flora and fauna begin to reappear on its slopes, with the ash settled into soil nutrients. But there are some damages so severe that dismal effects can remain for many years, a near permanence that can be recognized and absolved, but reversed, if at all, only by single-minded and diligent effort. Such is the concern with certain damages to the earth inflicted by us, unknowingly at first, but then culpably. The air and water are of special concern here, the land less so (though still urgently) because its utter immediacy to our lives insofar as we build on it, walk on it, grow on it, enjoying its solidity and textures, makes us somewhat more attentive to its well-being. We need water to survive, of course, and many of us often enjoy its surrounding embrace, floating and supporting us in ways more relaxing or invigorating than the land. And air we need most of all, surviving only a few minutes without it when the brain balks and begins to close us down. But the air is not seen or shaped or walked on, too taken for granted to enter often into our consciousness, even when badly fouled in our cities. And water, though seen and touched and tasted, usually gains a recognition only a bit more conscious than the one we give the air, even in locales where it does not run at our whim in faucets but must be sought in running streams and rivers. At least in English usage this preference for the land is perhaps best witnessed by the fact that our very name for the planet also functions to draw the following equation: earth = land, or soil. So, when we note the damage done to all three—land, air, and water—and set on the religious agenda for the coming millennium a healing of these, most of this task will likely be directed toward a finer and more urgent consciousness of the quality of air and water we require than toward the land. Such distinctions should never be facile, however, since for all of life the three are interwoven in an ecological symbiosis that forbids any attention to one without effects, sometimes serious effects, on the other two. The issue we are raising, rather, is one of emphasis, not exclusiveness.

There is a sense in which the earth is still gestating, and it seems that we are not the child to be born but only one developmental stage in a long and complex process. To some this image is a source for species pride, in the presumption that we represent a critical contribution that Earth's child will inherit for grace and benefit. To others, myself included, it is a source for species humility, in the acknowledgment that we are not the high point of creation, a terminus in the evolutionary process that portends no other, but rather a link along the way to what is coming. Yet in either case, the image also implies that things can go wrong during this gestation, a change in the womb-environment which, left unaddressed and unhealed, can trigger an abortion. It seems to me that religion urgently needs to re-teach this image, no longer glibly dismissing it as atavistic "paganism" (literally, the religion of country folk working the earth); that the image regards with utter seriousness our responsibility to the life of future years; that it establishes controlled growth as the mechanism for achieving healthy birth; and that Judeo-Christianity recognizes this in the Genesis narrative of the seventh day when the fullness of creation is finally achieved in a Sabbath peace that pervades the earth and all its inhabitants. This day, of course, will never be literally reached, even in countless turns of millennia, but is described instead to make imagination aware that *something* will succeed us, the creatures of the sixth day, but that we are in a position to prevent this from being a Sabbath peace, much like a fetus become restive in a damaged or soured womb seeks unwittingly to escape or terminate further growth. Then the mother, whatever her hopes or efforts to the contrary, is left only with tears. And while a science gone stale in its abstractions might belittle the expression of this sentiment, when recast into its own lifeless jargon it understands its truth to the bone.

The Land

Earth is the third planet from the Sun, a medium-yellow star of remarkable stability that has attached to itself eight other discovered planets and a host of comets, asteroids, and dust. Our best estimates indicate that it began to be formed primarily from gases and a percentage of dustlike particles swirling around an increasingly massive core about 4.5 to 5 billion years ago, and is consequently about the same age as the Sun itself. It is suggested by many theorists that much of these gases and particles are the remnants of at least one other star that previously existed somewhere in close vicinity to where our solar system now is, and then exploded under the pressures of gravitational collapse—as we noted in the last chapter, a fate our own Sun will someday undergo if our current data and speculations on stellar evolution are correct. As it cooled, the gas eventually solidified, forming all landmasses above and below the oceans, with regular increments to these masses still occurring, principally through volcanic eruptions and a settling down of cosmic dust from the upper atmosphere (but with regular erosion, too, primarily from wind and water). The lands above water, the continents, compose about one seventh of the surface of the planet, and are in slow but massive movements atop a series of tectonic plates at various depths below the surface. Earth is about 25,000 miles in circumference, 8,000 miles in diameter at the equator, and has one natural satellite, the Moon, much smaller than itself, with no water and only the thinnest veil of atmosphere, but nearly identical to the planet in age. All life on Earth is confined either to the surface or very shallow subsurface of the land, or to the water, with the possible exception of some very light, primitive, and continually airborne forms like bacteria and viruses. The planet is in a stable, slightly elliptical orbit around the Sun at a distance of around 93 million miles, taking 365 days to complete a full turn. Its various colors are caused by the way the chemical components of objects absorb, distort, and reflect light, and its seasons, where they are pronounced, are due to its spinning on its axis at a 23-degree angle to the plane of its orbit. Life-forms, according to the four characteristics I offered in the last chapter, emerged roughly three to four billion years ago and for about two thirds of the time since then were very simple in organization, the vast majority, if not all, likely being one-celled entities frequently congregating into large colonies, and water-bound. Human beings emerged from a complex evolutionary development from invertebrate to vertebrate to mammalian life-forms, and while we need to nourish ourselves from the water, we cannot live unaided within it. Our domain on the Earth, therefore, is quite circumscribed, and even on surface land must in differing places and at differing times be assisted with altering degrees of rigor.

Yet we assault this land relentlessly in that peculiar intellectual myopia that blurs the future beyond the current generation we happen to be in, and even here often not beyond the vagaries of an immediate profit or pleasure. Our assaults tend to be individually slight but cumulatively massive, though our nuclear weapons also make us capable of the spectacular violence the land can do to itself in geologic upheaval. We poison the land slowly with salts and other chemicals, degrade its strength by clear-cutting, gouge it out in open pits to satisfy metal and mineral needs or the needs of luxury in stones glowing red or green or crystal clear. The sweet smell of soil freshly wet gives way to asphalt and cement and artificial turf. This last, I'm told, can now be purchased with "earth fragrance, like the lawn in your childhood yard." Profanity has replaced sacredness in our attitude toward the land—the complaint of the great Aldo Leopold, the formulator of land-health ethics—just as the individual farmer is judged an old-fashioned relic to be gobbled up by entrepreneurs who value only the salability of a product, the perfect grain or fruit or vegetable, and not the land from which these grow except as a manipulable basis for agricultural greed. Researchers lend their cloying charms when they speak of a day when *all* the land will exist for whatever purpose we desire, since our food will then be grown in vats and reservoirs and atmospheres guaranteeing all needed nutrients with little or no soil required. In some perverse way Christianity may be a major culprit here, since it knows nothing in its traditions of a sacred land or sacred place, at least not one intensely or integrally linked to its self-definitions; there is no Israel or Mecca or Black Hills, and the closest Christianity probably comes to a similar locale is Calvary. Even the crusades were far more politically than religiously motivated, motivated more by colonizing and commercial strategies than spiritual ones. To say in response that for Christians "the whole world is ours, none of its particular places," has for much of Christian history been simply to extend this same motivation globally. For in not avowing special reverence for *this* place, a reverence that particularizes sacred presence in a single and fairly limited location, there is little motive for avowing reverence for *any* place (we must clearly acknowledge, of course, that in itself reverence for a single locale by no means guarantees an expanded reverence for the entire earth; but at least it gives the idea some initiative). It is only partly fair to lay the blame for this spirit of universal proprietorship and the failure to reverence the Earth on the Christian appropriation of the infamous and often misunderstood mandate in Genesis to "subdue" the earth; there is also the brute fact that as humans moved from small hunting/gathering societies to larger agricultural ones, they simultaneously moved from gaining sustenance *in* nature to gaining it *against* nature (it is in this latter situation that nature comes to be seen as recalcitrant, "wild," and needing to be "tamed" or subdued). Yet Christianity is just one illustration, though possibly the most rancorous and land-destructive, of similar observations that could be made of other religions under parallel influences from their own traditions and societal development. On the other hand, in its attitude of refusing a specialness to one place which no others possess, Christianity also offers a stunning clue to a marvelous reform it might assist in bringing about in the coming millennium if, as seems inevitable, our consciousness continues to regard the planet in increasingly smaller and more intimate ways as a single organism, the mother organism gestating life; or for those more comfortable with our other, sociological rather than biological designation, a single place, a village.

But another result is equally possible. There have been few things that have ushered in as much destructiveness in human behavior as the defense of land. Partly this is due to a spirit of proprietorship over land that is owned and under threat, but also, and more indefinitely, to a spirit of identity with the land. It is this latter phenomenon that particularly sustains so much of the rhetoric and driving motive of war, whether between nations, neighborhoods, or even households. To attack the land is to attack the person who has become one with it—and not usually in some secular mystic rapture that amounts to little more than a spiritual malaise too weak or indolent to seek an unseen God, nor in an appreciation of oneself as a representative of other life that might also live there, but from the brute geography of place and the security and stability this provides, as with the borders of a country or a homestead. At this point the spirit of proprietorship can re-emerge in force and, linked to the sense of identity, can carry with it this sad and telling truth: that many of us identify who we are with what we own, and assault on the latter is the same as assault on the former. The land is no longer sacred here, a gift or beauty unto itself, but an extension of ego wrapped in a shotgun narcissism that tolerates no counterclaims to personal or group ownership. Fields of life then become killing fields where we walk in jackboots, alert to our defense and little else, certainly not the voice of God that can speak through a forest or in the contours of a mountain straining high in a plain. It is no longer theology we think of, but strategies and tactics of aggression; it is not prayers of adoration that cross our lips but of boastful or terrified or whining petition that we may defeat our enemy. The dirt of the land becomes soaked in the same sweat that bathes our bodies in fright.

Part of the motive for the possessiveness many nowadays feel toward the land they occupy springs from an awareness that the earth is getting smaller: not literally, of course, but in the growing population occupying the most productive or pleasant portions of it—a sense of shrinkage, therefore, in addition to the increasing ease of travel and communication previously mentioned. A need for privacy becomes more thoroughly felt, more urgent, along with the feeling of security that privacy often produces. This need varies among human populations. Many Japanese, for example, appear to possess far less of it, at least as a structured requirement in their ordinary lives, than, say, many Americans. This is why the American, on viewing the relative smallness of so many family quarters in Japan, along with such accepted practices as public bathing, often registers incomprehension, or shock, at how the Japanese can live this way. The assessments are almost always negative; descriptive terms like "cramped," "claustrophobic," and "insect colony" are used with an easy facility. The Japanese counter-descriptions of the American need for privacy as "excessive," "selfish," "anti-community," and "spoiled" are equally harsh. Yet the mutual descriptions are both quite pointless, since the issue is not the fact but the *extent* of the need for privacy, nor of a land of one's own so much as a space of one's own. Every Japanese must have privacy, places for withdrawal and solitude, and will defend this forcefully, just as every American would do the same regarding his or her need for the community, sometimes the intense community of others. The issue, as we said, resolves itself into one of the respective degrees of these needs, not of their absence or presence. But as the possession of a private space of one's own in some fashion always involves the use of a land of one's own (though here not necessarily meaning proprietorship of the land, but free access to it) the land must again be safeguarded and reverenced for this purpose, even if it be but a city park in which one can walk at will, a segment of beach, a portion of meadow, or a small apartment sitting on top a tiny parcel of the planet's terrain.

If we presume as legitimate the metaphor of the earth as a global village—recognizing its instigation in the growing ease of travel and communication as well as growing populations—and confine ourselves to its primary intent, there is still another immediate and, in my judgment, critically important conclusion we can draw. It is that as our knowledge of each other becomes more accessible and widely spread, an intensification of pluralism will occur (as is already occurring now) that will lead to confusion and a corresponding entrenchment in defense of one's own sociological, political, philosophical, and theological visions. This is what underlies much of the above appraisals of Japanese and American citizens as they enter into growing and more complex contacts with each other. We also see it occurring among several of the larger religions: Roman Catholicism and Buddhism, for example, or, though still at the very early stages, Roman Catholicism and Islam. This confusion can make for fear that a way of life long held and revered is being threatened, which in turn can lead to outright hostility, or in the case of religions, if hostility is refused, a dogmatic deadlock beyond which further conversation is either abandoned or politely but ineffectively pursued. But these responses cannot be more than stop-gap devotions to distinct and unmalleable identities that the coming millennium will in its own turn demand that we finally abandon, if the global village that seems inevitable is to cease being at civil war with itself spiritually, intellectually, or politically—like a disparate ethnic or racial neighborhood whose members finally drive each other away, or in an exhaustion of antagonism, simply learn to ignore each other—and become a community.

Since I will be taking the issue up at some length in chapter 4, I will only note here that the gradual flattening out of pluralistic confusion into a communal identity contains the worrisome possibility of ideological rigidity—that is, a leveling out that permits no distinctiveness and is therefore something like an intellectual analogue to the state of entropy some scientists describe as the ultimate fate of all closed physical systems, a condition where there is no distinctiveness but instead an utter evenness in the distribution of matter and energy. And as these same scientists judge this as designating the final death of things, the condition of the complete collapse of all uniqueness save for the mere occupation of one "point" of space-time as compared to another, so a similar situation socio-psychologically would produce the demise of uniqueness, in this case critical imagination capable of questioning established paradigms of thought and proposing others in their stead. As a result, when I speak of pluralism leading to community as a global village gradually gets established through the growing accessibility of travel and communication, and the land concurrently becomes less and less a barrier to this, I am not recommending an ideologically complete society where creativity is shunned or even persecuted, an Orwellian or Bradburyan sacrifice of the individual rebel for the sake of the group's peace of mind purchased by intellectual paralysis and ritualized secularly and religiously by the demand for brute repetition of patterns of thought and behavior. In chapter 4 I will discuss this issue specifically within the distinction I will draw between moral absolutism and moral relativism, especially when assessing Jesus' doctrine on love. For now I wish only to suggest that the move from distractive or confusing pluralism to community, without slippage into a tyrannizing ideology, must be explicitly encouraged on any agenda for Christian religion in the coming millennium.

It is early summer while I am writing this, and the previous winter was a cold and arduous one for me. As is my custom, I went out for a walk two evenings ago, well after nightfall, and this time, instead of the stars, it was the sweet smell of soil, the land coming into its own again as a house for abundant life, that captured my attention. I was musing over the ideas in the last two paragraphs, and seeking some inspiration for what I wished to say of the land from my own religious tradition, when I happened upon a point where a small meadow filled with wildflowers became visible, wrapped in a moonlight that for a moment gave them a silver beauty otherwise gone in the sun's light. It was the notion of a promised land that came to me, the refrain of migration to a good place that weaves itself throughout the Old Testament, and specifically a memory of the text that speaks of Moses seeing the goal of the tragedy and comedy that was the Exodus lying before him, but that he was too old and weak and unworthy to enter. This notion of a promised land has to break the confines of geography and history and become more than the territory of a particular people. It must become the whole earth as we walk it, drawing into our mind the same sense of giftedness and gratitude for a promise kept which the ancient Hebrews felt for the land of milk and honey. A meadow can become a catalyst doing the same for us, though each of us, like Moses, will also know that walking an earth finally seen as a sacred place, a land indulgent in rich benefits and not to be blasphemed, will belong not to us but only, if at all, to generations ahead. And if we cannot believe, like the Jew, that it is God who grants this promise and whose fidelity makes it possible, then we must make the promise ourselves and seek a similar fidelity toward it. In this consent to the sacredness of the land, together with the intimacy of world-sharing our travel and communication technologies are making available, we can begin to speak of the planet not just as a coming global village, but in a description much older and religiously attuned, an *oikumene* as a gathering of all for common purposes and goals whose ecumenism is driven both by a desire for novelty in searching out each other's thoughts, and a communion that will safeguard this desire by reverence for it.

There is a certain point beyond which thought and speech cannot go. The Greeks called it *aporia,* and suggested that if any further effort was to be engaged at such points, it had to be not of the intellect but of the will. Something similar occurs in religions when describing the motivational power of faith as first seeking knowledge and understanding, and then at the moment of conviction, acts. It is for this reason, too, that religions tend to emphasize the importance of obedience as a process of interior discipline, an intense and undistracted concentration to achieve confidence regarding the meaning of an experience or proposition (in fact, the English word *obedience* comes from the Latin *ob* + *audire,* the intensive prefix emphasizing the meaning of the primary word, "to hear or listen or contemplate"). One can be presented with a ton of reports and analyses drawn from scientific observation of the land and our treatment of it, especially by mechanical rearrangement and chemical supplementation, and have it in mind that they should be taken seriously. But unless some process like obedience occurs, such reports will evoke at best only a momentary shock providing no basis for conviction. In these instances the experience of *aporia* either doesn't occur at all, or results in a stymied intellect unable to activate the will. Lamentation rather than action then follows. In the reflections here I have been presuming the reader's general knowledge of the alarming diagnoses regularly publicized by private and public national and international organizations regarding our use of the land; it is, after all, difficult to miss at least the critical outlines of such knowledge simply by reading newspapers or listening to television or radio coverage. What I have been engaging in, therefore, is what religious traditions call *parenesis,* that is, a challenge to the will based on knowledge already possessed; or, at a more primordial level, a challenge just to gain the knowledge. I can obviously not provide such knowledge here, at least not in its details—that is not the purpose of this book—but instead can witness to its availability, strengthen its legitimacy by encouraging the simple exercise of common sense when we see the land ravaged, and insist that a counteractivity of healing must occur. This is not just parenesis, then, but the kind that the prophets of every religion—especially Judeo-Christianity, Islam, Hinduism, and Buddhism—tell us we must make our own. Those ridiculing such prophetic parenesis as useless piety, idealistic nonsense, or out of tune with the hard reality of human need or greed, do not understand the very heart of religious engagement with the world and thereby do a flippant and radical disservice to the richness of their minds.

There has been a common idea that life emerged from the sea. We noted several paragraphs ago that its first forms combined molecularly into very simple types of bacteria, or possibly viruses, and algae, and that these were almost exclusively the life-forms on the planet for about 2 billion years, or roughly two thirds of the time there has been life at all. Recent suggestions, however, are indicating that life's emergence is far more closely linked to the land than previously thought, and scientists supporting this view speak of its beginning in an ambience of chemically appropriate and water-saturated clay, probably on the edges of shallow tidepools. Certainly our own particular type of life—vertebrate, mammal, primate—evolved on land, derived, some think, from an amphibian that in some time long past crawled up onto the surface of the land and made it home. But that initial ambience remains with us, not only in our need to drink water frequently to survive, but in the huge percentage of our bodies that is composed of water as well as the remarkable similarity between the fluid in which the enwombed fetus grows and seawater. But the religious mind, particularly one trained in Judeo-Christian traditions, will have likely leapt to the suggestion about clay as a substrate of life, since a common translation of the word used in the second chapter of Genesis to describe the material from which God formed Adam is "clay" (curiously, and probably for reasons of patriarchalism and to indicate the seriousness of the marriage covenant, the woman is formed of man upon worry for his loneliness). The creation of human beings on the model of God as an artist is frequent in religious mythologies, and in the last chapter we noted that it likely points to an understanding of the creative act *not* as drawing something from nothing but as giving form to what was formless, or more exactly said, changing its form in a radical way, much like the sculptor does to a chunk of marble or a collection of metals, or a woman does to living tissues in her gestating womb. The important point for the moment, however, is that in this rendition of the narrative, along with the notion of the promised land, we have—at least from the biblical perspective—still a further link between the land and our lives.

But there is another translation of the Hebrew term frequently offered in place of "clay"; it is the word "dust." This is a very intriguing translation, since to the Hebrew mind the smallest size that particulate matter could be reduced to was dust; that beyond this there was nothing. The Hebrews, in other words, never developed in their major scriptural traditions anything like the "atoms" of Democritean physics, the unobservable individual components that are only indirectly experienced as they congregate into tangible realities—or, for some adherents of the theory, as they can be directly sensed in smell, sometimes taste. The important point, though, is not whether the Hebrews aligned themselves with the Greeks on a *descriptive* level, but that they also thought that matter is always ultimately reducible to its smallest parts, and that here is where we can discover in a privileged yet not exclusive way the creative agency of God. In *ontological* descriptions, therefore, they would have had no aversion to Democritus' atoms—any more than they would to protons, quarks, and gluons—though they would have found little point in discussing seriously as the components of material objects particles that in themselves could not be sensed. This dust, then, brings us back to remarks made in the last chapter when noting that we are made of stardust—that there are elements in our bodies that were locked in the land as the residues of exploding stars were caught in the gravitational tug of our planet while it was being formed. We are made from the land, as it weds with water, and this fact remains whether the medium is gross, as with clay, or refined, as with dust, still more as with atomic, subatomic, or subnuclear particles. Somewhere in the lineage of both these parents, and in the marriage between them, religion must itself wed with science and look for God as life giver.

Genesis also states that subsequent to death we will return to this dust from which we came. Judeo-Christian tradition has had a predilection for understanding this as a curse, though the context itself justifies no such approach: it is a mere statement of fact premised on observations of the decay of corpses, eventually even the powdering of bones. From one aesthetic bias, of course, this image can indeed produce feelings of horror, of beautiful flesh distancing itself in a parade of rot from the life it has left, reduced finally to no sense-perceptive remnants at all. Embalming it, freezing it, locking it in tight coffins and tombs is scarce consolation, since these measures only delay the process whereby the earth consumes us in a communion that makes us once more a part of itself. In some contemporary ecologies this is seen as a marvelous irony, or a tremendous justice, in that the land we have brutalized and profaned so badly is the final victor conquering us. I am not entirely unsympathetic to this view, but it lacks a certain richness of meaning, first because it concentrates so thoroughly on the end of life, and secondly because it tends to be exclusively anthropocentric. My own preference, therefore, is to engage the wholeness of the image, "for dust you are and to dust you shall return," and find in it not a curse but a completeness, a rounding of the circle whereby we return to whence we came, and so an abandonment of all understandings of history as linear (in which death is a stop that leaves us behind) in favor of an understanding of it as circular—an apparent line only because death itself excludes our seeing the curve that guides it back to its source, which for religion is God. On this point a relevant though not yet unanimous science can speak to us as well: in the whirl of possibilities that brought us forth from stardust and ultimately returns us there, there exists a space-time continuum of endlessly self-generating proportions that can bring us forth again. Religions talk about this as reincarnation, and Christianity specifically as resurrection, though in either case an exclusive species orientation (only human beings can come alive again) must clearly be relinquished. These speculations will occupy us more intimately in chapter 5, where we propose for our agenda the outline of an understanding of God appropriate to them. But for now a contentment must arise for the simple idea that the end is like the beginning, but that this beginning can begin things anew.

Every early summer I attend to my two small gardens. I grow only flowering plants, and for years I used the land solely for the sake of their beauty; my attitude, in other words, was that of the utilitarian dilettante. Perhaps it takes a number of years of living before we can begin to appreciate the linkages between things. In my gardens this occurred when I realized that tied to my appreciation of the beauty of the flowers was the delight I had also gained from the feel and smell of the soil—and that without this the beauty of the flowers would somehow be diminished in its effect on me. I likewise began to notice more seriously that the gardens also accumulated beauty in formats other than flowers: insects of delicate colors and geometries, a beauty in lives that from first to last are drenched in violence. And the knowledge began to grow that the land was in fact a triple source for my pleasure in what it could bring forth in the bloom of plants, the small lives these nourished, and in itself, its textures and fragrance. And what this began to defeat was an attitude I now found particularly unsettling, except in the deepest intensity of love: that ancient vice that Christian piety calls presumption and a secular jargon calls taking something for granted. For years I had taken the land for granted—all the land, not just that of my gardens—with but rare appreciation when faced with stunning vistas that even my presumption could not ignore. But the gardens slowly taught me otherwise, and the land has become something whose importance I have now sought to convey in these pages. And there is one more thing, taken for granted even longer than the land, but the very thing that releases its fragrance, softens its feel, lets the flowers form and unfold, and brings the insects to them, all the many years using it, wasting it, presuming its availability and its health. I must turn to this one thing now, the second of the three components I have isolated in this chapter when describing the earth we experience. It is water.

The Water

What saves anything from dissolving as soon as it is formed is the enduring insistence of subnuclear, nuclear, and atomic particles on staying bound together, and then the way atoms bind together among themselves into molecules. As noted in the last chapter, physicists tell us that at the simplest levels of atomic organization this is due to the operation of two fundamental forces prevailing throughout the known universe: electromagnetism (e.g., the force that binds electrons to atomic nuclei) and the strong nuclear force (the force that holds protons and neutrons together in the atomic nucleus and holds quarks together in these particles). These two forces are further supplemented by the weak nuclear force (the force that generates ordinary radioactive decay) and gravity (the attractive force between any two masses), which is very slight and is usually considered a factor only in macrocosmic relationships, such as our bodies held to the earth, the earth to the sun, and so on. For the universe as we experience it, molecular bonding is paramount, the talent of diverse atoms to lock together in ever increasing numbers, *and to stay together,* that produces everything observable to our senses. This fact has been a constant source of wonder to scientists, and unraveling the mechanisms of the binding forces has been an obsessive interest of physicists since the time of Newton, above all in this century with the work of men like Max Planck, Niels Bohr, Werner Heisenberg, and of course, Albert Einstein. Captured in two questions, this interest can be stated, "Why do things cohere?" and, once resolving this in a description of the fundamental forces, "What causes the binding forces to behave the way they do?" All answers to the second question still remain theoretical, though considerable consensus has emerged that certainty will be found in the accurate analysis of the specific motions of the particles—wave, spin, and orbital motions in particular—and the exchange of energies these produce. But beyond this general consensus there still lie fields of tremendous controversy, and few scientists, I suspect, would share the view of Stephen Hawking that we are on the verge of a compelling or incontrovertible answer to the question. One of the issues that is clearly lingering in the mind here, for example, is whether the *entire* universe is subject to the same physical parameters we have so far been able to observe in only the very limited ways our technologies provide, an issue that frequently resolves itself more into a philosophical or theological than a scientific stance.

There is a spiritual or psychological analogue to the above coherence that causes the universe to achieve its distinct shapes and sizes, and it is found in the contents of memory. They also endure because their discrete elements hold together to form singular wholes that can themselves link together in what is technically called inclusive memory, or more commonly, a train of memory. Whatever the physical substrate is that enables the brain to achieve this ability—and in brain physiology it produces the same wonder in the biologist that the composition and function of the four elemental forces do in the physicist—two quite definite statements can be made about it. The first is that the coherence through which memory is achieved is far less reliable than that which holds macrocosmic objects together (for our purposes here, anything resulting from large-scale intermolecular bonding). This is why memory is capable of amazingly accurate representation of past experiences while at the same time producing significant distortions. The second statement is that just as we define the distinctness of an object by the coherence of its molecules, so we commonly define our identities as human beings distinct from each other by the coherence of our memories. This is why when memories loosen or deteriorate from illness or age, the affected individual in moments of analytic lucidity will frequently describe this as a loss of selfhood, a diminishment of a sense of uniqueness or of a fading into surroundings, past or present experiences, in which he or she is a component but no longer a reflective observer of them. Because we typically think that beneath a certain level of cerebral development non-human life-forms do not possess a sense of individual identity, we talk about such people as being like vegetables, just as we describe similarly those suffering a loss of consciousness in permanent comas. For many, unfortunately, the concurrent judgment also occurs that this has drastically reduced their value.

Water, of course, is one of the many coherences absolutely essential to our physical lives, not only as they are constituted (our bodies are well over 90 percent water) but as they are nurtured (we must continually replace the water we lose, and most of us can live only two or three days without ingesting an external supply). The coherence is on the atomic level, as every schoolchild knows, when two hydrogen atoms bond to an oxygen atom, making for a slightly blue color and a slight compressibility. This is *pure* water and is rarely accessible to us, since our *ordinary* water has other chemical elements attached to it either through "natural" atomic bonding such as the addition of a neutron to the hydrogen atom (which is otherwise a single proton and single electron) or through bondings imposed by us for purposes of health or, often carelessly, through some contamination of the water supply. While there are two hydrogen atoms and one oxygen atom in each water molecule, oxygen is nonetheless the dominant presence, possessing a much larger atomic structure and greater weight. Oxygen—in itself colorless, tasteless, and odorless—is in fact the most abundant of all the elements on the earth's surface, since it constitutes in itself and in combination with other elements such as hydrogen fully eight-ninths by weight of water on the planet, almost one half by weight of the rocks forming the earth's crust, about 23 percent of the air we breathe, and is a varying but large component of all organic, that is, carbon-based, compounds. The vast majority of water on the planet is found in the oceans, which themselves compose nearly three quarters of the surface of the globe, but which are all saltwater and therefore undrinkable by us and all land-dwelling animals and plants. While we draw other nourishment from the oceans in plant and animal forms, and until techniques for desalinating ocean water become financially more feasible on a large scale, our immediate concern is with so-called *freshwater,* found mostly in rivers, streams, inland lakes, springs (surface and subterranean), aquifers (a water-bearing bed or stratum of soil, gravel, or porous stone), and, supplying all these, rain and melted snow and ice. It is these last two, then, upon which we are most dependent for our freshwater, not just because they feed the other sources but because clouds are still the most spectacularly successful, though often unreliable, vehicles for moving them in an evaporated state over land. Without water, needless to say, there can be *no* life as we know it, and its discovery elsewhere in the universe is one of the principal and enduring goals of space technologies.

In the coming millennium there is no doubt that the major issue confronting our supply of freshwater is pollution. Everyone is aware of the contaminants that enter the rivers and lakes of the world every day—in some locales, technologically advanced ones, far more than in others—and how toxic it can eventually become. A blase attitude wishing to bypass the seriousness of this problem will typically do so in one of two ways. The first is to claim that much if not most of the damaged water ends up in the oceans, and that these vast expanses, precisely because of their very size, are able to absorb and "purify" through chemical reactions whatever amount of contaminants enter them, meanwhile allowing streams and rivers to continue flowing fresh from their sources. This stance is badly mistaken for at least four reasons. First, large portions of the water do not in fact make their way to the oceans; there are countless lakes, for example, that are landlocked and rivers that terminate in such lakes or in delta-like dispersions over the land. Secondly, polluted water can soak deeply into the ground and damage aquifers and subterranean springs. Thirdly, the source of freshwater in rain and melting snow can itself be thoroughly damaged, as recent experiences with acid rain have shown. Fourthly, the oceans themselves are not inexhaustible dumping grounds into which we can deposit without effect whatever wastes and toxins we wish—most immediately the quality, and in many cases the continued existence, of marine life is affected; more remotely, the quality of ocean-formed clouds is affected, thereby establishing a vicious circle of cause and effect between the source and final destination of most of our rain. The oceans as the scapegoat for much of our misbehavior in the environment is a grotesque image and a profound expression of immorality. And this judgment is only enhanced by the outrageous naivete that is unaware of *cumulative* effects. It is as if the pollutants dumped into the seas—let us say, from the latest oil spill, killing off as far as it reaches oxygen-giving phytoplankton and countless other life-forms—is *sui generis*, a singular event with parallels only to other oil spills, causing quick concern because brightly lit by media coverage, but if far enough away, soon forgotten.

A second way of bypassing the seriousness of freshwater shortages is to presume reliance on technologies that will successfully address the pollution. This is typically discussed in terms of financially viable desalination machines to tap the oceans, or reliably effective machines to filter freshwater from lakes, rivers, and reservoirs. This last is a technology many of us in the United States and elsewhere are already familiar with at any water processing plant near regions of sizable population. The United States, in fact, can take much credit in the way several of its individual states have effectively addressed water contamination at a given source: the gradual cleansing of Lake Erie comes immediately to mind, but so do efforts toward cleansing the Willamette River in Portland, Oregon, where I live. Many other examples could also be cited, though the list is not yet nearly long enough, and in many countries doesn't exist at all. But while these efforts are certainly to be commended, they tend to emphasize for praise the cleansing of the *water's* source, rather than the source of the pollution itself. Here much remains to be done, both in the United States and even more, much more throughout most other industrialized countries. And there is a further consideration, usually somewhat obliquely present in such recommendations. Ideas presuming that the oceans can absorb the results of our malfeasance toward nature, or that technologies independent of our behavior will soon enough resolve contamination problems, also tend to reinforce an overly profligate use of water within a freedom dominated by human pleasure and refusing or forgetting to look much further into the future than the current or succeeding couple of generations, surely not an entire coming millennium. It is this tendency toward a foreshortening of vision that an ethics guiding science must begin to address much more comfortably and conscientiously than has previously occurred—and not, of course, just with regard to the availability of freshwater. And religion must do so too, especially since in most of its forms, particularly Christianity, there has always been a willingness to look far into the future to perceive goals affecting present behavior.

The willingness to attend to a distant future is not the only contribution Christian religion can make toward present-day decisions. There is also the obligation of encouraging ascesis, as all religions must, and in their finer traditions, do. "Ascesis" itself is a word drawn from ancient Greek ethics and aesthetics, though what it intends to capture finds analogues in all other cultures. Its specific meaning is that of the regimen an athlete undergoes to achieve a competitive goal. In the sports arena the competitors are obviously other athletes. The regimen is one of an enhanced discipline that always involves degrees of self-sacrifice, with the most acute attention paid to proclivities toward physical or spiritual indolence. And so there are exercises, constant exercises of various kinds appropriate to achieving the goal. Additionally, because any ethic, including a sports ethic, is always generously sensitive to the appeal of pride, or what the Greeks themselves called *hubris,* there is an emphasis on particular physical and spiritual exercises leading to the practice of humility, whether or not one wins the competition. If there is anything in their teachings on ascesis that religions dislike more than a refusal of adequate discipline, a slovenliness indicating that one in fact does not take the professed goal seriously—words, in short, that are not loyally reproduced in deeds—it is the arrogant victor, the one who boasts of success without recognizing the assistance of others—above all, for the Greek and every other religious standpoint, the divine. If the goal is worthwhile, it is an ascesis demonstrating a commitment cloaked in humility that makes life worthwhile. Or differently: to the well-known Socratic maxim that "the unexamined life is not worth living," we must add another that the Hebrew prophets, or any religiously alert culture, would also affirm, namely (in the words of H. Rolston), that "the uncommitted life is not worth examining." Drawn from two millennia ago, the encouragement of this same twinning of maxims must continue to reside on any Christian agenda for the coming millennium, whether we are talking, as in the chapter titles of this book, of the universe, the earth and its land, water, and air, nonhuman life, human life, or the divine life we encounter.

It is foolish to deny or ignore the competitiveness we find in the world. Anyone even remotely observant of the ways of life can see struggle everywhere, not a pacific but a blood-letting kind. It compelled the unerringly compassionate Darwin to write in morose agony over the lack of peace wherever we seem to look, "Oh, what a book a devil's chaplain might write on the clumsy, wasteful, blundering, low, and horribly cruel works of nature!" We will talk about such struggles more thoroughly in the next two chapters. For now, though, there is another type of competition, certainly not the blood-letting kind, and not fully the athletic kind from which the notion of ascesis derives, but one that borrows from the second in a way more attentive to the concerns of Christian religion. For if the asceticism this religion encourages to reach its goals, especially its distant ones, requires discipline to succeed, it requires equally an informed awareness of those factors that are competing with us to secure our defeat. This is almost exclusively an issue of attitudes, and the ascesis involved is correspondingly spiritual, that is, a discipline in patterns of thought. And while this is obviously as true of the athlete—the appropriate mind-set is required to produce the appropriate exercise—there are two qualifications when the context becomes Christian living. The first is that the athlete's goal is relatively immediate and available for personal satisfaction: The athlete does not train for the benefit of future generations but for his or her own success; only secondarily might the knowledge gained through the training be eventually taught to youngsters of the next generation, when one's own glory days are over. Secondly, unless the athlete is a member of a team, the ascesis is privately or singularly engaged without regard to the need for communal coherence toward victory; any victory or defeat can only be an individual conclusion. This second qualification, therefore, makes the ascesis of the noncommunal athlete completely irrelevant to the concerns of this chapter, since victory in maintaining an ascesis that will assure the *continual* availability of something like freshwater or a fertile land and healthy air is not only a distant goal—and, unlike the final conclusion of an athletic competition, one that can be lost if the ascesis is subsequently ignored—it is also a goal that can be secured only by a group effort, no matter how heroic the discipline of this or that individual participant may be.

Most religions, and Christianity in its profounder traditions, have consistently recognized this second qualification in their clear preference for understanding the human community, even the whole world or the whole of creation, as organic. The controlling metaphor is the human body, with the commonsense observation that none of its individual parts can function successfully unless maintained in symbiotic community with other parts. Take any one of them out of this community, its web of interactive relationships, and its purpose utterly ceases. An eye or ear, heart or stomach removed from the body and laid on a table is reduced to a clump of tissue useful only for the secondary purposes of morphological study. Only as a member of the whole does the individual organ become competent in it contribution to life. These facts have impressed the formulators of religious doctrines as remarkably appropriate toward understanding the intent and obligations of human living. And while most of them, especially within Christianity, would be reluctant to gainsay the importance of the individual, any more than we would the eyes or hearts or stomachs of our bodies, it is clear that this importance nonetheless resides entirely within the relationships to other members of the community, even when this community is so truncated as to include only God: the tightened and inhuman community of Nietzsche's "saint" and all others like him. All religious notions of a corporate personality—a cosmic Adam, a universal Brahman, a Body of Christ—are built upon this premise, and all strictly egalitarian ideologies—presuming to locate autonomous value or dignity in the individual exclusive of communal placement and function—are inherently divisive of human community insofar as they attempt to flatten out differences so that any individual becomes "in essence" the same as every other one in a spiritual monotony that makes the worth of the whole no different from the worth of the one, which in sad cases can catalyze the most confused or criminal behavior. Whether it is vice or virtue we seek, the seeking is assured its most thorough success when we do it together according to our own contributing individual talents.

The ritual signifying acknowledgment that someone has been judged competent to be a member of the ritualizing community is in many religions similar to the baptismal practice in most forms of Christianity. There is a sponsor, someone guaranteeing the rightness or worthiness of the person's membership as determined by accurate training and the proof of this in corresponding deeds (if the one to be welcomed is an infant or child, the sponsor is usually the one assuming responsibility for this training and monitoring the deeds). There are statements of commitment to the way of life being professed, followed by ones of promise for the life so lived, that together commitment and promise establish a covenant between the individual and the community, preeminently including God. There are also celebratory statements of thanksgiving, ones that serve, at least in Christianity, the further purpose of uniting one intent of baptism with the defining intent of the eucharist, a ritual whose very name derives from the Greek verb for offering thanks. Additional statements convey hope for strength of will in seizing opportunities to express the commitment while resisting those that might obscure or deny it, so capturing the two qualities, strength and opportunities, which St. Paul suggests (or so it seems to me) are the defining traits of grace. Above all there is the use of water to signify a bathing and rebirth. Throughout religions, baptismal rituals—or their analogues in rites of passage—are probably the most sacred use to which water is put. The bathing intends to signify the abandonment or washing clean of a previous way of life that is inevitably understood as a less worthy one, even wicked or innately perverse, as in old Christian doctrines of original sin (in a peculiar offense against the God of Jesus, these doctrines extend this wickedness or perversity, this distortion of orientation, even to newborns). The metaphor of rebirth represents the final act of this abandonment, in which the water now functions less as a vehicle for cleansing than as an analogue to the water in the womb, whose release heralds the child's first birth. At the central moment of the ritual the individual is therefore immersed in water and then emerges from it, though to avoid logistic complications or potential embarrassment in such a procedure, it is also quite common to be satisfied with simply pouring some water over a part of the body, almost always the head. At the conclusion of the ritual reminders of what has just occurred are pronounced, and these are usually followed by a festive celebration. Water has again become the key element in understanding the emergence of life, symbolically now rather than biologically.

There is more. In the grip of extreme instances of joy or sadness water again plays both a physical and deeply symbolic role. I am referring to tears. While many other animals possess tear ducts, as far as we know only in human beings can tears become an aesthetic expression of profound emotional release or the trauma of robust laughter. Otherwise they function, as with other animals, as a cleansing mechanism for the eyes, and we may anticipate a concern of the next section by noting that they are therefore a prime indicator that the air we are breathing is foul. As noted at the beginning of chapter 1, this double symbolic function of either sadness or joy/laughter is universal among human beings, much like the closed fist of anger or victory, and provides an access to communication between cultures that spoken language frequently does not. To stem their flow, then, as in the insistent counsel of many parents toward young sons, is not only to deprive the individual of a privileged outlet for emotional tension and struggle, but in a clandestine way to refuse a communality in humanity when symbols expressing it are rare and to be cherished. Religions even know of weeping deities. And while a Christian doctrine preferring to avoid such depictions as too anthropomorphic and so demeaning to divine dignity has had its way with most theologians, Christian artists have often seen tears as expressing best our linkage to deity, even *the* linkage in the person of Jesus whipped, crucified, and dying. In popular Christian piety tears have also been viewed as a favored medium of healing, as in purported vials of the tears of Christ or cloths on which they've fallen that populate some European Catholic churches. Sometimes, however, tears also just happen, somewhat spontaneously and without identifiable cause, and then they tell us not so much of a oneness we share in matters of sadness and joy but of a oneness in the way life seeps out of us, ineluctably as with water poured from a jar, a harbinger of final emptiness, death whose ache we wish healed with new life.

Water is also a key ingredient in other of our activities—ones now required rather than optional as in baptismal rituals—that can also possess a profoundly symbolic function. Eating comes immediately to mind, and while we can certainly eat without an overt use of water (though covertly, of course, everything we eat is predominantly water), its use in flavoring, softening, and above all cooking techniques contributes much to the range of foods we can not only tolerate but enjoy, and whose anticipation is enlivened by filling the air with enticing fragrances. Little need be said about the sense of community meal-sharing can provide, or about its utilization in many religions as a sacred act celebrating this community, as in the Christian eucharist, or its parent, the Jewish Seder. Biologists also tell us that part of the appeal of sharing food is not so much in the sharing but in the food itself, the release of chemicals and the concentration of metabolism for digestive purposes that produce a sedative effect or sense of well-being. This may also explain why anger seems more deeply felt while we're eating and shortly thereafter, especially if the person we're angry with is at the meal: the anger must become more intense to overcome the ameliorating effects of the food. The appeal of an ancient wisdom, as captured, say, in Jesus' admonition, "Do not let the sun go down on your anger," is possibly recognizing this, since the main communal meal in many cultures is the evening one. It is for a similar purpose that overeating or eating too quickly is criticized, since it can produce discomfort, outright pain, or excessive weariness destructive of the pleasures of attentive communication between the meal's participants. And eating alone obviously prohibits such communication by its very definition, and having to do so on a consistent basis is a heartbreaking complaint of many, particularly on those days a culture has set aside for communal celebrations like birthdays, anniversaries, and religious festivities such as surround baptismal rituals—all of them to some degree acts of thanksgiving, which being alone makes harsh by being unshared, often driving the lonely to seek even the anonymity of a crowd, as in a restaurant, to remaining in silent isolation from one's own kind. Less oblique in its symbolic value than water-cooked food shared at a meal is the sharing of a beverage for purposes of pleasure or nourishment. But precisely because the biological demand for liquids is far more pervasive than for solid food, their intake is far more frequently engaged alone, in all societies the quick drink of tap, well, river, lake, or rainwater being the most common manifestation (contrary to a peculiarly American bias, it is still water and not such "purified" or "safe" beverages like wine and ale that people everywhere drink most abundantly). As with food, various beverages also infiltrate many religious rituals for purposes of communal bonding, and are standard components as well in such profane rituals as the American cocktail hour and the endorsement of achievements on toasting someone, glasses held high and then gently touched before drinking. Like the sharing of food, however, the use of beverages can also be a medium not of camaraderie but of anger, perhaps more pointedly since water is by far the more important immediate need for survival than food. To spit on someone thus originated as a curse that the person would die very soon, before he or she needs to drink again. And to throw a beverage in someone's face functions similarly as an act of utter dismissal of the person's worth, as worthless as if he or she were dead. Finally, like eating alone, drinking alone can also be indicative of profound loneliness, as with the excessive caffeine that keeps one energetic and interested in tasks or people, or more damaging, the alcoholism that makes them tolerable. A gluttony in these cases will also produce discomfort, outright pain, and, despite all contrary claims, an eventual weariness of mind and body that are the hallmarks of most rampant addictions.

There are other destructive dimensions to water that are independent of the dietary misuses to which we put it when constructing our stimulants and soporifics. Its movement in floods, glacial flows, rain torrents, and blizzards are obvious examples, each as potentially damaging to life as when the land moves. The ambivalence of nature toward life's well-being is a notorious problem in theology and dominates as the nemesis in that particular branch called theodicy. As I will be remarking in chapter 5, there have been a variety of proposals addressing it, and I will be siding with one of the least widely known—and for many familiar with it, least acceptable because of ancient biases it seems to offend. Nature's ambivalence, however, also functions for some as an aesthetic offense, and the rage of waters is particularly unnerving. Images of placidity, clarity, and health metamorphose into fury, unpredictability, and death when the beauty of a mountainside suddenly gives way to avalanche, the river breaches its banks, the rain and snow grow strong and start pummeling the life out of things. We prefer that what is beautiful remain so, and transformation into the awesome forms renegade water can take enhances this beauty only from the safety of distance; up close, to a person trapped in one of these transformations, the awesomeness is no longer beautiful but dumbly terrifying. This is why rain drowns the wicked in Noah's story—once it starts, no screaming can halt it—and why in apocalyptic imagery throughout religions flooding is almost always an ingredient, along with fire, which belongs to the air, and earthquake, which belongs to the land. The three components that have defined the earth for us in this chapter turn against our perversions, and the aesthetic sense chokes in disbelief. Water, in which we gestate and bathe, seek nourishment and a floating rest, directs toward us the one power over it we do not possess by nature's chance. We cannot breathe in it.

There is a wisdom in old religions—ones deeply attuned to the earth and the relationships life has with the land, water, and air—that seeks to provoke gratitude in us. You still find it in those religions that have been touched only lightly by the massiveness of modern technologies, or in those refusing the compromises that convictions like mastery and proprietorship toward the earth tend to encourage, or in those greeting such convictions with ambiguity or acknowledging them with a dismayed resignation. The old wisdom, though, is beginning to gain new vigor, a sympathy toward it and a sense of shame for the arrogance that caused its dismissal or forced it into foolish compromises. This gratitude is not merely a spirit of thankfulness—that doesn't bring it beyond the response a proprietor or master might also make—but a conviction that we must return something *in better condition* than when we received it. It is the failure to understand this dimension of gratitude that has perplexed so many Christians upon hearing Jesus' parable of the talents, and why the householder became angry when the one man returned the exact number of talents the householder had given him, having buried instead of invested them (a talent is a monetary unit). Yet it is not a parable of anger over profits lost because of the man's indolence, for then it would be a perplexity indeed, since the householder, as nearly all commentators hold, is an analogue for God. Rather, it is a parable of anger over the man's negligence of the full spirit of gratitude. We not only take life from water but make it work for us as well to improve that life through such things as waterwheels, steam power, hydroelectricity, and so on. Like the man in the parable, the past millennium has shown too much of negligence in our gratitude toward the water of the earth, not just by not leaving it better, or even the same, but very much worse in its purity and health. In the next millennium Christian religion must abdicate whatever complicity it has had in this failure, and with harsh resolve insist on its redemption.

The Air

When I was in my early forties, I developed a rather serious asthmatic condition, a chronic one exacerbated in the spring and summer by severe allergies. For those who have never suffered an asthmatic attack, it is like this: imagine your breathing is quite labored after unaccustomed exercise, and you are forced to breathe through a straw. It is a frightening experience requiring self-discipline so that the fear doesn't initiate a hyperventilation that only worsens the situation. The experience, like similar ones, I imagine, of close drowning or smothering, brings to consciousness in a elementary way our dependence on air, a demanding, sometimes harsh dependence, since we can live without it only a handful of minutes. And thus we have moved in this chapter through a series of constrictions defining the earth as our habitat, from the land to the water to the atmosphere, and with each there appeared a more intense motive for the gratitude I described above. Furthermore, if we are setting the outrage of our polluting behavior, our proclivity toward defiling things, as one focus for religious responsibility toward the earth, then the air we breathe should probably have priority, not only in itself as the most immediate need of the three, but because much of the pollution of the land and water originates in our defilement of the air. Speaking like this, of course, presumes some criterion for assessing the quality or health of the atmosphere beyond itself, since air by strict definition is the assemblage of any gases in the atmosphere above land and water. That criterion for us is the bringing forth and cherishing of life, one of whose components is respiration. Everything alive in some fashion breathes; and what it breathes, no matter how intermixed chemically, whether above or below water, is what we will call air.

Yet the air I will be primarily concerned with is the air that we and most other land-dwelling animals breathe in unassisted ways simply by living on the earth. When not defiled it is an invisible, odorless, and tasteless mixture of nitrogen (78 percent by volume), oxygen (21 percent by volume), and trace amounts of argon, carbon dioxide, and other gases, as well as water vapor and dust. It is the oxygen, of course, that is so critical to our life, and removing it from the air is the primary function of the respiratory system, in most animals performed by the lungs or their equivalents. Upward from the earth's surface, the air decreases in temperature roughly one degree centigrade every five hundred feet, and gradually thins out in a dispersion of its components that makes the gathering of oxygen into the lungs more difficult, and at a high enough altitude this causes unconsciousness and then death. (Descending in water also decreases the oxygen supply while increasing the water pressure. This allows for sinking only short distances before deleterious effects begin to occur in the human body.)

The primary sources of oxygen in the air we breathe are the evaporation of water, some exudation from the land, and very importantly, the respiration of plants (which depend primarily on the nitrogen and carbon dioxide in the atmosphere). At sea level the pressure that air exerts on a body is about fourteen pounds to the square inch, which internal pressures pushing outward in a healthy organism assist to counterbalance. At a certain density of pressure the body will implode, and at a certain diminishment of pressure it will explode (in many cases in either situation the skin or carapace would effectively make this a rampant internal hemorrhaging). We should also add that oxygen is a fairly unstable element, and that as it interacts with other elements or compounds it becomes easily combustible, producing light and heat, most typically manifested as fire. In many classifications of earlier centuries this result was so integral to the understanding of the physiology of the Earth that fire is often listed as a fourth "essence," along with land, water, and air. Of the four it was the one treated with the greatest ambiguity as a source of both benevolent and destructive effects and the one needing the closest attendance when being used.

Some sources of air pollution are "natural," and also tend to be catastrophic, as with volcanic eruptions, violent windstorms, and, though many would not think of it as such, pollination (we could also mention the introduction of large amounts of oxygen itself into the air of the planet some 2 billion years ago, a massive and killing pollution for many life-forms then existing). I suspect that in popular knowledge the most spectacular example is the meteor that many experts tell us was a major factor decimating life at the Cretaceous-Tertiary border in geologic history some 65 million years ago, including all living species of dinosaurs. There is little argument that the major culprit was the dustlike debris settling high in the atmosphere and impeding photosynthesis sufficiently to cause a radical disruption in the food chain. But much of air-breathing life and some of water-breathing kinds would have perished almost immediately by the mere act of breathing and the mortal congestion, then suffocation the debris caused in the respiratory system. But these natural sources of air pollution, while there is nothing to prohibit their occurrence, will not be our concern here, which instead will be the kinds resulting from the workings of human ingenuity. These are almost exclusively exhausts: from factory chimneys and those of homes where wood-burning stoves and fireplaces are used, to jet engines, coal-burning furnaces and electrical plants, air conditioners, aerosol sprays, insecticides, herbicides, and of course the ubiquitous automobile. Literally millions of *tons* of deleterious chemicals and particulate debris are spewn into the air every year, and a substantial percentage of it virtually never settles back to the land or water. In many places—large urban areas—it can actually be seen as that floating gray-yellowish-brown obscenity we call smog. This is what hundreds of millions of people breathe every day and make their own, coughing, hacking, and choking, oblivious of any awareness that other life-forms, innocent of all behemoth and malfeasant technologies, are suffering even more.

Some of the prognoses regarding present and, if continued, future effects from our errant technologies are so alarming that the consciousness of many either withdraws completely from contemplation of them, ridicules their seriousness, or metamorphoses them into the imaginably manipulative terms of science fiction. Ozone, for example, is an allotropic form of oxygen (it is a molecule composed of three oxygen atoms bound together) that blankets our planet with particularly delicate concentrations at the magnetic poles. It is a basic ingredient in the shield that protects life-forms from the otherwise devastating effects of solar radiation. In recent years everybody has heard of the rip in this shield above Antarctica, a large rupture that seems to be cyclic or pulsating in its growth and withdrawal patterns. It has produced in many people one of the three above responses, which is a particular aggravation to those taking the phenomenon seriously because each response is intensified by the fact that there is no indigenous life in the locale beneath where the rupture is occurring—which has made it psychologically a very distant, abstract problem. It is a never-never land neurosis that's coming to the fore here, the idea that because the problem does not impinge upon the quality of our immediate environment, such as it is, it might as well exist nowhere. Christian religion has as one of its most serious burdens in the coming millennium the discarding of this attitude, to be assisted by a long wink toward its otherworldly concerns for the sake of this world. Either it does this or it becomes an accomplice in strengthening the neurosis. To be sure, there are naturally occurring phenomena that partially explain this "tear in the fabric of the heavens," and science instructs us in these. But it is equally certain that the controlling phenomenon is the pollution we are pumping into the air, especially carboniferous kinds, and it is functioning like a skin cancer, now active, now in remission, that will eventually thin and then rip ever larger gaps in the ozone layer unless radical therapy is engaged to halt the progress, though the damage done, as with the cancer, can apparently never be fully healed.

In Judeo-Christian mythology we are told that two things distinguish the act of creating humanity on the sixth day as recorded in Genesis. We saw something of the first in our earlier discussion of the land: that in one translation God is understood as functioning like an artisan taking clay (land, or soil, mixed with water) and shaping the human form. On none of the other days is any divine activity other than speaking explicitly employed (the "separations" of the first, second, and fourth days are the result of the words spoken). The second distinction is that God bestows life on this clay by breathing into it. For our concerns in this chapter, therefore, the Genesis myth is stunning in its power because it portrays humanity as constituted of the very same three factors we have isolated in our discussion of the earth, and so establishes an intimacy of relationship between the two, humanity and the earth, not shared in the myth by anything else. An understandable but lamentable warping then occurred in the tradition-history of this mythology. I am referring to the sense of mastery this relationship produced in adherents to the myth, along the lines of a patriarchally dominated understanding of the marriage covenant in which the husband is presumed to be the more skilled, clever, and controlling partner. Nor, if we refuse the influence of this conjugal interpretation, does anything in the myth suggest that we are the children rather than the masters of the earth, as in so many other religious traditions; instead, we remain a privileged handiwork on the model of technological advance whose role, since God is understood as the actual owner, is that of proprietary stewardship (see, for example, Genesis 2:4–4:6; Psalms 8, 19, 74, 104; Isaiah 40:12–31, 45:9–13, 48:12–13; Jeremiah 27:15, 32:17; Proverbs 3:19–20, 8:22–31). In an apparent dislike for the wayward applications of this image, however, and as a counterpoint to the marriage hermeneutic, Jesus isolated in his own teachings not an earth/child but a God/child metaphor in which all of earth's living forms, and not just human beings, are by implication the children of God (there is a beautiful strand of this in Old Testament Judaism, along with that of proprietary stewardship, though it never wins the day as the controlling tradition). Yet in an alarming aberration of fidelity, his followers continued to relate in terms of mastery to the earth in a belligerent and destructive fashion that no parent would ever tolerate among the children in a household, at least if the parental presence was not lax, indifferent, or itself wickedly supportive of what was occurring. Applying this latter description to God's own parenthood, however, is something that Christian religion must always find repellent, refuse to justify by that catch-all of inconsistencies we label "paradox," and seek to do without.

A second warping in the tradition-history of the Genesis story is at root just as old as the first, but in specific application much more recent. It emerges with the suspicion that our technologies have gotten out of hand, first because of the foregoing proclivity toward mastery and power, and then because of a failure of ideologies, especially ethical or theological ones, to provide a benevolent intelligence to the proclivity. This is the warping that occurs whenever we seek to blame others—in this case God, as the cause of our creation or emergence from evolutionary process— for why we act and think as we do, rather than assume final responsibility for it ourselves. It is the same warping that occurs when the primal couple in Genesis refuse the task of accountability when confronted with their misdeed. That automotive power, for example, based on self-contained combustion engines has provided an enormous surge in human mastery of the planet is beyond dispute. But an ideology of its applications is only now understanding the defilement of the air this mastery has produced while proposing benevolent adjustments to lessen and eventually eliminate it in the coming millennium—though success here, as in all similar cases, is again going to depend on something like that consciousness of ourselves as a global village discussed earlier in the chapter. What the Genesis story is telling us, in other words, is that if we do in fact enjoy an intimacy of created being with the earth, and if we also continue to fail to provide a benevolent ideology (toward which a critical contributor must be religion), then our abuse becomes a form of self-abuse, a contempt whose furthest reach is suicide. At times I am of the mind that this furthest reach is in fact a part of our nature, that we are the lemmings of the family of primates, and that our destruction by ourselves, given how many other life-forms we have destroyed for the most obscene and species-infatuated purposes, would not only be an exquisite irony but an exquisite blessing on the life-forms surviving us. There is nothing, after all, especially in religions that are willing to cast a cold eye on human behavior, that guarantees our uninterrupted survival as a species. And no species we know of, once extinct, has ever come alive again in this world. But this melancholy, so intensified by the refusal of blame and the assumption of species responsibility, will await further exploration until chapter 4.

For the religious mind sympathetic to the Genesis myth there is a further intimacy it suggests besides that between the earth and humanity. For the very same word, *ruach*, which is used to describe the life-bestowing breath of God is also used (along with the Hebrew *nephesh*) to describe the Spirit of God, and hence is a designation for the divine itself. The story is telling us that as we are in some ways of the earth, we are likewise of God. Moreover, the *ruach* is the *creative* Spirit of God, and we've already noted that the Hebrew word for the act of creation, *barah*, means a giving of recognizable form or consistency to what is now without them, *and* to do so in benevolent ways. The myth consequently proposes at least the following two inquiries for assessing how we participate in this creative talent. First, does our activity conduce toward a diminution of chaos, or its increase? We suggested in the last chapter that this is also the fundamental question distinguishing symbolic from diabolic activity, to which we may now add that opting for the former—that is, creative and symbolic activity as diminishing chaos—has been the clear and constant claim of most proponents of technological development. Against this claim, however, the second criterion at once comes into play, namely, has our creative activity been benevolent? When joined together so that the two inquiries become basically one, there can be no absolute or resounding judgment, no unqualified affirmation or denial, as might occur when only the first question is asked. There have been blessings and curses in our activity, technologies that have united as well as divided us, creating both harmony and discord. And so I am going to center my own response in a judgment of *weight*. Here too, however, further reflection will have to await succeeding pages, though my basic response has by now been clearly implied: a cold eye judges the weight of our behavior tipped heavily toward chaos and the diabolical, frequently in spectacular, usually in trivial but cumulative forms. In our present context I find this confirmed with every sour breath I take in many large urban areas, and on many days here at home in a city that regularly advertises its pride in its cleanliness of land, water, and air. Yet I am not an escapist who might flee this in deserts, mountains, or sea islands, at least not permanently, nor a robust activist in meetings, demonstrations, tours to argue my case, since my health does not permit it. And so I write: of melancholy and worry-filled thoughts that we have aborted both the earth and the God within us, and that religion has languished too lazily in the process.

While the *ruach* continually appears throughout the tradition-history of the Old Testament as a creative presence, it also appears as a communicative presence. This is the whirlwind from which God spoke to Job, and the mighty wind as harbinger to the still small voice that addressed Elijah. Just as in the Genesis myth it is the *ruach* of God that communicated life to clay, and the life to hear the words of God, so in these other stories words are spoken that communicate humility to Job and confidence to Elijah. In this sense, then, the communication is also empowering. And while it preferred a vocabulary more comfortable with Greek terminology (ruach is replaced by *pneuma*), Christianity also understood this idea from its start. In the structuring of Christianity's baptismal liturgies, the celebrant was instructed to breathe on the water, which in flowing over the catechumen, as noted earlier, both communicates and empowers a second birth, a new life initiated and in the future sustained by responsiveness to God's word, or more specifically, God's call. And so in this example we reach still a third characteristic of creativity: What it communicates and empowers is always something new— whether it be a new arrangement of ideas when thinking or words when speaking, marble in sculpting, emotions in feeling, a child in hope for the future. It is the *ruach,* the breath, the air, that makes these traits possible. Without it there is nothing, not even death, since there has been no life. And this is as true in the creative beauty of a religious myth as it is in the creative discoveries of a wondrous science. In this way the myth and the science are telling the same truth about creativity.

Probably the most sense-provoking manifestation of the air on our planet, even more than the wind, takes place when combustion occurs, that is, when there is fire. As with respiration, it is the air's oxygen that is the critical factor here; decrease or remove the oxygen and a fire diminishes or dies. It would be difficult to overestimate the influence fire has had on human development: as source of warmth and light, making days and nights more tolerable and conducive to activity; as a weapon; as contributor in the production of various types of ash for soil fertility; as a cauterizing healer of wounds; as a mesmerizer toward feelings of relaxation; and for religions particularly, as a symbol of power. It was for all these things that Prometheus had to suffer the wrath of Zeus: Prometheus who gave fire to humanity and thus made them less dependent on the goodwill of the gods—Prometheus, the Titan martyred to the beginnings of human technology, its freedom from power we couldn't control. And fire, too, that the Jews preferred in the depiction of the greatest of divine epiphanies in their history, the ones that came to Moses first as surrounding yet not consuming a bush when God's name was revealed, and then as an awesome pillar on the heights of Sinai when God's law was revealed. The imagery is twofold in purpose: as fire is, so God is both (1) reliable when attended to with devotion, and (2) unpredictable when not. Setting aside the theological polemic also implied in the image (one driving the search for any image implying that our God is more powerful than yours, and hence more worthy of worship), this call for devotion is always legitimate. Even outside the context of religion it is legitimate—now to the reality more than the symbol of fire—since for decades we have known how to amplify many times over the effects of combustion fires by nuclear fires, producing not so much a flame-igniting unpredictability if treated cavalierly as a heat-igniting one of such monstrous proportions that even the blue-white heart of a flame would seem cool as ice. A lack of proper devotion here can only generate a more severe unpredictability, and with it a far greater potential for uncontrolled destruction.

Of all the power fire has given us, however, and all the ways it has liberated us from the harshnesses of life, I suspect none is as important as the nutrition it has made available to us. There are many food items we simply would not be able to eat if we were not able to cook them; the stomach would either rebel outright and disgorge the food, or the digestion process would cause such pain that continued ingestion would become masochism. I mentioned in the last section that water is frequently an element in this cooking. But this obviously presupposes fire, as water alone can only soften food, or with seasonings flavor it, or as ice preserve it. But with fire you can not only boil your food, you can roast, bake, or broil it. There is also the issue of enjoyment. Paleoanthropologists tell us that as far as the fossil and pictographic records can be deciphered, there emerges a clear preference among early humans for cooked food (especially meat), even when the same food was digestibly tolerable uncooked. Along with this there is a consistent portrayal of communal life in the pictographs, especially around an open fire (though killing still remains a far more dominant motif). In many societies, of course, electricity has extended this ability of fire, as have certain other noncombustible forms of heat, though in the world overall it is still fire that is the most common and manipulable medium for cooking. But even while blessing us with his presence, Hephaestos, the god of fire, remains a fearsome presence in our old tales of the gods, dwelling deep within the world in ancient tribute to his most powerful manifestation in volcanic eruptions. He is to be feared, therefore, as well as petitioned for what he controls. For while Prometheus gave fire to humanity, the reach of the gods is long, and the humility before stolen gifts demanding.

In all these remarks, as well as those of the preceding chapter, there has been an implication that I should now bring out. It is in fact a recommendation, and it pertains to encouraging a reemergence of natural theology as a worthy task for the religious consciousness. I would locate this reemergence at the center of any agenda for Christian religion in the coming millennium. By natural theology I mean reflection on God that draws its dominant impetus from reflection on the world, or more widely, the universe, as a place of sense experience. Christian theology by and large withdrew from this venture in the closing decades of the last century because of its conviction of God's utter transcendence and the implied correlate that looking for God's presence in the world, with the spectacular exception of Jesus, explicitly contradicts or demeans that presence. Yet this stance is immediately at odds with any companion claim of God's immanence, which suggests that knowledge of God's presence is accessible only as we discover it in the world, with Jesus no longer a spectacular exception to our search but a primary example of it. A second motive for the negligence is the fear or suspicion that natural theology seduces the human mind toward the deification of the world or select parts of it, too easily leading to neopaganism or neopolytheism— and thus to an assault not just on God's utter transcendence, but more specifically on God's utter simplicity (meaning the inaccessibility of God because there can be no "hints" or "traces" of God that might diffuse this simplicity into a suggestion of complexity within God's very being). As discussed in the last chapter, a third reason is that from the time of the Enlightenment until the emergence of neo-orthodoxy in this century the intellectual competence of Christian theology was damaged badly by its contests with science, to its often petulant embarrassment. "Once burned, twice cautious" has thus been the guiding maxim, and natural theology has been indicted as the culprit that might readily lead, should it be encouraged, to further embarrassment.

To those still hypnotized by this intellectual ambience, much of this book will be dismissed as an attempt to resurrect a theological discipline better left buried—that we should not look for God's presence in such things as land, water, and air, the components of a planet circling a star in a seemingly endless universe of stars, but only in those revelatory intrusions of God in human history that we believe occurred in a uniquely concentrated fashion in Jesus, anticipated or corroborated in the prophets, seers, shamans, and priests of other religions. The air we breathe literally to survive is relegated to insignificance, or to the fanciful and iconoclastic imaginations of poets, as a conduit to knowledge of God, and we are told instead to breathe the air of the words of the saints, a figurative breathing that we need for spiritual survival. It is obvious that I have no interest in denigrating the witness that saints have provided, and I don't really oppose the metaphor of breathing the air of their words; their witness is an irremovable datum in any approach to learning of God, and only a foolish mind would ignore or demean its crucial importance. But when I breathe the fouled air of many cities I don't need a saint to tell me of the perversity, shortsightedness, or indifference that has produced it, or, oppositely, that as it is given and left undefiled the air is a blessing. What I need the saints for is to aid me in understanding human malfeasance—something of pride and greed and sin: the sense that there is something wrong—and in understanding the source of the givenness of what we have defiled—something of purpose and providence and God: the sense that there is something right. For every religion taught to us knows that God is first discovered in the workings of the heart and mind as we each ponder our experiences of the world, in musings on both the good and evil, virtue and vice we discover there. The teachings of others cannot provide this discovery for us, therefore, but only assist and enhance what we must discover for ourselves. Yet a transcendence that diminishes immanence will always tend to make this discovery quite abstract, perhaps intellectually satisfying for some, but motivationally sterile. Reading and hearing about the air's rottenness may shock us, but shock of itself is a weak motive for redeeming the sin. For this redemption to begin, which means for theology to become a natural theology, we must first go into a city from the freshness of a meadow or seacoast, or anywhere touched only lightly by the exhaust of our technologies, and breathe.

There is something more to be said before I close this chapter. I have been emphasizing in my remarks the role of religion in confronting the human rampage against the earth, its land, water, and air. And I will continue much of this in the next chapter when contemplating plants and animals. But as a counterpoint to this critical function, religion must also extol the earth's beauty, the wonder and enchantment it draws from us. To do so adequately, however, requires some grappling with a notion that is not only essential to the contours of any religion, but in the minds of many defines precisely and exclusively religion's primary function. The notion is that of ideals, and the function is to set them forth clearly and passionately as the standards whereby we should live.

The word *ideal* comes from the Greek *eidolon,* which is also the source of the English *idea* and *idol.* Its definition has two parts. The first is that an ideal is something we perceive as beautiful, whatever particular criteria we employ—though an intuitive judgment based on a consensus by others is a common factor in these criteria (it would be unlikely that we would find something beautiful that no one else does). Beauty itself we can define according to Webster's dictionary, not only because this presumably represents the common understanding, but because I can think of no reason to attempt its improvement: "*beauty:* that quality or aggregate of qualities in a thing which gives pleasure to the senses or pleasurably exalts the mind or spirit; physical, moral, or spiritual loveliness." Yet this definition is not sufficient for our purposes here, since then beauty would remain fundamentally abstract, producing aesthetic pleasure as it delighted the mind and heart, but nothing more. Instead, beauty starts functioning as an ideal when it breaches this abstraction and begins to control behavior. Now it is no longer passively enjoyed but pursued; it begins to affect the decisions whereby we contour our lives, and, as with all beauty once it becomes an ideal, we find a longing in ourselves to spend as much time as possible with it. A Beethoven sonata may strike us as beautiful, but it becomes an ideal only when we go beyond the aesthetic effect to an ethical one: when we realize that a serious engagement of the music has begun to determine our sense of the rightness or wrongness of how we spend our time, or at least considerable portions of it. The same could be said of any other art form functioning as an ideal, or of a particular pattern of virtue, a career, or another human being. It is beauty, I would say, that can drive our lives in ways and to an extent that truth and goodness cannot, unless they too are first judged beautiful.

It is the *beauty* of the earth, therefore, that can impassion us toward its well-being in ways that other considerations, including the very powerful one of utility, cannot. And the passion takes on a direction—it is not willy-nilly, anarchic or anomic—that I have been suggesting should attend foremostly to the land, water, and air. In the process, as with the pursuit of all ideals, we must first identify those things that both assist and obstruct the pursuit. And for this Christian religion must always be more directly reliant on the dictates of common sense and the data of science than on those of revelatory scripture—so that when common sense tells us, for example, that automobile exhausts as they emerge in billows of blue-gray smoke are going to have *some* deleterious effects on the health of the air, and science goes on to delineate the chemical marauding specifically involved, we are aware of at least one obstacle any pursuit of the beauty of breathing well must seek to overcome. Other obstacles will obviously be uncontrollable for the foreseeable future, like the spewings of a volcano, or meteor bombardment, just as they are in the pursuit of more individualized ideals: the violinist whose hand is crushed irreparably must seek music's beauty in ways different from playing it, or a sad foolishness results. Such uncontrollables are brute data, and as such a fate we cannot go against. Our concern, however, must be with the controllables, not volcanoes and meteors but such things as (1) factories, (2) jet and automotive engines, (3) herbicides and insecticides, (4) the wasting of water, land, animals, plants, and energy in a wealth of conspicuous consumption and discard, (5) our rampant overpopulation and species-centricity, (6) tolerance of political and religious leaders toward military and industrial organizations whose policies damage or ignore the environment, (7) the education of children—and all the other devices and life-styles we have created but not mastered while mastering the earth. If the unharmed violinist is to be faithful to the ideal of her music, she must forswear whatever impedes its fair pursuit, or else the beauty will entice only partially or periodically, something like a retreat from the round of a daily life whose ideals in fact lie elsewhere, or one in which there are no ideals at all. It is the same *in attitude* for the earth's beauty as an ideal that lies before us.

And in attitude, I am convinced, it is the same with religion. If the

English word *religion* has a similar source in other languages (the Latin *religo*, "to bind" or "to draw together"), and if the fundamental object of all religions is God, then this binding to God is the same as the passion that drives us in pursuit of our ideals, and to the enhancement of all that assists and the diminishment of all that obstructs this pursuit. What I am saying is that for Christian religion to be an enduring force in human hearts and minds, God must be perceived not first as true or good or powerful or just or merciful, but as beautiful. God must be perceived as an ideal—the way we sometimes discover in such overwhelmingly theotropic individuals as Jesus: "theotropism" is a God-leaning that, like the heliotropic, or sun-leaning, behavior of many plants, always seeks movement that lets it absorb most fully its need. If in the last millennium, therefore, and in several others before it, we find a preponderance of fear in attitudes toward God, or indifference or confusion, religion in the next millennium must redeem this by speaking of God's beauty, extolling and emphasizing and glorifying it before all else, so that other traits, should we be compelled toward them, as Christianity indeed is, will have their proper warrant and justification in the one thing that must endure beneath what encourages and beyond what questions them. This is the epochal insight of Augustine, and should stand both as an expression of what God is when we seek deeply into divine things, and as a warning to every religion in the world. Augustine confesses in the familiar lament that makes him great, "O Beauty, ever ancient, ever new! Too late have I known Thee, too late have I loved Thee." This beauty of God, though: for Christians it is unbreakably linked to the beauty of Jesus, for whom the beauty of the earth provided kindness and insight to parables capturing the heart of his vision.

It is time now to move to the next chapter. I have written it with deep affection and an abiding concern, because while the earth itself is of a beauty worth pursuit, and the defilement of its land, water, and air a profound act of contempt, it is in the inhabitants of the earth, the life it houses, that I find its most concentrated beauty—not its human life, however, toward which chapter 4, with touches here and there in the other chapters, will describe my worried ambiguity—but the life of its plants and other animals, our partners in a life-experiment which, if God's beauty encompasses a largesse of creativity, is also taking place elsewhere in our universe.

Chapter three

PLANTS AND ANIMALS

OUTSIDE THE WINDOW in the room where I write there are three small honeysuckle vines. In the spring they bloom with small, trumpetlike flowers filled with nectar and exuding the sweetest fragrance I have ever experienced. Sometimes I will pinch a few and let them lie in my mouth to see if the taste is as sweet as the fragrance. It always is. Shortly after the bloom hummingbirds begin to appear and take nourishment from them. I am told by a biologist friend that hummingbirds do not winter here in the Pacific Northwest, so I am always amazed at the precision of their awareness that it is nutritionally safe to come back here. I am also told that they might come earlier, or even chance the winter months, if enough humans provided them with a nectar surrogate of red-colored sugar water. But enough humans do not, and from many of these I have heard as the petulant excuse—which serves them across the board with plants and animals, not just hummingbirds—that they do not have time to waste on such matters, or that their money is better spent elsewhere, on their own needs and delights, and the hummingbirds can fend for themselves. It is a tightfisted and small-minded attitude, a denial of a chance to witness beauty, and a mockery of the goodness I once saw in an achingly poor Navajo family whose members would deprive themselves not of a few teaspoons of sugar to nourish hummingbirds but of chunks of bread and cornmeal for raccoons and small deer. The way my memory has linked the honeysuckles and hummingbirds outside my window to each other as well as to the Navajo family and the small animals outside their hogan provide an initial focus for my concerns in this chapter. I certainly know that not all such linkages are benign or mutually advantageous— that against the hummingbird who is fed and then scatters the honeysuckle's pollen, or the small animals that are nourished and then teach a human family the meaning of tolerance and generosity, there stand countless other examples of parasitic relationships that benefit only one partner while damaging the other, or still further examples wherein not just one but both partners are damaged. But they all affirm the single idea of a mutuality or communion of relationships throughout the earth that undergirds every ecological vision, whether it be a secular one that speaks of the world's health or a religious one that speaks of a common creation and benevolent providence.

Trying to define life in a univocal and complete way, one with which everyone would agree, is a fruitless task. Aside from biological considerations, there are psychological, philosophical, and theological ones that come into play for everyone in varying degrees of sophistication. I wish to bypass for the moment these latter considerations, since they are concerned more properly with the *quality* of life than with its brute fact, and for the time being stay with the biological determinations. In the last chapter I mentioned four of these: metabolism, growth, reproduction, and autonomous abilities of adaptation to immediate environment. This last consists primarily of the components that concerned us in the last chapter, the land, water, and air. I myself am not much satisfied with this description, and for two reasons. First, at a certain level of smallness or intensification any living thing can be broken down to the molecular and then the atomic and subatomic matter that composes it. At this point two options are available: either to refuse the designation "life" by maintaining the above four characteristics as essential, or to expand the designation. In recent years my ever stronger inclination has been to choose the latter, and elsewhere I have suggested four other and far more basic characteristics to life's definition: movement, duration, novelty, and relationship. Physicists have for the most part been delighted with this, biologists defensive, philosophers skeptical, and theologians aghast, though less so if they come from traditions like Hinduism and Buddhism rather than Judeo-Christianity or Islam. In the next millennium I'm hoping that these characteristics are taken seriously on the agenda of all religions, both for purposes of understanding the presence of divinity as a living presence in the whole of the universe, and for the second reason I've offered them, which is as follows.

It is my conviction that it is only when we abide by some such description of life as just offered that the whole of creation can be treated with a common dignity—one based on the assertion that it is the *life itself* that matters, and not its particular format—thereby allowing us to intensify the concerns not only of the second but of all the chapters of this book. The description would require a sharing of life on the scale of the entire universe and would provide an attitudinal component to the physical facts of our sharing quarks and protons with everything that is. The reluctance to do so may likely stem from a sense that worth is found in what distinguishes rather than what unites; certainly this has been true in much of human history and is at the root of most of our arrogance and violence. It is the type of reluctance, now grown to recalcitrance, that greeted Copernicus and his sympathizers when he offered the observational geometry that dislodged the earth from the center of the solar system (though not the solar system from the center of the universe). Offense was taken not so much because the geometry and mathematics could be denied as that the new idea assaulted the sense of dignity that arose from the belief that *our home* was at the very center of things, not circulating it in an orbit, and since there can be no sharing of a center, unique. As Copernicus's view came to win the day, consolation was sought in the idea that while the planet was not the center of the universe, we ourselves were the apex of creation, unique from all else because of the chance that drove us qualitatively beyond all other things in an unrepeatable fashion, or because of a divine intrusion doing the same. But then this second dignity was put in question and obscured by Darwin and his immediate predecessors. Finally, human dignity denied twice, it stayed alive in protestations of our freedom, our being liberated in ways unknown to any other life-form because of brain capacity, or, for the religious mind, God's favor. We were the captains of our fate, the masters of our soul, until Freud insisted that we weren't even masters of our dreams or the neuroses locked deep in the very brain we extolled.

The cultural traumas that occurred in Christianity because of the discoveries and insights associated with these three men—the dislocations of human dignity and feelings of uniqueness in the universe—need, I think, to be taken a step further in the realization that any dignity or uniqueness we possess is exclusively individual, because at the most fundamental levels of existence we are together, one, of a common parentage of the same particles. To be sure, at a certain point in macroscopic development, reached quickly in molecules, we can begin to make distinctions and divide those individuals sharing them into distinct groups. There can be no argument with this. But all notions that these distinctions somehow imply ontological diversities, such as those assessed in terms like "inferiority" and "superiority," must be abandoned: the science denies it, and so should all philosophical and theological ideologies. These claims can be made only relatively, and any observer outside or within the group may well judge them differently from other observers. The conclusion, then—the absoluteness of life, and the relativity of worth of its individual formats—is something I would place on any agenda for Christian religion in the coming millennium. Even the heartfelt protest of Christians that God graced humanity uniquely in the incarnation of Jesus misses the mark. For the consistent tradition from the earliest days is that this incarnation occurred not because of our worthiness as a species but because of our wickedness. The belief is that God's benevolence could absorb even such a magnitude of evil into itself and bless it, including the bloodletting, choking agony of crucifixion. The most corrupt form of religious arrogance lies in the claim that God consents to me, or to us, in loving ways denied everyone or everything else. When the author of 1 John said that God is love, he captured a truth that neither he nor anyone else should have ever qualified in the extent of its offering, save that God loves more intensely those who love least: not to show their superiority, though, but to show their need.

So, distinctions are to be made within the context of the traits of life I have offered (its movement, duration, novelty, and relationship) as they determine its relatively different formats—like the one that specifies these four traits into the more distinct ones of metabolism, growth, reproduction, and autonomous adaptation to immediate environment. It is with this secondary specification that I will be concerned in this chapter, dividing it into three parts, respectively concerned with the cherishing of life, the profaning of life, and being in communion with life. From the perspective of our own lives, the human format that life has taken, this will continue a general context of appraisal also used in the last chapter when discussing the earth. As with the planet itself, its land, water, and air, our lives are also embedded in unbreakable relationships with plants and animals. We've already noted, for example, the contribution of plants to the air's oxygen content that is necessary if we are to survive in any but the most tightly controlled artificial environments; and we could note countless similar contributions, though none, of course, as initially and perduringly necessary as oxygen, offered by animals. To my way of thinking this point is profoundly pertinent, since it gives us a clue as to how we are to approach nonhuman life-forms, such as we may likely find elsewhere in the universe, or for the concerns of religion, God. For we can hardly expect an attitude that habitually neglects plant and animal life, when these are known to be critical to the survival and well-being of human life, or is hostile or completely utilitarian toward them, to adopt some other enduring stance regarding extraterrestrial or divine life. Or at least we can hardly expect it unless the discovery produces a conversion experience, which means, according to the etymology of the word (*con-*, an intensive prefix, plus *vertere*, meaning "to turn"), not just a slight turning in how one thinks, but a radical one, like turning in the opposite direction from which you were heading while on a walk. It is the same with similar attitudes toward God, and Christian religion, one of whose defining tasks is conversion, obviously has a thorough interest in these matters.

The most archaic biological life-forms we have discovered are "precursor" plants, forms of bacteria or cyanobacteria that have developed either no ability at photosynthesis or a very limited one. Paleobotany is tracing these forms further and further back in Earth's history, and current though somewhat controversial analyses are now dating the rock in which they have been discovered at about 3.5 to 4 billion years old. Moreover, not just one but several species have been isolated in the record. These claims have perplexed many scientists, since a common theory has been that to emerge from the primordial "soup" life would have needed more than the billion years or so from the time the earth began to solidify, and that a single species would have had an exclusive claim to its characteristics. But the history of science is rife with such unanticipated disclosures, and while we might commiserate with those whose researches and theories would be rendered useless or highly qualified by them, it is also these very disclosures that make science a continually lively and imaginative enterprise, unlike, unfortunately, much of the history of Christian theology. But quite like this history, that of science also shares a multitude of examples where the discoverers of new data, like the discoverers of new insights, are initially greeted with accusations of insufficiency of technical education, ineptitude of interpretation, or outright deceit in what they present. Perhaps this is what we must expect, since in science as in religion novelty that damages acceptability (of paradigms, of doctrines) must be forced through a crucible of doubt—not just by the discoverer, if he or she is a conscientious thinker, but also by those to whom the novelty is offered—before it can be granted tentative reliability, that is, something upon which further thought can be premised.

There is no doubt that photosynthesis has to be very high on any list of developments that has secured the success of life-forms. It is the process whereby green plants transform the energy of sunlight to produce carbohydrates from carbon dioxide and water. Essential to the process, and this is the reason why only green or green-filamented plants can accomplish it, is chlorophyll (found in small, oval-shaped bodies called chloroplasts and chemically similar to blood). It is activated by photons (a discrete particle of energy, or quantum, transmitted by light waves; the energy is imparted to a charged particle in the chlorophyll molecules when the photon collides with it, and in the process oxygen is released). It is still generally acknowledged that all plant and animal life is ultimately dependent on photosynthesis for food and oxygen, even non-green "plants" such as yeasts and molds through becoming parasites or saprophytes (the former attach themselves to living organisms, the latter to dead and decaying organic matter). The exact chemical nature of photosynthesis is still not fully understood, though it has been accomplished in laboratories without intact green plant cells; finally mastering it in a technologically, financially, and ecologically workable way would obviously cause vast improvement in food resources. The earliest life-form, most likely a bacterium, that developed the distinct green pigmentation of chlorophyll would have been the first photosynthetic plant, as long as enough photons penetrated the atmosphere to provide the energy for the process. Yet not a great deal of atmospheric debris is required to slow down or paralyze photosynthesis, as recent discussions of the meteor impact contributing to dinosaur extinction because of food loss suggests. At a certain point of diminishing plant growth and reproduction, all other life-forms on the planet are threatened, save (with a very large "perhaps") some of the above parasites and saprophytes, certain types of bacteria and viruses, a selection of primitive and dark and deep sea dwelling organisms, and whatever else might survive in very advanced and technologically secure "greenhouse" environments.

When many of us think of the necessity of plants to other life-forms, we tend to do so in terms of the food chain. But the previous remarks also indicate their utter necessity to the oxygen content of the air we breathe. All land animals (as far as I know) are in fact aerobic—that is, require close to the 23 percent by weight of oxygen the air contains—

with the exception of some few species adapted to living in high mountain altitudes where the percentage is somewhat lower. Most sea-going animals also require substantial amounts of oxygen in their environment—which they have, since seawater is about eight-tenths oxygen by weight—though there are some forms deep in the ocean near volcanic vents that appear to be anaerobic, needing very little or no oxygen for adequate respiration. But they would be flagrant anomalies to a safe general statement of the substantial oxygen needs of all animal life. All species of plants, on the other hand, have a very reduced oxygen need when compared to animals, or compared to their own need for carbon dioxide. And so the most amazing symbiotic relationship exists between plants and animals, the "exhalation" of the former providing oxygen to the air and that of the latter carbon dioxide (the plants keep almost all the carbon during photosynthesis as food material). This is the principal reason why all life as we know it is "organic," meaning biologically based on the carbon that plants ingest from photosynthesis and animals ingest by eating plants and/or each other, all up and down the food chain. In common usage "inorganic" has consequently come to mean inanimate or "dead" matter. What we discover, in other words, right at the first inklings of simple plant and animal forms is what my own definition of the characteristics of life includes, but the common biological one does not, at least not explicitly: namely, relationship. In the cherishing of life this fact has the controlling role to play, just as it does in profaning life.

There is, of course, no cherishing of life whenever it is abused: the oxymoron of a cherishing abuse might serve some purpose in a peculiar poetic sentiment, but in behavior it indicates self-contradiction and maladjustment. This description implies an ethical judgment premised on a series of norms that require continual evaluation and application. As far as we can detect, only human beings are able to engage the communal or individual self-reflection that this process—similar to the obedience we previously described—requires. We speak of cherishing when the norms are acknowledged in behavior, and abuse when they are not. The difficulty that has plagued the history of human intellect resides precisely in the norms, both in their formulation so as to bind a society together as a community, and then in relating them to the differing norms of other societies so as to avoid destructive conflict. And it is in this process, I would say, that there finally emerges what seems to be a truly universal or common norm of all societies, namely, the achievement of a lasting peace. To be sure, this immediately places us in an awkward context, since the very definition of peace can itself be a cause for discord. Yet I think there is one ingredient to it that obliges us all, no matter how consistently or not we submit to it, and that provides the primary rubric for assessing whether or not peace is being honored in our behavior. That ingredient is the cherishing of life, with its converse in the judgment that peace is threatened or dissolved whenever life is profaned. A delicacy of mind is required here, insofar as a *mutuality* of violence is not the point at issue, but rather damaging or killing violence *itself*. When you are walking along and for no reason other than your indifference or deliberate malice rip a plant from the soil or crush an ant underfoot, you have denied the norm of peace—though no one, certainly not the plant or insect, will boost this act into a mutuality of violence toward you. Discord does not require violence between two parties, though it may certainly include this. It exists whenever life is abused, and perhaps its most unnerving expressions occur in the banality of the indelicate mind that rips a plant or crushes an insect without a thought.

We cannot be naive in these descriptions. As I noted at the beginning of the last chapter, the Sabbath peace that Genesis proposes as the high point of creation is not within our talents to secure. For there is built into us and all life a degree of innate destructiveness that will always prohibit the fullness of the Sabbath peace, and which demonstrates itself most obviously in our need to eat and the indeliberate violence we manifest, as when the plant or insect are now destroyed not with deliberate or indifferent malice but accidentally. If the inclusive definition of life I have been proposing is also employed, then this innate destructiveness would likewise show itself in the violence of earthquake, flood, and windstorm. Only a complete slippage into fantasy, the free play of imagination in world-utopian scenarios playfully or neurotically engaged, can conjure up the removal of the destructiveness that so thoroughly surrounds us. What this means when we also assert cherishing life as the norm for securing peace is that all existence is characterized by what I would describe as biblical tragedy. Unlike Greek tragedy, which locates the source of tragic deeds in a character flaw—usually ignorance, as when Oedipus unknowingly weds his own mother, or pride, as when Narcissus boasts of his beauty as godlike—biblical tragedy occurs whenever the choices before us are all evil, *and we must choose*. This is what confronted Jesus, as it did many of the Hebrew prophets before him, when he had to choose either to remain faithful to his convictions and be executed, or to deny them and suffer the self-contempt of disobedience. The biblical perspective could have never assented to the Greek view because it asserts that while we are surely all flawed, the tragedy resulting is not an ontological designation of human existence but an ethical one. Nor, by implication, could the biblical perspective adopt the further Greek view that qualifies ethical accountability for behavior in the assertion that the end justifies the means. Rather, the evil we do is *always* evil, no matter what our motive or how accidental the deed. And the proper response is always repentance, though one, of course, sympathetically attentive to motive and accident.

The notion of biblical tragedy is not unique to Judeo-Christianity; we find it throughout the religious traditions of the world. It attempts to capture the idea that we are locked in our finitude, that this is a "fallen" state not because any other has actually existed but because we can imagine other ones, and that redemption must take place within this finitude or fallenness. What all this means is that there is a degree of inevitability to the evil we experience and ourselves commit, and that the religious consciousness is required to be continually aware of this and simultaneously committed to contrary acts of good according to our norm of the cherishing or enhancement of life. While we must still kill to eat, therefore, as one expression of our finitude, some corresponding good deed (what the Old Testament calls a *mitzvah*) should occur to balance this death in an act of care for other life. This "should" again indicates that we are involved here in ethical considerations. Improving the environment, taking into one's home unwanted animals, the culturing of plants: just as there are innumerable ways we can damage and destroy other life, so there are innumerable ways we can heal and preserve it. Yet throughout this dialectic, this give and take, the ethical consciousness must remain aware that all our efforts at healing and preservation do not justify, that is, excuse or rectify, the initial damage or death. For life is not an abstraction, as we are sometimes seduced into thinking to pull the sting of the ethical judgment or ameliorate the tragedy in our choices. It is, in fact, *that* plant, *that* animal, *that* life I have scourged or ended, and no subsequent behavior should attempt to bless the deed or blend its evil with indifference or an abundance of good deeds. The evil stands; my response must acknowledge it, but cannot camouflage or eradicate it.

As in chapter 2, there re-emerges the question of weight. For the good can increase its presence only as it grows stronger than evil, only as the weight of behavior is on its side. Here we are in the realm of the will as it operates within our finitude. Or differently: what our finitude has made of us is a *fate*; what we make of ourselves within this finitude is a *destiny*. The peace that cherishes life, therefore, cannot be the result of our fate, since it has interwoven within it, if we were correct above, the inevitable destruction of life. For even if we were someday able to synthesize our food completely from inorganic compounds, and could do so for all other biological life-forms, there is a legitimate question raised by geneticists as to whether any of the species involved would remain the same or evolve into something else. Added to this would be the need to overcome the many other ways we deliberately or inadvertently damage and destroy life—spanning the gamut from the bacteria found throughout our bodies to the insects and other animals smashed by our transportation vehicles, until a point is reached in all such considerations where the impossibility of denying the fate becomes compelling, and continuing to exercise the mind on the issue becomes exclusively the fantasy of a benevolent imagination. But the destiny: this is another matter altogether, and it is our choice. Fate provides the confines within which our destiny is chosen. For religions this distinction has always been critical, and it has been destiny more than fate that has been their abiding concern—a fact that must remain lively on any agenda for Christian religion in the coming millennium. It is destiny that provides the arena for assessing the choices we've made for the achievement of peace through the cherishing of life. Where many religions have gone askew on this issue is through an abrogation of concern for earthly life in favor of an afterlife, with a corresponding bias in understanding the dynamic and object of that virtue we need in a singular way at the end of this millennium: hope. I want to spend some time on this, both because the object of our hope is integrally related to the destiny we choose, and because an overall assessment of human destiny in trying to achieve some judgment on what I've been describing as the "weight" of human behavior vis-à-vis the normative value of peace, inextricably involves the fate (we are part of their fate) of countless other life-forms.

Hope and the Cherishing of Life

I have taken up the issue of hope in other publications, though here I

will be refining my position so as to apply it to our concern for nonhuman life. Yet I must also remark as a cautionary note, since it will influence
my analysis, that I am in full accord with St. Paul when he states in a
wonderfully unqualified judgment that love is greater than hope, just as
it is greater than faith (1 Cor. 13:13). This judgment has been frequently
misunderstood in the tradition of Christian piety, as it is in similar illustrations from Buddhism and Judaism. It is not a judgment that faith and
hope are unnecessary, but that they achieve their proper meaning only
within the context of love. Or from a slightly different angle: love is the
overarching phenomenon of which faith and hope are lasting constituent parts. We will be able to work this out more fully only when we discuss the doctrine on love in the next chapter. For now our concern is
simply to state the premise that hope is legitimate only to the extent that
it expresses love, and it is the neglect of this premise that has issued in
the misunderstandings noted above. The reflections will proceed according to three dominant approaches to hope I have drawn from a variety of
religious traditions, though in accord with the intent of the book I will
isolate for emphasis Christian tradition. The approaches are: hope as
absent (or hopelessness), hope as escape, and hope as mission, this last
representing the proper relationship between hope and the love I will
describe in the next chapter.

The first approach is that of hopelessness. It is born from the refusal of
the imagination to construct possibilities other than those confirmed by
common experiences of tedium, failure, and pain as traits pervading the
world, particularly intense among the poor, the ill, the aged, but to some
extent present anywhere we look—especially for pain and savage death,
among animals. It is the same emphasis we find in Dante's great *Inferno*,
which for him represents the human condition far more accurately than
his *Purgatorio*, let alone his *Paradiso*: the vice and destitution, squalor
and scatology that characterizes most lives before death, makes them
hopeless, and provides thereby the catalyst for his descriptions of hell.
But while for Dante a hopeless life is a hellish one, for the Greeks it is a
realistic one, bolstering, among other results, their well-known preference for viewing personal, communal, and world history as cyclical, my-
thologized exquisitely by the great poet Hesiod, though also found in
the more dispassionate analyses of philosophers. It is Hesiod who tells
the story of Pandora, the irresistibly beautiful and curious woman designed by Zeus in his anger at the Titan Prometheus (whose name means

"forethought"), and given as a consort to his brother, the foolish Epimetheus (whose name means "afterthought"). As part of her dowry she possesses a jar in which all the Olympian deities have put a woe for humankind, since Zeus knows that the most effective way to hurt someone is to hurt that person's beloved—in this case humanity, for whose benefit Prometheus has stolen fire from heaven, as we noted in the last chapter. He also taught humans ways to deceive the ruling deities, specifically through sequestering for their own food the choicest portions of a sacrificial animal while camouflaging the remainder with the animal's skin. (We run into the same peculiarity here as in other religions, including Judaism: that the fragrance of burning animal flesh is somehow pleasing to the divine.) What interests us is that hope (*elpis*) is included in the jar, a woe because it leads humans to think that they can become gods, and so merit divine wrath for their pride (this is *hubris*, or pride as the specific claim to divine prerogatives). Yet of all the woes, it alone is prevented from escaping, since in a second meaning hope is also the ability to anticipate events, especially future sufferings that can then be avoided. It is an extraordinary myth, very intricate, this tribute to the genius of Hesiod, and it provides one of the elemental reasons for viewing history as cyclical, since a future that cannot be anticipated in its novelty and unpredictability can only be reliably controlled when construed as the repetition of a past already known—to which the Greeks will add as further justification the obvious cycles they observed in the birth-life-death-birth of plant and animal populations as well as the transits of the Sun and Moon. A similar experience of hopelessness is also found in the Old Testament book of Koheleth, at least those parts not touched by a later editor too depressed by its vision and more faithful to the common Hebrew view of the passage of time as linear. It is this notion of time's linearity, of course, that then allows the postulate of a goal, a divine providence leading toward it, and so the consolation that the suffering we experience is understandable, or at least acceptable, as a need toward achieving it. The classic analogy here is Augustine's. The whole of history, he says, is like a mosaic, which when seen up close (the only way we can see it) is filled with sharp and abrasive stones, but which when seen as a whole (the way God sees it) is of supernal beauty.

A second approach to the experience of hope is what I am calling hope as escape. This is by far the most common approach in religious mythologies and theologies throughout the world, certainly in those sources that influenced the formation of early Christianity and in those that were influenced in turn by a later, more doctrinally set Christianity. In almost all its formats this viewpoint requires belief in an afterlife whose general description everyone knows: a miraculously endowed space-time where the virtue of the good is ultimately redeemed and blessed in heavenly joy while the vice of the wicked is condemned and punished in hellish pain. In some few traditions where the notion of an afterlife does not develop, it is death itself, and the hope that it be nobly met with neither joy nor fear, that is the escape. In such traditions, though, the virtuous life still tends to be prized more highly, the viceful one scorned more deeply, because the former contributes more obviously to an education in the nobility desired at life's final moment, even when this moment brings death by one's own hand. However, aside from the brute desire of most people to continue living immortally, which these less common traditions do not satisfy, there is also the problem of the virtuous sufferer whose ordeals on earth are completely out of proportion to his or her minor immoralities, *when this is accompanied* by a fervent trust in God's absolute justice. If there is no resolution of this conundrum before the individual's death, and if God's justice is indeed to be honored, then belief in an afterlife of reward or punishment becomes the handiest cognitive device to secure the resolution. Parenthetically, it also satisfies the ancient concern of where to "house" God mythologically, as well as God's angelic servants and demonic adversaries.

The tremendous difficulty with this whole approach is that it utilizes hope not just to escape the suffering of this life in a new life of bliss, but also to diminish or condemn earthly life as little more than a preamble testing worthiness for the new life. A contempt for the earth easily ensues from this, with one of its more malevolent consequences being what we would call today the ecological crisis, including the chronic and deliberate abuse of nonhuman life-forms. I'm not certain how far I would want to draw the consequences of saying so, but the development of a belief in heaven, along with a misunderstanding of the Genesis mandate that as "the image of God" humans "subdue" the earth, has been a singularly vicious culprit in our marauding of the planet, a major perpetrator in our betrayal of what Whitehead called "world loyalty." It is becoming increasingly clear to many that our home and its inhabitants would likely be much better off if human consciousness had never conceived a heaven or drawn itself so closely to it as God's home. Thus, in a shocking twist of common pieties, and in alignment with the minority traditions above, a more pervasive virtue, a greater care might exist in human behavior if in fact we behaved as if there were no afterlife—or if we still must assert one, that it brings us back to the earth from which we came. The obvious caveat here is that this approach could also lead to a sybaritic depression that scorns care for the sake of pleasure, including the pleasure of a willful death.

A third approach to the experience of hope is the one I prefer, indeed the only one I consider legitimate from the tradition-source of Christian religion in the teachings of Jesus—though I admit that in certain circumstances of my life each of the first two have also appealed. It is what I call hope as mission. Here it is precisely the earth and its inhabitants that are the object of hope, particularly when we share the vision of the second approach that much of what we see of life on earth involves suffering. Unlike the second approach, however, this one is not concentrated exclusively on ourselves or select groups we care about, nor on employing hope as an escape mechanism blurring pain in raptures of heavenly joy. In Buddhism it is the approach of the bodhisattva on the verge of nirvana, a final release from suffering, who refuses this release and continues living for the sake of diminishing the pain of others. The mission is to *all* life, and to all its pain, and the commitment to assuage this pain as much as possible. But again a familiar critical point is reached, at least in my own regard: as a species we are weighted too heavily toward malice, not just in our finitude, our fate, but in our destiny, our choices; we are individuals not concerned enough for the whole—not just the whole species but the whole of life—because of a self-infatuation that cannot break the bonds, or breaks them only intermittently, of proximate self-interest. I do not say this as someone apart from the judgment, but as someone on whom it is intimately made.

There is a further dimension to this same point that is the more essential one for our present concern. It reads like this: if we are incapable of redeeming our world, yet continue to affirm a hope whose mission is exactly this redemption, then the world needs the persuasion of God. I am partly happy with this conviction, since it weds me to an ancient, consistent, and urgent theme in every religion I know of, and that surely will perdure on any agenda for Christian religion in the coming millennium. But I am also partly unhappy, not with the conviction, but with the suspicion that some readers will take it as merely a rehash of old ideas, especially, perhaps, those caught up in the appeal of science, its methods and results. I am stuck here and cannot find a way out, since merely a clever rewording of the conviction won't obscure its age for the perceptive reader. And I'm not sure this is advisable anyway: first, because ancient ideas, including ancient religious ones, are not by that simple fact useless to a contemporary culture—this is the judgment of an adolescent mind; secondly, because this whole book speaks of my willingness to challenge ancient ideas when I find them inappropriate or unworkable for a contemporary culture—this is the judgment of what Yeats would call the "cold-eyed" mind, or what I would call the eye of theological realism. To redeem our failures we need a persuasive act of God, or as a Christian would say, *another* persuasive act of God, this time more thoroughly effective. But in my judgment this hope can do nothing more than exist; to this point in time it has never seriously affected human behavior with sufficient weight to overcome our evil with good, and, left on our own, I don't believe it ever will. Consequently, this is my only telling argument against all schools of Christian theology that premise their encouragement of human betterment on our capacity to conquer human-caused evil through determined, and if necessary, violent effort. My objection is not first to the violence, though Christianly its use is abhorrent, but to the presumption of the effectiveness of human effort roused to action by devotion to justice and blessed into success by God's compassion. Has God been sleeping through all previous millennia, and the saints among us too, persuading no kindness?

Science can assist us with enormous effect if we understand hope as a mission commitment to the world. In fact, its healing and agricultural technologies alone could obviate much of the pain we observe, and the so-called soft sciences like psychiatry or psychology, alone providing therapeutic analysis or together with a humane use of chemicals, can lessen or dissolve for many the spiritual crisis hopelessness can create. And if the many scientists I know are a reliable indicator, such uses of their science is a paramount concern. But Yeats's cold eye must also be cast on the same sciences that cavort to produce technologies of monstrous destruction, or recommendations for the experimental uses of such things as psychotropic drugs and disciplines of behavioral alteration that leave nagging uncertainties as to the virtue of the scientists and an inevitable fear of megalomaniacs of any type, but particularly those in control of arsenals, schools, and churches, who would hesitate little to employ them. Furthermore, hope as mission also turns us directly back to the concern of this chapter, and as the stance of the last few paragraphs indicates, not because the benevolent treatment of plants and animals can benefit *us* all the more, since then it functions merely as a form of species-conceit, but because they are other life-forms that are likewise caught in rounds of pain and destruction that, when addressable, should be addressed. There is no choice in this *if* the cherishing of life is indeed the primary trait of peacefulness, and this peacefulness the controlling goal of religion, or any ethic that seeks the whole world's good as more than a passing dream, a hopeless extravagance of imagination, or a fantasy of escaping from present responsibility.

Yet the hope we are talking about must remain limited in its effects, not only because of our finitude and the constraints it places on us physically (as in our need to eat) or intellectually (because the effective use of intellect is interwoven with these physical constraints), but because it functions as an ideal and hence can never be fully possessed. Why, then, continue? This is a legitimate inquiry, and it becomes especially pertinent whenever cultures find themselves overly involved with issues of achievement or success. Every religion I am familiar with addresses it according to what Jesus designates in his own religious tradition as "purity of heart." In my judgment it is the luminous mind of Kierkegaard that has provided the most telling analysis of this phrase: namely, purity of heart is to will one thing. What he means by this is that if we look to the motives for why people do the good, we discover just two fundamental ones. The first he calls double-mindedness, or doing the good for the sake of a reward. The reward can be of a type we anticipate while alive, usually with small patience for delays, or, for every religion asserting the possibility of a blissful afterlife, heaven. This represents basically a childish motive, since the equation good = reward, and its counterpart, evil = punishment, provides the most effective pedagogy in the moral training of children. The sad and inevitable problem that emerges, however, is that every growing child soon learns that a switch of terms in the equations often represents more accurately the experiences the child is having, such that doing good is frequently punished (the contempt of peers, failures in self-satisfaction, and so on) while evil is rewarded. At this point every worthy parent tries to oblige the wisdom of religion and teach the child to do the good simply because it is good, whatever its consequences might be. Yet this further pedagogy appears for the most part a failure, and people maintain themselves in double-mindedness rather than single-mindedness. Double-mindedness therefore becomes the control over how they structure for their lives what we've been calling destiny.

Single-mindedness toward the cherishing of life is rarely distorted in religious parenesis (preaching designed to incite, challenge, or console toward an ideal in ways that refuse qualification), though in practice (and nonparenetic preaching) it very often is. The *auto-da-fe* of medieval and Reformation Christianity would be a case in point: the execution of heretics after absolution to ensure their heavenly life. So would all religious wars slaughtering parts of populations to establish the remainder (after due catechesis) in a righteousness also earning heavenly life. Such events constitute a dangerous memory for us, these distortions that presume to tell what is needed to procure God's pleasure. They are dangerous in the sense that forgetting them makes their repetition more likely, thereby excluding the only peace whose character we can in fact establish for ourselves: not a heavenly but an earthly peace, not an eternal but a temporal one. The situation for science is far more ambiguous, since single-mindedness in its regard pertains almost exclusively to unveiling reliable facts about the physical universe, whereas in religion it is an ethical perspective directed toward doing the good. This is the ambiguity men like Einstein and Oppenheimer felt when the facts about nuclear reactions were applied to weaponry. The passion of these men was directed toward the discovery of the intricacies of matter and space-time, the motivations that caused the universe to be the way it is, and to discern, in Einstein's words, whether the universe was friendly or not. They were abhorred when their own scientific single-mindedness was betrayed by applications that denied the ethical single-mindedness that they thought must also prevail over our behavior. The difference between them is that Oppenheimer finally consented to these applications, whereas Einstein never did. This is the same bind some other scientists have found themselves in, particularly biologists and chemists, but twice-felt because of the experiments they deem necessary to establish reliable facts: the damage and death done to the experimental life-forms themselves, notably the mammals, and then witnessing these facts employed for further purposes of destruction in commercial and military ventures. I league myself, therefore, with those among these scientists who propose the following considerations, and I would recommend that in the coming millennium Christian religion adopt identical or similar ones as well.

1. The first consideration has to do with the scientists themselves. There is nothing prohibiting a scientist from being as thoroughly committed to religion as to science, and nothing that obliges him or her to ally indiscreetly with one or the other when values come in conflict. If the value is as integral to world well-being as peace, and if this peace originates in the cherishing of life, the scientist must maintain a single-mindedness whenever the specifics of research or application begin to offend this value, just as he or she must if the specifics of religious doctrine or practice do. A thousand enticements can pull strongly away from this commitment, as well as a type of distorted single-mindedness that compels the scientist to complete a task once begun (perhaps the most powerful enticement of all, especially when linked to fame or financial reward). As in the case of Oppenheimer, this was the terrible bind several scientists found themselves in when building the first nuclear bombs at Los Alamos. The rest of them, however, along with many of the military and political personnel, were ethical cretins whose vision did not extend beyond swift victory for the purpose of establishing the United States as the unassailable and so unquestionable military-industrial-political power in the world.

2. *All* life is to be cherished. When research or application denies this with regard to nonhuman life, the value of both is to that extent abrogated. Scientists are as ethically accountable for what they do, rather than what they say, as anyone else. And any secular divinizing of science (with scientists as the new priesthood) that attempts an exemption from this principle is a sacrilege, a demeaning of intrinsic worth—in this case, however, more against the hallowedness of life than against God.

3. In many areas of research and application computer simulation can replace plants and animals (each year between 100 and 200 million animals are killed in laboratories throughout the world). This is one of the singularly most important advances in experimental science and should be encouraged. Yet this same encouragement also raises the very serious question of whether these simulations can become so exact as to become the equivalent of the life itself. This is a difficult issue, and there is nothing approaching a consensus among scientists regarding its resolution. There is little doubt, however, that in the coming millennium computer technology will become vastly and

more intricately sophisticated, so as to allow behaviors that today are still dreams. Christian religion will have to be very cautious here, and this, I suspect, through three stages. The first is the stage of enchantment—where we now fully are—and it has the danger of establishing an intimacy of relationships with machines that threatens the generous pursuit of relationships with other people and other life-forms, the bonding that takes place in the sharing of experiences. This is already a common and serious complaint in our culture, applied especially to young people in the classroom, adults in business or professional environments, and both in the home. We are being dehumanized by our own machines whenever an excessive companionship with them is counterinfluencing their primary intent: to free us from tasks for greater time spent with each other. It is a situation that for many astute observers is getting alarmingly out of hand through initial infatuation with a clever technology, the little effort involved in establishing companionable contexts with computers, and a growing rebellion against the "human world" as too demanding, too frightening, too inconsistent, too self-centered, and too boring.

The second stage is that of confusion—where we partly are—and it has the danger of disorienting us because of a failure to apply a satisfying ethics assessing the extent to which we wish to establish our dependence on computers. I suspect the foremost illustration here is the effect of computerized technologies on the job market in countries like the United States. We are not at all certain that we approve of the way these technologies are disattaching people completely or even partially from their work, and so from their sense of contributing to the world. It is a frustrating situation for many and tends to produce feelings of absurdity about the purpose or integrity of their lives. (A different situation is occurring in education: the computerization of knowledge making whole libraries available from all over the world to individual scholars inclines them to limit their fields of expertise and intensify their research to a precision that will make impossible—or, if the precision allows no exceptions, disreputable—the one thing that education in so many areas even now desperately needs: the insightful and imaginative generalist).

The third stage is that of either identity or rebellion—where we have yet to come—and signals that a conviction or operative decision has been reached. "Let us give ourselves over as completely as possible to the technology" is the decision for identity, proposing a cybernetic future where even subjective immortality—as in the theoretical suggestions of physicist F. Tipler—becomes possible via our machines: a placement within a computer network so refined and encompassing that the simulated identity we exhibit is the one we've always experienced, though edited appropriately to bring out the best in us, and our joys. On the other hand, "Let us give ourselves over no further to the technology," is the decision of rebellion, proposing now a limit to intrusions on our identity for fear of losing it in a forgetfulness induced by the attractions technology offers (like Tipler's subjective immortality) and a sense that this forgetfulness is a betrayal of our place in the universe, or religiously, an offense against God. It is toward this last sentiment that I myself am inclined, though not from the theoretical objections some scientists raise regarding the limits to which computer technology might stretch, but from ethical ones recognizing that up until now even our most praiseworthy technological goals have frequently had a way of getting perversely derailed by human vice, or failures of adequate forethought, so producing our unending capacity and willingness to ruin things. This is my same discomfort with the galloping speed of current DNA research into genetic manipulation. Having said this, however, I will admit that a contrary view also has its appeal for me, namely, that an increasing computer dependence, particularly in visions blending computer technology and the biology of genetic research in the production of human cyborgs, would with proper ethical care toward the cherishing of life at least be of potential benefit to nonhuman life forms too used to our rapacity and indifference. Transforming ourselves deliberately into a new and more benevolent species does not depress or frighten or anger me—if I thought for one moment the benevolence could be guaranteed.

4. But as long as we remain biologically identifiable as what we are, our fourth consideration remains pertinent: our finitude traps us in the need for organic nourishment. With increasing precision and success, however, chemical and biological research is offering us not just visions of our future but synthetic diets here and now that not only do not require plant or animal death, but will likely prove healthier for us. As with the previous point, this research should be greatly encouraged, especially if eventual product costs are kept at a minimum to

ensure availability for the world's poor. It is better, after all, to eat a synthetic gruel nutritionally complete than the slop, even when tastier to the accustomed palate, that many in the world do. The well-to-do opponent who says to all this, "But I want my steak," could be educated out of existence within a few generations.

5. A fifth consideration acknowledges that while computers can be used to simulate life-forms for experimental purposes, there may be some procedures that will still require the living plant or animal. There are two major criteria to be employed here. The first is that *under no circumstance* is the organism to suffer pain (I put the comment this way because there is a growing number of experimenters who insist that *all* living plants and animals respond to certain stimuli in ways best interpreted as an experience of pain—though commonsense observations have told countless people this for millennia) and that any procedure that cannot guarantee this must be abandoned. Obviously this criterion applies more thoroughly the more the nervous system or its equivalent is developed as a receptor of pain; if there are no indications whatsoever that pain is being endured (with the above comment in mind), the criterion does not apply. In this regard we should also mention the suggestion that animals other than humans cannot feel pain because as a biological phenomenon pain also requires self-consciousness. This is a major concession to foolishness, and is denied every time we witness the agony of an animal in the control of a vicious or indifferent experimenter—just what does the witness think is going on in the animal if not pain?—as well as in our own spontaneous response to experiences like a sudden burn. Even as we involve relatively simple life-forms in the experimenting, a deliberate and humane research program must first determine the extent to which pain is possible on the basis of lesser pain already endured, and then build into the experiment its very quick alleviation, and no death. This first criterion is undoubtedly disturbing to many readers, some of whom will dismiss it out of hand. But the second one will likely be even more disturbing. It insists that all experiments on a life-form must have as a controlling purpose the increased knowledge and/or benefit of that life-form itself. This applies especially if the experiment is being pursued for the primary benefit of some other life-form, such as us. If we need to experiment for the purposes of cherishing human life, therefore, medical experimentation above all, and we have

insufficient data indicating that the use of other life-forms will benefit either them or us—then if the experimentation is still judged necessary, it must be performed on human beings. It is ethically wrong, even in medical procedures, to presume that other life exists solely for our free use and benefit.

6. A final consideration recognizes the problem of population control. Should the previous five considerations ever be seriously enacted, especially the second and third, the most obvious way of avoiding an overpopulation of life-forms for our feeding and experimentation is to let the remaining members die naturally, or, if there is concern that a species once alive should never be allowed to become extinct, methods of humane sterilization of select members should be employed. This last is also the wise counsel of many organizations regarding the abundance of cats and dogs in pet-oriented cultures. Since willing abstinence during fertile periods seems beyond the talent of most human beings, similar procedures may also be required eventually for rampant human population growth—though again, a species-centrism, often a species-conceit, makes this suggestion abhorrent to many. Yet if other methods of population control—excluding, from my perspective, abortion, war, and such options as lottery terminations—are not willingly engaged, this one appears the most effective option left. Chemicals carefully monitored and released into the air and water could also assist nonlethal birth control over more inaccessible populations such as insects. It is extraordinarily difficult for me to write such comments, since they seem to indicate not a cherishing but a tight control of life, especially the comment on sterilization (which, additionally, is an issue of painful controversy in my own religious tradition). My position is that it is the higher value to prohibit the beginning of life if the existence of too many members of a species seriously *threatens*, not just inconveniences, their own quality of life or that of other species. The same principle, however, also prohibits me from recommending any method of control once life has begun, that is, once an organism has begun manifesting the majority of the four biological traits we have been employing in this chapter (reproduction must generally be excluded, since it almost always waits upon a degree of metabolic growth after birth). This principle applies, given these traits, even if the life is not yet viable outside the mother. What we must encourage is prevention of the very beginning of life for the

purposes of population control, but never its destruction once it has begun.

A memory of mine nags at the close of this section. When I was a young boy I once captured a number of fireflies, put them in a capped jar, and brought them inside to show my father. He was a man who often surprised me by his sensitivity to life. It was night and he said we should go back outdoors where we could better appreciate the beauty of their light display. We did, only to have him point out the many other fireflies in the yard and to ask if I didn't think they were more beautiful in their free movement than the confined ones in my jar. I knew at once they were, he looked at me as if to say, "Then set them free," and so I did. When he smiled at this and decided to say something outrightly, he theologized the issue by asking if I thought God loved me more than the fireflies.

To this question, as to the one about their beauty when flying free, I knew the answer at once, said no, and he smiled again. This memory nags at me because for many years afterward I denied my response and my father's smile by thinking my superior worth to a firefly was inarguable, and my response a child's innocent fancy, my father's smile a facial poem for the moment. Now I am not so sure, not sure at all, that my child's response was not the correct one, the smile not an aching hope, one of a mission to the cherishing of life that he wished me to demonstrate even more faithfully than he. Several years ago I also heard a renowned physicist, Stephen Hawking, say that anything that happens in one part of the universe, no matter how small the scale, affected to some degree everything else that happened in the universe. It too has been a nagging memory, since it expands to the largest proportions, now in a poetry of care that for a moment translates the physics of indeterminacy, every act whereby we cherish life, and oppositely—to which we now turn—every act whereby we profane it.

Educating One's Conscience

To profane something means to debase it by an unworthy or wrongful purpose; when religiously employed it means to violate or treat with irreverence, or to blaspheme. Like the cherishing of life, therefore, to profane life presupposes acceptance of an ethical vision that we are free to honor or offend. In chapter 5 I will be suggesting that a powerful motive in the construction of such a vision is how we understand God. For now, however, I want to mention two other motives, both obvious, but only one of which—the one, unfortunately, least convincing to many—appears able to persuade human behavior across cultural boundaries. The first motive is disciplined education. By the time you are twenty years of age and have always been taught, or taught preponderantly, that plants and animals exist solely for purposes of human use in pleasure, entertainment, food, and clothing, it takes a seriously engaged pattern of doubt or a catastrophic conversion experience to alter the ethical control of the education. The recognition of this appears constantly in the complaint of those who do cherish life that the one who profanes it is not acting so much out of malice as out of ignorance, or perhaps better, from a narrow-mindedness of ethical vision that the individual has not had sufficient reason to expand. The formative importance of early education has always been acknowledged by ministers of religion because of its quick and lasting influence over the young, so that to whatever extent religious education has taught a cherishing of life limited to only select forms, such as other human beings and God, it has been a major contributor to the profanation of all other forms. That Christian religion has a profound obligation to teach the young must remain on any agenda for the coming millennium, with some special urgency in our own culture in the United States. But *what* it teaches must include not just doctrinal content but an encouragement to continue this education in analytic and critical ways outside the formal structure of schools and programs: to become, in short, diligent and confident in educating oneself. This encouragement is above all the task of theologians.

The second motive is conscience. To a considerable degree the role of conscience in structuring an ethical vision is guided by the first motive, the type and extent of education one has enjoyed. A deeply ingrained education during formative years can convince the individual that the values taught are ontologically anchored, a part of one's very being such that fidelity or infidelity to them becomes fidelity or infidelity to oneself: a conclusion enhanced if the same education and same values are also shared by many others. This seems to me a legitimate orientation toward understanding the meaning of conscience. But I also think there is something else, perhaps best described as an internal sense of rightness and wrongness of behavior toward other life-forms. A brain physiologist given to speculation might describe it as an imprinted residue of experiences we've inherited from prehuman species before the persuasions or chance of evolutionary direction or randomness led to us. There is the possibility in us of a genetic memory that intuitively identifies us with other life-forms through a complexity of neurological linkages, which in turn is embellished by the knowledge that all life is derivative from the same source in particular atomic and molecular arrangements. This does not compel us to cherish these other forms, any more than we can be compelled to cherish ourselves, but it can elicit a reluctance to actively profane them, a feeling in Whitehead's sense that we would thereby be profaning ourselves. This is a phenomenon we discover throughout our behavior: not a clear preference to do the good, but a definite preference to shy away from deliberate evil. Both preferences are frequently weak, especially the second, and their presence as controls is difficult to articulate, but religion has had a tendency to do so in terms of innateness—the analogue to the equally difficult and slippery descriptions drawn from the notion of genetically transferrable neurological linkages in the brain. What many people "know" is that when they are standing between a tree and a boulder, there are stronger feelings of intimacy with the former than with the latter, and that to damage a tree is somehow of greater ethical concern than to damage a boulder.

The description of conscience I'm offering here, as the intuited intimacy between ourselves and other life-forms as well as the product of education, is what the prophet Jeremiah is getting at in his distinction between the law written on our hearts and the law written on stone—or what a Navajo shaman once described to me as an untutored and tutored sense of right and wrong. These descriptions are as handy as any others, and to them we could add not just the previous notion of genetic memory but also Jung's concept of the collective unconscious. All of them are saying basically the same thing: that just as we are not a *tabula rasa* physically when we are born but the inheritors of a vast history of life-forms, so we are the same in the working of the mind in its reliance on the brain. We are not fated in this latter inheritance, as fate was previously described, but these intuitive realities are factors in our destiny, providing "impulses" in the choices we make. Christian religion is usually comfortable discussing this phenomenon more in terms of God's spirit or presence working within us as an autonomous agency (Jeremiah's "law written on the heart"), and genetics or psychological patterns as its mediator or secondary cause. What these comments are suggesting, in other words, is that judgments against the profaning of life are not solely a matter of aesthetic discernment, since this can only sometimes break the confines of the individual's biases, but of a discernment of conscience, an irksomeness in the mind that propels us away from neutrality and gives us the feeling that we have the *right* to be heard because to some degree we are identified in our own life with the issue. It is the same feeling many have toward the issue of God, and so a taproot into people's minds that Christian religion should continue encouraging in the coming millennium, far more vigorously than in this one, when far too often the religion has been defined almost exclusively in terms of propositional assent, the way one might assent to a theorem in geometry neither understood nor persuading one's behavior.

There is a process whereby conscience can be enlivened and made powerful over an individual's life, and I draw it from the pedagogy of conversion we find throughout religions. It has three stages, and I'll offer here a brief description of each. A similar process can be detected, though with much different content, in the movement of scientists from one explanatory paradigm or model to another. However, I will want to concentrate only on the religious process. The first and most critical stage is evangelization. It has two parts, and in each the controlling experience is beauty. In the first part the individual becomes attracted to a particular religious vision (defined according to the famous three "C's" of Hegel: the religion's creed, or system of belief; its code, or system of ethics; and its cult, or system of worship) because of how he or she observes its adherents treating each other. The behavior is judged according to a defining quality of all beauty, that is, its lovableness, or more basically still, its loveliness. The second part involves the individual's observation that this behavior is indiscriminate. It has nothing of the flavor of a gnostic sectarianism or species-centrism about it, and is freely expressed toward *all* life. To the individual's perception, in short, there is a universality of application in the behavior that the observer concludes is extended even to himself or herself. This is what an old Christian tradition captured as one dimension of prevenient grace, the awareness that in some way I am already a part of what attracts me. And the tradition is undeniably accurate in also understanding this experience as essential to a desire for more thorough participation. A conscience well-formed in the cherishing of life has become such because other consciences so formed have provided experiences of beauty in both words and deeds that seduce an abiding interest. The observer is thereby led to the self-identifying conclusion: that is the way I would like to be.

The second stage is catechesis. Through evangelization the interest of the observer has been enlivened and an impulse of conscience has provided a sense of obligation to pursue the beauty experienced. In religion this stage is predominantly one of education, undertaken at the desire of the observer to understand why those observed behave as they do (secondarily, the ones observed seek confidence at this stage that the observer is understanding them correctly). This is the way it always is with beauty, as we noted when discussing ideals. Appreciation alone is enough only when the beauty remains abstracted from one's life; when conscience stirs a sense of obligation toward it, appreciation seeks knowledge of the beauty—which means spending time with it that is informative, analytic, and critical in purpose. (In human relationships this can be a difficult task if the perception of beauty is not mutual in the partners, or is mutual but not growing in interest at the same rate; in both cases the one partner will feel overwhelmed by the other's attentiveness and likely begin to complain of it, usually to the other's surprise.) In religion the analytic and critical components take place both by way of direct communication with those already committed to the beauty—education in the formal sense demanding a spirit of open-minded docility—as well as by an internal dialogue, a talking to oneself regarding the quality of one's knowledge of the creed, code, and cult, and the greater thoroughness this knowledge requires for their fuller appreciation—education in the informal sense demanding a spirit of clear-minded humility. This second stage never ends, since a point is never reached with any beauty that is functioning as an ideal where *all* knowledge of it has been gained. There will always be more ahead: a generative permanence of new historical data, insights, and possibilities coming to light in ways that require the obedience we earlier described as a giving over of oneself to a concentrated and undistracted study, meditation, or prayer.

The third stage is conversion. I've already noted that the word *conversion* derives from a Latin intensive verb meaning not just "to turn," but "to turn radically so as to be going in a completely other direction than you were." In our context it represents the moment of conviction, an experience of certainty that what you have found beautiful and have given devoted attention to over an extended period of time, is now something of a part of you sufficiently powerful that you are markedly different from what you were before. Some psychologists will talk of this as a "peak experience," philosophers will describe it as a compelling insight, a mystic might talk of *metanoia,* a carpenter of change of heart. A scientist, departing the terrain of ethics but still in that of knowledge, might talk more abstractly of a new theory or new paradigm. But he or she can also identify with the whole foregoing process: a perception of the beauty or elegance of a new interpretation of data, the full-hearted research it elicits, and then the moment of conviction that the interpretation is accurate and a new theory or paradigm established. In its attitude toward the livingness of things the converted conscience thus moves from the intellectual/emotional easiness of profaning life to one of cherishing it. Yet this ease of attitude does not necessarily procure an ease of activity, a putting forward of the attitude in deeds. Conscience at this point then becomes an accuser, the gadfly Socrates talks about, because we have a spontaneous dislike for discrepancies between thoughts (or words) and deeds, unless a clever and finagling casuistry talks us out of it—though to a truly converted conscience this never lasts. For the discrepancy still aches under the tight bandage of our casuistry, and we know that only an unwrapping of it will speed the healing process.

Of many examples of such discrepancies in my own experience, I will give one that occurred not long ago. My book, *Bless the Beasts,* had just been published, and I was at a bookstore signing copies when a woman came up to me with tears in her eyes saying how much she had enjoyed the text, especially the chapter on the therapeutic effects of animal care. I couldn't believe my ears, because there she was standing in front of me draped in a full length chinchilla coat. I became very angry, and asked her to stop her praise. The self-centeredness of her remarks concerning what her pets did for her, the assertion that "of course" she only kept pedigreed animals, and the obscenity of the coat made me harsh toward her in that nervousness of outrage that Camus so forcefully describes. To breed and raise animals only to kill them for their furs or skins to satisfy the vanity of the rich or the depravities of current fashion is an absolute profanation of life, and in my judgment as a Christian theologian, a sin. There are times and situations of biblical tragedy that infiltrate all our lives, when all the choices we have are evil, and I am aware that many millions of people must still take life to clothe themselves adequately. But I am equally aware of two other things: that when all the choices are evil, you decide for the least evil among them, such as an animal already dead from other reasons rather than a live animal for your clothing; secondly, and more importantly, I am aware that technology has advanced sufficiently to provide synthetic materials fine and adequate enough to clothe the whole world. A monied woman, or man, draped in animal furs is a barbarity to the eyes of any conscience seeking peace through the cherishing of life. And a religion that ignores or ridicules or blushes at this judgment is an accomplice.

There are other barbarities, and most are familiar to the informed reader. The cosmetics industry in American and European countries earns many billions of dollars every year. A huge number of the products involve the killing of plants for their ingredients, and many involve the killing of animals. The latter fact in particular is usually camouflaged on the label by descriptive terms that very few people are aware point to fluids or liquified parts of animals. The manufacturers know that if they were precise or blunt in these descriptions, many people would be repelled by the product. And so a distancing occurs either through the use of technical jargon or, very commonly, euphemisms. Much of the educated buying public probably has at least a subliminal awareness of what is happening, but as long as the distinct and common words describing the ingredients are not used, concern becomes softened and usually muted. What educated man or woman knowing of the plight of many marine mammals wants to hear or read without these verbal obscurities that oil in their favorite facial emollient comes from the heads of whales? The banal excesses of human vanity, linked to a proclivity to avoid challenges of conscience because life is thought to have too many challenges already, guarantees the success of the word games on the packages or in the advertisements. A more outrageous obscurantism occurs in keeping from the public the cosmetic experiments performed on living animals, with rabbits, cats, and dogs being special favorites in the laboratories. Grading toxicity levels in eye liner, eye shadow, and mascara by dropping burning and blinding chemicals in rabbits' eyes, and then out of "humaneness" for the brutalized animals killing them, is a monstrous ugliness and hypocrisy on the part of those involved, and something of the same on the part of those using the products but refusing to hear of the experiments. Dogs and cats punctured, sliced, and dismembered around the world to test "regenerative" liquids and ointments, along with purported aphrodisiacs requiring parts of an animal for the mixture's success, are further illustrations of how for the sake of self-infatuation we curry and support the profanation of life. And in those few countries where there are laws prohibiting such ethical obscenities, only a happy naivete would not know that they are honored far more in the breach than in the keeping.

Military maneuvers and weapons testing link activities profaning non-human life to those whose purpose is to profane our own. Scattered bombings of so-called uninhabited land, or nuclear detonations underground "where they do no damage," are deceits. So are naval operations that imply in promotional films and pamphlets that because we can see no life on the water, it isn't there, though the vast majority of it in fact lives just below the surface as much as 90 or 100 feet down. Test firings of weapons are also frequently trained on live animals, as are chemicals and fumes for biological warfare and mechanisms of torture. A general once commented on these facts before an animal protection organization, but did so not in a context of shame or a bothered conscience but in one of pride for his country's military technology and continuing research in ways to kill. At the time he boasted particularly of the potential for laser-based weaponry in satellites circling the planet, and also of work being done on a bomb capable of destroying all life within the parameters of its immediate and residual effects, but leaving buildings intact. When asked about the animals being slaughtered during tests, he replied in a manner—though he didn't know it—also suited to such Christian thinkers as Origen, Alan of Lille, Thomas Aquinas, Luther, Calvin, and Karl Barth, among countless others: that it made no difference, since a higher life-form, human life, *American* human life, was being safeguarded in the process by a policy of "aggressive peace and protection," and that most of the animals killed in laboratories and on testing sites would die anyway from lack of care. Given the quality of his response, no one dared ask him how he thought these animals have so far survived without us.

I wish to extend these critical observations to include food. Everyone, of course, is aware of the human need for certain proteins and other nutritional requirements that are most easily, or at least most habitually secured by eating various kinds of meat. I noted earlier, however, that these requirements can also be met on a vegetarian diet, and that many physicians and nutritionists agree that such a diet is in fact the healthier one because of the absence of animal cholesterol, the increased concentration of certain vitamins and fibers, and so on. I also mentioned the research currently being done on the similar and even greater benefits of synthetic foods. But until these other options become more widely available and/or acceptable, meat will remain a standard component in the diets of many cultures. To this situation I can only reiterate my previous comments on finitude and biblical tragedy. My specific concern, therefore, is with what I would call "exotic" meats, the killing of a whole variety of animals simply to satisfy the curiosity or catholicity of self-indulgent human palates. In some parts of Asia, for example, monkeys are gagged and bound and the top part of their heads forced through a hole in the middle of a table, where it is then lopped off with a machete so the brain can be eaten warm. And baby or child animals, with scarcely a chance at life, like ducklings and fawns, are served as grotesque delicacies; veal is the flesh of a child cow, and infant lamb stewed in wine or milk is considered by many exquisite to the taste. I know people who have told me they will eat anything once, save human flesh, and speak as if this were a point of pride with them, an expression of adventuresomeness that they would never detect in not eating meat at all. Toward these animals they would never attribute the idea—though because they are Christians they do to Jesus—that the animals' life has been ransomed for the health of their own, and that the appropriate response is a profound but sad gratitude. Christian religion, and religion in general, has work to do here in the coming millennium.

My observation of naivete could be turned against me, with the statement that I am the one who lacks realism if I think the foregoing judgments and recommendations will be taken seriously, or as anything more than sheer idealism, or what some philosophers call the pathetic fallacy (a misplaced pity, sorrow, or concern). I am sensitive to this comment, and sometimes even toy with its legitimacy myself. No one needs to remind me of the harshness of the world or of human vice: these will both come quickly forward in the next chapter when I assess ourselves as a failed experiment in evolution. But for the moment I will note that I have already taken my stand on the side of idealism, though not as foolish fantasy making, the way the word is often used, as above, but rather as the pursuit of beauty in recognition of limits, of destiny in the context of fate. I know that for some readers the suggestions I have made for the coming millennium are so unlikely of fulfillment as to be virtually useless. But that is not the point, since fulfillment, achievement, complete success are not available in the pursuit of ideals, and any proposal or insistence that they are has simply not understood the character of ideals from the start. Instead, the issue is one of degree of implementation, or as I've otherwise put it, of the weight of our behavior, or of the passion of our striving. If judgments and recommendations regarding *this* issue are dismissed as fanciful or unrealistic, then so be it. That person and I are heading in different directions when assessing the capacities of human desire. And though I think we will surely fail in seeking peace as the cherishing of life, and profaning life will be our undoing, until then we can show what worthiness we do possess by continuing to strive—like all other animals who merit our admiration when inevitable extinction still does not prevent many from seeking the ways of vitality still available to them. The difference is that one of the ways of vitality open to us but apparently not to them is the way of ideals, the liveliness of beauty and its good pursuit.

Encouraging the pursuit of ideals is the responsibility of religions everywhere and at all times. Yet religions have also regularly demeaned themselves by a discrepancy between the words and deeds of cherishing life—and here as elsewhere in the book, I am isolating for concern the teachers and formal magisterium of the religion. The discrepancy becomes especially alarming when it manifests itself at the very heart of a religion in its styles of worship. I am talking about the sacrifice of human or nonhuman life, literally or metaphorically, particularly as it presumes to demonstrate gratitude to God in the context of self-interest. A common expression of this is the first-fruits sacrifice, whose pure intent is to signify in the destruction of select portions of field or flock, usually the first-ripened or first-born, that all the plants and animals, in fact all life, belongs to God. It is a horrendous theology that underlies the practice, the idea that death in the context of worship is somehow pleasing to God, *and* that because of this God will bless the field or flock even more abundantly with new life (this is the self-interest, which in some religions, as with primitive Judaism in certain circumstances, applied even to the first-born of a human couple). It is to the enduring praise of teachers like Jesus that they prohibited such sacrifices among their followers. In fact, several Christian scholars now suggest that the most offensive deed to ordinary piety Jesus committed when he confronted the merchants in the Temple was not the overturning of the tables and driving them out, but the freeing of the animals purchased there for sacrificial purposes (a practice his own parents engaged in to meet the purification requirements after his birth). Jesus, like Gautama, didn't want the sacrifice of plants or animals. He wanted the sacrifice of the evil in human hearts, with no surrogate ways around it. Christians cannot claim much success at this task, but at least the sacrifice of plants and animals has never been a part of their formal theological traditions and is found only where Christianity has been blended with other traditions to produce the hybrid sociologists call Christo-paganism, as in the practices of voodoo and Santeria.

Nonetheless, the cherishing of life has had a consistently more faithful acknowledgment in religions like Buddhism and Jainism (the latter, as the former, being a heterodox version of Hinduism) with their doctrine of *ahimsa*, noninjury, than it has ever had in Christianity, where nonhuman life, though not ritually sacrificed, is for the most part treated with indifference, contempt, or the aforementioned self-interest (almost from its beginning this attitude can be laid at the door of Origen in the early third century, as against the attitude of his great predecessor Irenaeus). Even in discussions with Christians involved in animal care I very rarely hear their commitment described as the result of religious obligation—except in reference to the example of St. Francis, in a somewhat oblique and no doubt unintended confirmation of Nietzsche's judgment that Francis is the only true Christian who has lived since Jesus. But a Buddhist or Jain would do so at once. The Christian attitude is perhaps demonstrated nowhere quite so explicitly, and aside from brutal deeds nowhere more uncomfortably, than in the utilization of animals as personifications of evil. Even though the Genesis narrative of the primal couple doesn't support it, the serpent, functioning as a tester, an adversary as in a court of law, was interpreted from the beginning of Christianity, following a popular Jewish exegesis, not only as evil but as Satan himself, much like the Beast in the book of Revelations and the common portraiture imagining him with distinctly animal appurtenances like horns, a tail, and as with serpents, vertically contracting pupils. For centuries there was also an identification between cats and the presence of evil (perhaps because their pupils also vertically contract), culminating in the superstition that they were the preferred familiars of witches. Ravens and birds of prey also fell into this category with some frequency, as did goats and spiders. Rats were universally reviled as demon-inspired carriers of disease, and anything living underground was thought to do so because of a preference for dwelling closer to hell. Many of these outrageous images still control the immediate response countless people make toward these animals because the mythologies and superstitions are so embedded in the art and preaching of Christianity (as they are in other religions too), despite the fact that not one of them has even a remote anchorage in the teachings of Jesus. And where this contempt or fear does not exist, as in the sophisticated theologies of commentators like Barth and Bultmann, indifference does, or at best a human-oriented utilitarianism. There are many who follow the ways of St. Francis today, but with the possible exception of the Dalai Lama of Tibetan Buddhism, not one of them has world renown.

The profanation that goes on throughout this whole development sounds a peculiar psychological signal, the kind telling us that we are radically defaming what is good—or at least sinless—to convince ourselves that our lesser virtue is better. The success of this maneuver, of course, lies in the fact that animals, let alone plants, can't defend themselves against it. It is similar to the individual who is otherwise poor at speaking except when railing against God. Then he or she becomes passionately eloquent, words and damning phrases coming quickly to the lips (a bravura performance, worthy of a high-priced lawyer)—all because God will not answer back. I've seen the same thing with women, battered and abused by spouses and children, when tormenting the family dog. It is not that animals like this cannot appreciate the meaning of set words and phrases or by their own methods communicate; they can. But in situations of hostility from a human being, when the dog or cat is the surrogate for the human who deserves the anger, the growl or the frightened whimpering, because it is verbally bereft, is taken with the same spirit as silence in ancient laws: as consent, in this case to the legitimacy of the abusive, accusing, and condemning language. We blame the dog, as Christian tradition blames the serpent, because we refuse to blame ourselves. There is deep pathos in this, and the shame of ethical failure that occurs whenever innocence is maligned by deceit. The most powerful and lasting image of evil I have ever seen was not a serpent, raven, cat, or spider, but an utterly malevolent man with a smirk on his face after brutalizing his two-year-old son.

I am going to suggest in chapter 5 that just as Plato's thought largely controlled the philosophical and psychological format of Christian theology for its first millennium, and that of his student Aristotle for much of the second millennium, Whitehead is an excellent candidate for doing this in the coming millennium. Woven throughout his philosophy is an implicit psychology that encourages the appreciation of a metaphysical view of the universe that seeks to establish the interlocking being of everything that is, a process of inheritance and bequeathal from every entity to all others—or what he calls the adventure of the universe as One. It is a wondrous vision he offers, and it is gaining an increasingly sympathetic response especially among scientists, with theoretical physicists being the most outstanding illustration. The appreciation of his vision, however, like the vision itself, is not just cognitive but affective as well, a matter of "feeling" when this is understood to include both learned and intuitive content. Such feeling is exemplified at its highest pitch, so far as we know, by human beings, and therefore ought to call forth from us the most thorough response. This notion of "calling forth" is very ancient and directly or implicitly undergirds every understanding of vocation with which I am familiar. I am particularly alert to its description among biblical prophets, and devoted much space to it in a previous book, *Christian Commitment and Prophetic Living*. Yet its presence in Whitehead's thought is far more expansive than in most of these prophets, establishing a vocation not just to other human beings but to the whole of creation, since there is nothing done that does not impinge in immediate or remote ways on everything else. There is a hidden ethic here, in other words, that depends not first on an arbitration of the good or the true, or even an aesthetic of the beautiful, but on a metaphysics of the wholeness of creation—one that includes in privileged cognitive and affective ways, because of the intimate linkage of human vocation with them, plants and animals that metabolize, grow, reproduce, and adapt on this earth together with us. If superiority is sought in this relationship, then, it is not because it is possessed by either one of the partners, but because it resides in both due precisely to the relationship. In this sense there are no inferior relationships, which in turn gives us access into the concern of the next section: the communion of life.

Values and Violence

In religions that never develop a notion of the afterlife, and in the finer traditions of some that do, the question of death is forced to take on a much different complexion than the usual one, "Is there life after death?" I call these traditions "finer," however, not in the sense of better, but to indicate that they pose the inquiry with greater refinement so that it is one every human being can ask, even those who will entertain no possibility of life after death. This finer question reads: "Is there something for which I am willing to die?" In some strands of biblical tradition it is judged the most important question a person can ask, since its answer provides the enduring commitment that guides his or her life. To this I would add that it also provides one of the clearest indications of the extent to which we seek communion with others: a sense of identity is constituted between myself and those I am willing to die for such that their absence, like death, denies this identity altogether. This is surely something of what Jesus is getting at when he says, "No greater love than this has anyone, that you lay down your life for your friend." The friend in the statement provides the commitment in your life, or that to which you are utterly bound in self-identifying communion. If we add at this point our previous description of ideals, then the friend represents your perception of beauty at its highest pitch, that for which you will strive without qualification. This is why the death of love is perceived throughout the world's literature as involving a type of death of self—not always in the literal sense, but in the awareness that what drove the very intent of your life is now gone, and only an emptiness, or nothingness, the blank abyss of poetic imagination, is left.

Yet this notion of giving up life for one's friend can in fact have a literal application. This is what occurs in every case of martyrdom to a cause or person, some of heroic proportions and an intimacy of sentiment, as when Jesus dies for the God he preached, some more spontaneous though no less heroic, as when a woman saves her child from a speeding car at the cost of her own life. It is clear from such examples that the word "friend" is functioning generically to describe anything lovable, just as the word "enemy" in the mandate "Love your enemy" means any-thing you find unlovable, not just what is trying to damage you—and that this lovableness toward an enemy also does not need conscious at-tention before it is enacted. If we combine these two understandings of friend and enemy we can then conclude that at least in the teachings of Jesus, the profoundest expression of love is when you lay down your life for your enemy. The importance of this identification cannot be under-estimated in any cherishing of life that is also Christian. It is, for ex-ample, the surest mechanism for achieving an absence of war, though among individuals and groups soaked in a sense of ideological superior-ity, it is also the most abhorrent, tasting of indifference or lack of prin-ciple when, to the contrary, it demonstrates the most intense and prin-cipled cherishing of life I know of. If you will not kill an enemy, if you will die for the enemy who in the alchemy of love has become a friend, then war as *mutual* destruction cannot exist and the destruction becomes plain savagery, a massacring bloodlust. Of such behavior, of course, we are also quite capable, and among animals the only ones—with the pos-sible but unproven exception of other primates—apparently capable of it in premeditated ways (by which I mean our talent for abstraction and forethought guaranteeing confidence of success in the behavior, or differently, its near total dissolution as a gamble). An entomologist once told me that of all insects the praying mantis is apparently the only one that will kill neither for food nor any apparent posture of threat from its victim. Yet the animal does not plot or plan its brutal revelries. There are no fantasies, no wounded feelings, no ethics involved; there is just the attack, and then the dying. Theologically we might say that God's suc-cessful persuasion of the world into animal life involved risk on God's part, because with this success not only nurturing but also killing strate-gies emerged for purposes of survival, gain, and domination.

We can presume that the vast majority of animals do not possess a reflective self-consciousness, by which I mean the ability to formulate abstract notions such as that of a continuing identity (like the soul or self in theological/philosophical traditions, with accompanying intellectual talents like the notion of cause and effect and the logical structures of mathematics), or that of pursuable ideals (like goodness, beauty, and God). This is why I am reluctant to assign their behavior ethical designa-tions such as cherishing or profaning life. This is a heated controversy among ethologists, usually centering on questions of the altruism in animal behavior. Is the baboon who sacrifices his own life to warn the troop of an approaching leopard being altruistic or submitting to the genetic dictates of the survival of the species, in a similar way that the reproductive urge does? I don't know the answer to this question, and many scientists confess the same because sufficiently reliable evidence is not yet available. What I do know is that all life is subject to its finitude, and that when our ethical categories are applied to the behavior of nonhuman life, we again find situations where all the choices are evil, but that a choice must be made: the individual baboon dies, or the troop is marauded; the thistle chokes off the dandelions, or itself becomes weak and stunted to an early death; the virus kills your cells in order to reproduce, or itself perishes. But just as I am reluctant to assign these life-forms an awareness of ethical categories of cherishing or profaning life, so I am reluctant to do so of the metaphysical category of the communion of life. Yet this reluctance by no means requires that *we* cannot look to these life-forms for illustrations of each of the categories. This is similar to the distinction J. McDaniel makes between a moral agent who can be held responsible for behavior toward other beings, and a moral patient as anything worthy of ethical regard, both in how it is treated and how we can learn from it, and as such deserving the respect and care of moral agents not just as an object but as a subject to itself (and hence possessing intrinsic value). We in fact acknowledge this distinction every time we assess our own behavior in the light of what we observe in animals, sometimes in criticism—as when the communion of life in a bee colony is used to describe the seemingly mindless and rote activities of a particular human group—or sometimes in praise—as when this same communion becomes a model for cooperation when an individual sacrifices selflessly for the sake of the community.

The notion of intrinsic value in plants and especially animals needs further clarification beyond the theological avowal that it exists because the whole of creation is derivative from God. I would like to pursue this briefly in two stages. The first pertains to Whitehead's distinction between entities as monarchies and democracies when this is applied biologically. A biological monarchy is one wherein there is a clearly defined and functioning center for the reception of sense data and responses to them. This is what we usually designate neurologically as a brain. A biological democracy, on the other hand, is one where there is no such clearly defined and functioning center. For Whitehead this is the major distinction between animals and plants, as well as the major criterion for assigning greater intrinsic value to animals and, among animals, to those with more developed neurological centers. In a world where biblical tragedy prevails, for example, and we must kill to eat, this criterion provides a basis for deciding what our food will be. The second stage pertains specifically to animals (though a minority of scientists would also apply them to plants) and criteria for concluding that as monarchies they are subjects with interests of their own (a furthering of intrinsic value). I will again depend on J. McDaniel here, who himself is depending on Bernard Rollin's excellent work, *Animal Rights and Human Morality*, though I will make some minor amendments. The two of them list five criteria. First, there is the evidence of neurophysiology, that is, the ability to respond to external stimuli in ways that indicate interests of the organism as a unified whole. Second, there is biochemical evidence of mechanisms permitting alert consciousness of what is happening to the organism. Third, there is behavioral evidence, demonstrated especially in movements of thrashing about and/or vocalizations indicating the animal is experiencing pain. Fourth, there is anatomical evidence indicating the presence of sense organs that permit some degree of consciousness in determining how these organs are utilized. Fifth, there is the evidence from evolutionary theory suggesting the implausibility of denying that any organism that has a nervous system manifesting biochemical processes that in us allow consciousness, and that withdraws from the same painful stimuli or other dangers that we do, and that has sense organs, is not, as each of us is, a subject with interests of its own. These five criteria, along with the distinction between organisms as monarchies or democracies, indicate from their anthropomorphic basis that knowledge of ourselves and some of the biological motives whereby we assign ourselves intrinsic value can again be applied to secure reliable knowledge of other living things.

To my mind, therefore, anthropomorphism can be an effective way of relating to nonhuman life. And this is so not only in the above sense of providing illumination in understanding other living things biologically, but as a way of securing a more thorough awareness of the metaphysical communion of all life. It is, if you will, our privileged avenue into this appreciation because it takes the most competent knowledge we have, knowledge about ourselves, and applies it to the less competent knowledge we have of other life. Anthropomorphism, in other words, is a form of analogical thinking providing a mutual knowledge both of ourselves and, in terms we can understand and assimilate in familiar ways, of the other. Religion has always made much use of this procedure in its attempts to describe God, in both the subtle workings of philosophical theology and the more immediate and pictorial ones of mythology. And we do so for the very same reason I believe we should maintain an analogical approach to nonhuman life: to achieve a sense of communion or identification. Yet in an image I am taken with, that of two overlapping circles, we must also remain explicitly aware of those areas of separateness (as in our forgoing examples) that provide pluriformity and distinctness, including, for religion, the distinct human preoccupation with God that other life-forms apparently do not possess. Aware of this proviso, then, and in opposition to a modern bias especially prevalent in the relationship between Christian theology and animal-care issues, I would suggest for the coming millennium an intensification rather than a diminishment of anthropomorphism as a critical method toward achieving greater consciousness of the communion of life.

While it may indeed have a literal application in certain instances, then, describing love as giving up your life for your friend nonetheless achieves its greatest compass in a metaphorical application to the spiritual life. This puts us back into the context of Jesus' criticism of animal sacrifice (if we have understood the "Temple incident" correctly) and his concern that sacrifice be done, but that it be drawn from one's own life, especially the sacrifice of sin, and not from the lives of others. It is a self-directed move he is calling for, an inward one that identifies obstacles to the pursuit of ideals and in fidelity to one's destiny as his follower attempts to overcome them. An identical teaching can be found in the sermons of the Buddha and most other great teachers of religion. In our present context, for example, we must sacrifice whatever aesthetic appeal there might be in all artistic expressions that, without anthropomorphic allusion, personify evil in animal form: as if the animal in its own life were morally evil. This is most urgent in the aesthetic education of children. I have lived long enough to know that the adult conceit claiming that childhood experiences exercise little or no control over life except when we permit them is badly mistaken. And since most of this portraiture has been done in the context of religion, with Christianity as its foremost practitioner, I am calling for an aesthetic reformation in the coming millennium that will relinquish these personifications in the uses of music, painting, sculpture, the language arts of metaphor, simile, and analogy, and so on. We must also sacrifice the easy attitude of indifference, especially when it seems the only recourse for the sensitive mind overwrought by human savagery toward nonhuman life. And in the spirit of the *oikumene* that the world truly is, we must sacrifice all notions of superiority to other life-forms, while simultaneously sacrificing the uses of our technologies exclusively, or nearly so, for our own benefit.

I have sometimes heard a peculiar rationale opposing the above viewpoint, one that presents itself as incorporating a more profound service to the cherishing of life. It has to do with the strengthening of adaptive ability through the imposition of stress factors; in this way there is assisted the natural stresses that allow only the fit to survive when competing with them (forgetting, of course, that cooperation is also an evolutionary-adaptive requirement, and very often a more effective one than competition). So we should not worry overmuch about the damage we do to the land, water, and air, the pollutants with which we are engorging the whole world, since their presence has already caused the most amazing genetic adjustments in viruses and bacteria, flies, fleas, and mosquitoes. This is the stance most at home in hard-boiled military and corporate ideologies, and sometimes in a naive religion, though here the same situation is analyzed more in terms of God's testing the worthiness of life-forms to endure than in terms of genetic adaptation (which would function only secondarily, if at all, as the means or method of the testing). On three occasions I have also heard proponents of the ideology take the obvious next step, suggesting that such imposed stresses will also fortify the descendants of our own species; that to curtail these pollutants is tantamount to contributing to evolutionary weakness. There then followed diatribes against the "eco-freaks," as one of them put it, whose obsessive interest in the cleansing of the planet and the care of all its life-forms was a sin against the future strength of living things, and thus no cherishing of life at all. In all three cases the listeners' initial perplexity at the remarks gradually gave way to about half of them indicating agreement, though the consensus here was that because such an ideology was not politically correct, they preferred to keep their agreement to themselves in most forums. I was stunned by the glibness of all three discussions, but alerted once more to how persuasive and clever we can be when justifying even our most serious flaws, and how willing we are to gainsay, ridicule, and threaten other viewpoints, even ones of virtual unanimity among the competent observers of a situation. I might add that one of the speakers was a priest-scientist.

I imagine that if we had the greater possibilities toward genetic mutation and physical adaptation that viruses, bacteria, and many insect species apparently have, we might be able to take the comments of the above speakers a bit more seriously. For one thing, however, we can't reproduce ourselves to even a minuscule fraction of the pace and numbers these life-forms can, making survivable or successful mutations more likely. Nor are we as genetically simple as they are. In fact, all the evidence we have indicates that the more complex an organism becomes, the less successful it is in adapting to environmental alterations, even slow ones measured in decades, centuries, or in some cases, millennia. Instead, it simply becomes extinct, as with about 97 percent of species that have existed. Yet in our own case the situation is different, qualitatively so, because while no natural mutations have succeeded for hundreds of thousands of years, they can now be induced into the population by our genetic science: a radically different issue from that of nonintrusive species weakening or strengthening due to spontaneous gene-shifting or mutation. This is an extremely complex and delicate topic, and as I indicated earlier, our talent at genetic manipulation, though still in its infancy, is not even close to having a guiding ideology or ethic. What we have so far is basically one primitive maxim with two different emphases: we will do nothing that will damage our own species (to say "threaten" is an extension of concern not yet fully acknowledged at this primitive level), and we will do everything to benefit our own species. The pathos in this primitiveness is that it expresses a robust hope that has no adequate support in our current knowledge. We can make calculated guesses, perhaps of tremendous sophistication, but we cannot say for certain, as we cannot for naturally occurring mutations, if one crafted in a laboratory and released into our environment will not itself undergo an independent and threatening mutation at some later date. I am therefore ambivalent toward genetic manipulation, not so much because it is unethical as because it is dangerous. And if a previous generation saw threat in the work of nuclear physicists who gave us unleashed fire as Prometheus of old, this generation should see the same in the work of biologists who would give us unleashed life as Pasiphaë of old—Pasiphaë, the mother of the man-beast, the minotaur.

In my judgment it is a primary task of religion to sound a warning similar to the above, as it is of any humanism intent on safeguarding avoidable dangers by a satisfying pursuit of educated forethought before the pursuit of action. At this point religion might find itself in legitimate dispute with science, particularly its theoreticians. For what most theoretical scientists desire is to see their discoveries put into practice: this is a leitmotif throughout the history of science in all its branches, and it represents a fair expectation since the practice is understood as the needed final proof. But terrible chances have been taken in the process, gambles that speak more of impetuosity than adequate forethought, or of pressures placed by powerful authorities external to the science, political/military ones especially. To my mind, when confining ourselves just to public record, one of the most frightening of these centered on the great theoretical physicist Enrico Fermi. Until it was actually exploded, Fermi thought that the surface detonation of the first nuclear device might ignite the atmosphere. His opponents were vociferous, both among the other physicists for theoretical reasons and the political/military leaders for reasons of strategy to end the war with Japan as quickly as possible. The point I wish to isolate is that when someone of Fermi's stature raised this frightening possibility, all further procedures for exploding the device should have been halted by his colleagues, and the aggravation and hostile posturing of the political/military personnel on the scene should have been resisted. But there was pride involved, a professional pride in the predictions of the other scientists—most notably, after a wearying battle with his doubts, J. Robert Oppenheimer—and only the actual explosion, the putting of theory into practice, could rest the case. The event obviously proved Fermi wrong, everyone relaxed. And in the time since, as often happens, a foolish hindsight has frequently made light of the issue. But what matters is what those involved, especially the scientists, thought *at the time,* and whether the gamble, no matter how serious or far-fetched they judged Fermi's caveat, was ethical.

A similar situation prevails in the field of genetic experimentation, with one major proviso. There is no urgency to this research as there was at the end of the war, except for whatever urgency corporate leaders may impose to be the first to develop any new and saleable technique; most of the larger, up-to-date laboratories are owned by private corporations. I certainly would not diminish the pressures this situation can put on a scientist, but there is little of such bedrock considerations as patriotism, the quick end to extended slaughter in a current war, religion as the rightness of a way of life, ideologies of superiority in governmental forms (democracy versus tyranny). Some of these might be remote considerations, intensified by a quasi-hysterical jargon of technological preparedness in order to extend the scientists' passion beyond the satisfactions of successful research or monetary profit. But there are no enormous numbers of human lives at stake, and very few of the researchers care about the nonhuman life their experiments are damaging and killing. What these and other concerns I've noted in previous pages are telling us is that one responsibility integral to the character of Christian religion is to confront these situations and call a halt to them until an adequate ethic premised on the cherishing of life as a *comprehensive* as well as immediate value achieves a general consensus. It is not that this ethic must emerge out of the conversations of all, or of their representatives in council. This can happen, as many examples drawn from the congressional history of this country would indicate. But it is just as likely, as the history of religions amply illustrates, that it will emerge from the teaching of one, taken up by an initially small but committed group, and received by others intuitively as correct. Christianity itself is certainly a foremost example of this process, as are Buddhism, Taoism, and Islam.

Throughout these pages I have spoken repeatedly of intuitive experiences. Because they have played a critical role in all these instances, I would now like to attempt a description of what they involve. Everyone I've spoken to on the issue agrees that intuition exists, and all claim to have experienced it. But when inquiring as to its nature, vast webs of confusion, along with quick failures of precise terms, typically result in sudden statements like, It's just there; something happens in your mind and you become convinced of the rightness of an idea or feeling. I've tried to escape this imprecision by studying masters of the intuitive sense—mystics from a variety of traditions, some of its philosophical exegetes like Hegel, Lonergan, and above all Schopenhauer and Santayana, and many, many poets. I've also examined work done by psychologists and brain physiologists, and from all this emerged with a feeling of dismay that didn't advance much beyond the above statements. So I decided to look to myself, knowing that all the descriptions I read were in my memory, circling around until they came to their own accord on the issue. What I decided to do, in other words, was wait to see if I could have an intuition about intuition, a peculiar phrasing, but capturing one of the few things all the analyses agreed on: intuition's suddenness. I think I may have experienced this—of all things while planting portulaca in my garden—and while the description now seems quite simple and commonplace to me, it is critical in capturing the source of much of my own thinking. Intuition means that we cannot *fully* analyze the workings of the mind; the mind continues with its computations while our conscious thinking is directed elsewhere, until these computations themselves come into sudden consciousness at their completion. By this definition we may say that intuition functions intellectually in much the same way that spontaneous mutation does biologically.

It is intuition understood in some fashion as this that percolates subliminally in our awareness and gives us "feelings" about experiences which at some later point in time may emerge into a more definite and describable idea. We can repress these feelings, and if we do so powerfully enough we can obstruct their emergence into consciousness. This much seems clear from both theoretical and clinical psychology, though no repressive maneuvers are apparently powerful enough to guarantee that the intuited idea will *never* come to clarity in conscious awareness. I remember walking beside a colleague one day as a small spider crossed the path in front of us. Her gait was such that her shoe would have crushed the animal, yet she intentionally jerked her leg and avoided the killing. She was a biologist, but the rare kind who had a serious avocational interest in theology. As it happened, we were discussing how ecological concerns had infiltrated the writings of a number of contemporary theologians, and that two of the dominant motives for this were reappraisals of the Genesis creation narratives along with the Pauline doctrines on Jesus as a new Adam and his salvific effect extending to *all* creation. We had discussed these same themes several times before, and I had no reason to think she had abjured her timeworn view that the rest of creation existed for the uses of human need and pleasure, including the intellectual pleasure of biological research into the puzzles of life. I called her attention to her sudden awkward move, and asked why she did it. The question perplexed her, and her initial response was a confession of ignorance, "I'm not sure," then following immediately upon it, "I just had a feeling that I shouldn't do it." When cautioned that the reason was perhaps a sensitivity to my presence with her, she was certain that it was not, and then turned the conversation back to its previous topic. It is these and similar experiences all of us have had that give us an inkling of how intuition operates.

It may have been the whole composite of many discussions her mind was computing, even though her conscious attention was on our immediate conversation, that caused the directive—still only a "feeling" to her— interrupting her gait. Two of the three psychologists and one of the two brain physiologists to whom I related the above story were comfortable with this interpretation. But the other psychologist and brain specialist were more in accord with a view that I myself have also become more sympathetic toward over the years. It is centered on an idea that I've noted before but which has never gained popularity enough to garner serious financial assistance for its thorough study by a large enough number of professionals. I am growing more convinced that a further reason why my colleague did not step on the spider, and possibly the dominant one, is that the intuitive function of her brain was computing not just memories of her own experiences, but inherited memories buried in the labyrinth of her genetic makeup, possibly in the memory of all her cells— since genetic science teaches us that we can indeed speak this way—but very probably in those brain cells whose particular proclivity is precisely the storage of memories. Very few biologists seriously entertain anymore the idea that our brains are a *tabula rasa* before we begin educating them after birth; instead, the vast consensus is that this education begins at some point prior to birth. This is the safe because generally acknowledged position, premised on the bias that a certain degree of brain complexity is needed before memory can begin to persuade the behavior of the organism as a whole, or notable portions of it. Single-celled organisms, or indeed any not manifesting this degree of brain complexity, are thereby denied memory in how they behave, and similar behavioral patterns are consigned to rote action or the very simple imprinting of primitive neural structures. Yet if we take a cue from Whitehead, to assert that memory occurs in a society of cells does not preclude its occurrence in every individual cell independently of this society; or more exactly, it could occur within the cell's own society as an entity, in its genetic structures, and ultimately in the society of its subatomic particles.

I am enchanted by the above proposal, since it again interlocks all life into a communion that is more than metaphorical, but has a physical/ metaphysical basis as well—an idea likewise appreciated with exquisite sensitivity, and a special delight on my part, among peoples like the Hopi and Lakota (Sioux) of North America and the Jains of India, though it is also present in Christianity in individuals like St. Francis and even a diligent dogmatist like Gregory the Great, as when he writes that there is "within us something of the birds, of the flowers, of the stones." Earlier in the book I was concerned with this basis at the primordial level of the being of all things. Now I think we can give it further content in at least the minimal sense of describing a mechanism—memory—whereby the inheritance of each entity binds it to all previous and successive ones, and that in some life-forms this mechanism achieves self-reflective rehearsals of its content both in deliberate and directed thinking as well as in intuition. This assertion of a shared inheritance is also a commonplace in religions. In some, like Christianity, it is confined throughout most of the tradition to the generations of humanity, with a special emphasis on the inheritance of sin through the mere conception of a child. Fortunately these traditions are for the time being in disregard, because inevitably they link sin and its effects to nonhuman life as well— a presumption of the universal importance of what humans do. In other traditions, like Hinduism and Buddhism with their doctrine of multiple births, the progression of inheritance also includes nonhuman life, which partially explains the notable reverence they have for these other forms, and in which memory (though in most of the traditions, not a self-reflective one) is active in the passage from one form to another as a determinant in what the reborn form will be. We should not let the foundational myths and doctrines of such religions, simply because they were formulated well in advance of current doctrines in science, dissuade us from a search for a communality of fact and intuition between the myths and science. This is to develop a bailiwick attitude that has never served the communion of life, in this case an intellectual communion among ourselves as we seek communion with all else to serve the purposes of a prevailing peace.

The therapeutic effects of plants and especially animals in the repair of human feelings is publicly and widely enough acknowledged to speak not just of a communion between ourselves and other life-forms, but of a healing communion. Children demonstrate this all the time when they seek out animals for preferential company instead of their own kind whenever bothered or psychologically wounded. And this is one reason why when others note a child's abuse of animals, even small abuses, a warning is being sounded of serious psychological disruption. Studies of convalescents have also verified the healing assistance of animals, particularly ones that can be held and stroked to their obvious pleasure. And of special poignancy is the well-attested relief that the care of animals can give to the elderly suffering from feelings of rejection, loneliness, and perhaps a too thorough concentration on self. This last example is a particularly sharp concern to me, and in our context of care for nonhuman life I find it satisfying to expand this context by adding to our agenda the absolute obligation to provide for *all* the needs of the old. In Judeo-Christian tradition this is captured with exquisite clarity in the fundamental law code influencing the whole of this tradition's ethics. There is nothing in this code that names specifically your spouse, your child, even yourself and how you are to behave toward them, but only God in the first three of the commandments, and then following these immediately in the fourth there is this: Honor your father and your mother. There are no qualifications attached, no exemptions offered, and it is the only one of the ten that has a promise attached: that you may live long in the land. And if their own children disobey, the commandment requires in its application that others honor beyond their own biological parents all who have also given life to others and now need their own lives cherished as the end of their years hovers nearby.

In the context of the old at the end of life I will bring an end to this chapter. As the years go by and the more I learn of the earth, its inhabitants, and the universe in which they exist—our three concerns in these first three chapters—the more I think Christian tradition is in error when it proposes history as a temporal line issuing in an absolute term. I am more sympathetic to the image of it as a circle, though not one of endlessly repetitious cycles that do not alter from one beginning to the next, but more like a spiral in an infinite density of movement, duration, novelty, and relationship: what I have offered as my own characteristics of life, which are the same as the characteristics of everything that is. Perhaps a more accurate image, then, might be that of a swinging pendulum, which can swing neither at identically the same speed as it moves from one side to the next nor come back at each full swing to identically the same point—which makes this image also like that of a pulsating heart. In the spiral, the swing, the pulsations lies the communion of life in which we are all caught, and perhaps explains why many of our old, who are close to the end of one rhythm, feel such profound attraction for the young at the beginning of another. An intuition encourages them in this. But while the rhythms lock us into a communion with life as a wondrous fate, how we act within this communion is a destiny, a function of choice. And this brings us finally to our fourth chapter and fourth concern, the least appealing of them all, humanity.

Chapter four

HUMANITY

THERE IS NO doubt that of all biological life-forms indigenous to earth, ours is currently the most influential. Scientists argue as to what makes this so, though all agree on at least four things: first, and of unquestionable predominance, is the brain, particularly its size and organizational structure; second is our bipedalism; third, and related to the second insofar as bipedalism generally frees two of our appendages from assisting locomotion, is the excellent manipulability of our hands with their opposable thumbs; fourth is the structure of our vocal system, permitting a large multiplicity of sounds and eventually words. From these four derive most other traits also recognized as contributing to our influence, though to varying degrees each is dependent on the first, the exquisite complexity and talents of our brain. In this context the ability to conceptualize and create tools of survival, and then "speak" of them to others, are almost always given a preeminence of place, the premise being the prior ability to form abstractions from variant experiences that allows us to relate them in purposeful ways: the heavy stick is an effective device for individual or group protection and aggression; sharp points are repellent or killing in their hurt; put the two together and the stick becomes a spear. Also frequently noted as a contributor to this influence is the long dependence period of child humans, along with certain deprivations—such as the absence of claws, powerful dentition, and speed against predators—all of which encourage group behavior. Being omnivorous, adaptable to wandering, hierarchical in group organization, and willing to slough off the demands of the weak, deformed, and aged; having an innate propensity toward offensive violence in order to accumulate beyond what is needed—all these, too, are frequently cited as contributing to this influence, along with the serendipitous weakenings or extinctions of other life-forms that would have restrained or obviated our advance to dominance.

Yet this assessment of dominance is not absolute or indefinite. Certainly at the level of the individual we are quite limited, nowhere near as robust, for example, as tortoises, and little able to make our way in life as successfully as many solitary animals. Grouping appears to be a necessity. But even in very large groups we are still not as dominant as many presume. The demonstrators of this tend to be of very small size, no longer the dinosaurian monsters that helped to keep our predecessors in the mammalian line globally insignificant. I am referring to viruses and bacteria, especially the former. It takes no imagination to realize what would happen to our species if the AIDS virus, or a successor, mutated and became transmissible by air. And the largest of any life-forms capable of threatening our stay on the planet is not very large at all, but even more lethal than the very small ones. And in a peculiarity of evolutionary adaptation, it appears to be the one life-form of all of them that we are the least adapted to. It is ourselves. Alfred Wallace, the contemporary of Darwin who proposed similar evolutionary observations as he, was deeply perplexed by this fact. He sometimes thought that it related to the size of the human brain and the inexplicability in terms of evolution of its rapid development: it should have developed only enough to give us a slight survival advantage over other animals, and not so grossly as to produce its degree of talents not needed for survival. Darwin was just as perplexed, and the time frame he and Wallace usually presumed did not permit the existence of "missing links" that would trace out a much more gradual development. Even today when we have identified fossils of bipedal hominids several million years old, there is debate as to whether sufficient time was available for the brain's development, its amazing educability and plasticity of function.

It is not that there are no other animals who have brains equal in size to ours or even larger; there are, just as there are many other animals possessing the same characteristics we previously mentioned (bipedalism, opposable thumb, etc.). The difference, rather, appears to be one of relationship in at least two senses. The first is that the size of our brain in proportion to the rest of the body appears excessive to the needs of internal control, unlike, say, a whale, whose brain is much larger. This excess seems to be what allows for unique degrees of ability at abstraction, imagination, memory, and communication, though the initial registrations of these in the first few years of life also seem to be one reason why physical autonomy comes relatively slowly in our development: the brain is still small, and since others take care of our physical needs during this period, it can devote itself to familiarizing, controlling, and learning to harvest these abilities fairly soon for purposes of self-interest. The second relationship, and by far the more telling one for our species survival and dominance, has already been touched on: the ability we have to draw relationships from disparate experiences to form abstract possibilities whose realization we can work to secure. As far as we know, no other life-form can do this with the abundance, precision, and technical application that we enjoy. An arrogance on this point should be avoided in the awareness that the working of genetic mutation ultimately brought it about. This suggestion is a particularly unpleasant one for the religious consciousness of many, but the scientific data are too reliable to deny it. Any person arguing for the presence of God in the evolutionary development of our species cannot intelligently forswear these data so as to postulate a direct and privileged interruption, or a series of them, to account for our distinctness in creation. This is the way Wallace went with his perplexity about our brain size, whereas Darwin chose *agnosticism*, a word coined by his greatest defender, T. H. Huxley. God works always within the ambience of the facts of creation—or from a different angle, God's work establishes the facts—and it is in the capacity of our brains to draw novel relationships between these facts that our primary distinction lies.

It is this residual capacity of the brain allowing it to revert back on itself in reflective consciousness that thus appears to underlie the beginning of human devotion to relationships of little or no use to immediate or extended survival. Art emerges early as one of these relationships, as, apparently, does music, mathematics, and almost definitely, religion. This echoing effect of brain-consciousness—observing the world and having the observations bounce back in retentive ways that are then interwoven with each other to produce not just ideas but articulable ones that can then be tested against the similar observations of others—is where I locate the origin of explicitly human intellect and discursive language and reasoning. Eventually, when these ideas began to become more inclusive, when proximate similarities conspired toward the notion of general similarities, and inductive logic was born, abstraction became not just available to human thought but its defining component. It is as an abstraction emerging from observations of similarities in the dependence of all things on the presence and power of other things that I will suggest in the next chapter the idea of deity arose. To utilize concerns from chapter 2, the process may have gone something like the following. As I observe my own reliance and that of other living things in my immediate environment on land, water, and air, and having heard the same from my neighbors, as they have from others, so as to conclude generally to a reliance of all living things on land, water, and air—I then ask of their origin, or on what they themselves are dependent, and religion begins to appear. In short, I am sympathetic to Schleiermacher's proposal: Religion arises from feelings of dependence as these are abstracted to include ever widening observations that at some point seem to justify a universal conclusion. As far as we know, human beings are the only life-forms able (or interested enough) to do this; only humans have religion, just as, through the same process, only humans have mathematics and theoretical science.

It is with fair reason that our ability to abstract inductively has been greeted with ambiguity by many analysts of human behavior. The beauty in the talent is precisely the comprehensiveness it permits our thinking, the imaginative extension of experiences that underlies our capacity for theorizing. (The roots of the word *theorizing* go back to that singularly imaginative people, the ancient Greeks, who prized it so highly as to link it to divine behavior; *theory* and its various forms derive from *theos,* "god.") It is what allows us to contour our thinking toward convictions of universal compassion, tolerance, and mercy, toward assertions of common human nature, desires and fears. It is what encourages us, in other words, toward the formation, proclamation, and pursuit of *symbols* as whatever captures and drives us to cherish what I will designate in the next chapter as our unitive being. Symbols and symbolic behavior cannot exist without the ability to abstract, to leave the confines of the immediate for the compass of the universal. But there is a dark side to this as well, when the same talent for inductive abstraction becomes negatively bound: the harm that the father does becomes the harmfulness of the whole kinship group; the aggressiveness of the king becomes that of the nation; the lie the lover once told becomes a life-style. I need not argue the reliability of these or other examples; they are there in each person's thinking, and they have been there from human origins. And memory holds; it holds tight to our abstractions. The dog who knew only abuse from humans as a child animal, comes to distrust all humans. Only with persistent loving-kindness will the memory begin to fade; it will cease echoing back and forth in the mind in continual rehearsal and refreshment, as sharp ten years from now as today.

It is the above conjunction of abstraction and memory that accounts for much of the directedness our lives possess, and becomes as such a primary constituent of ethics. And for many people this ethics, cast and justified in theological or God-inclusive terms, then defines exclusively what religion is. I have an argument with this view and its exclusivity, and will outline my reasons why in the next chapter. But it does present us with a second conjunction—not an identification—between religion and ethics that is often a worthy one, and to which I would like to devote most of what remains of this chapter. Feuerbach and Freud insisted that religion is shaped by experiences of childhood dependencies that in adulthood are cast in more sophisticated terms for purposes of a cogency and security they would otherwise lack. And there is no doubt that in this they have captured an important psychological impetus toward religion that we should continue to acknowledge. Even Freud, by far the harsher of the two in his criticism of religion, could now and then see the benefits of constraints imposed by divine father figures. He was, after all, exquisitely aware of the utter malice we can perpetrate, and at a certain degree of severity would recommend anything to alleviate it. But dominating his view was that religion worked toward human deprivation, excuse-making for the most outrageous irresponsibility, and a lie in the soul that deprives us of autonomous dignity. The young and middle-aged Freud was at heart a Marxist romantic who thought that hard work, a mind attentive to the tasks at hand, some system of fair punishment and reward, a civil demeanor, and gratitude for the life we have without need for another afterward, would produce as close to an ideal society as we could get. In the darker musings of his later life, though, his *thanatos* (death) principle, with its impulsive as well as planned proclivity toward destruction, came reluctantly to dominate his view of human behavior, and he began to think that the humane life was simply one that could avoid as much suffering as possible without inflicting it on others. He never admitted it, to my knowledge, but in this he was a child of his Jewish forebear, Koheleth, without the latter's final reliance on the justice of God.

The Doctrine on Childlikeness

The parent-child relationship as a key ingredient in understanding the God-creature relationship is a commonplace in religions—though in most, as in Judaism and Islam, it does not define the enduring or effective relationship, which is that of two adults in a contract with each other. Yet in some, as with the teachings of Jesus (though hardly in the history of Christian theology and devotion), it is paramount. Jesus clearly insists that there are dimensions in the consciousness of a child that make the child pleasing to God as he or she is, and that our task is to identify and nourish them for the whole of life. In other words, he is proposing childlikeness as a constitutive part of any *spirituality*—a term that I would now define (somewhat lengthily, and borrowing from Hans Urs von Balthasar) as that basic practical or existential attitude that is the result and expression of the way in which a person understands his or her religious—or more specifically, ethically committed—existence; the way he or she acts habitually throughout life according to both intimate and ultimate decisions and insights. Yet Jesus is not being indiscriminate here; he is not referring to all the dimensions of a child's consciousness, to the child's petulance or self-infatuation, the indifference he or she manifests toward the world at large or toward serious reflection on the past or future, and so on. He is referring to other traits, ones on which I would now like to spend some time. Some readers may be offended by this, adopting a Freudian smile that presumes I will be reverting to the very perspective on religion that the great psychologist found so reprehensible: that I will be demeaning the religious sophistication of the educated adult mind by proposing a sentimentality better done without— the soporific and useless kind that portraitists from medieval to Victorian times refused to indulge by depicting even very young children with the faces, posture, and costumes of adults. But this presumption is wrong in its negative assessment both of the worth of child consciousness in itself and of its value as a context for examining adult behavior. There are at least four characteristics of this consciousness to which I think

Jesus is alluding in his teachings, and they are found everywhere children are raised, save in grossly abusive or deprived environments. They are: wonder, responsiveness, righteous anger, and persistence. What I want to do in the remainder of this section and the following one, therefore, is to work out the contours of a Christian spirituality that will move from a dimension of it only here and there acknowledged in Christian religion (the childlikeness just mentioned) to one more fully acknowledged (what I will be calling messianic servanthood) to one universally acknowledged not just in Christianity but in all worthy religions (the doctrine on love). It is my recommendation that on any agenda for Christian religion concerned with spirituality as I have defined it, each of these dimensions must be included as essential—by which I simply mean that in the absence of any of them we no longer have a spirituality we can claim as Christian.

1. Wonder has a double movement in the mind. At first it is a feeling of doubt or curiosity that poses inquiries regarding experiences; more specifically, questions are raised dealing with relationships among the experiences, both within them individually and among them collectively in type or similarity. By saying that this goes on in the "mind," I am simply using a singular term—though it has had a very tortured history in philosophy, as most things have—to capture what I described earlier: that excess of activity whereby the brain can take on additional functions to its internal control of body systems. Since wonder is therefore not an ingredient essential to the physical health of the organism, we frequently find it scarcely exercised, except in children, when its potential first appears almost simultaneously with language, in questions of what and why, effect and cause. For the child's wonder typically wants a thing first described (what it is), then its source (why it is), both of which he or she also needs explained in reduced conceptualities that often frustrate the adult, such as in attempts to explain clouds, or God. This is a major reason why anthropomorphism slips so easily into religion, particularly in the use of parental metaphors to describe God's behavior in terms already familiar to the child. Because of the extraordinary power of influences shaping the growth of the mind in early formative years, these descriptions tend to be maintained as a root source for later thinking, though they are by no means unbreakable. Moreover, if children in a particular grouping, a culture or society, have been educated similarly

during these years, then even with later sophistication these descriptions can also provide a powerful source of communality within the group, a shared "vision" of the world that is further intensified if there is also a shared history.

The foregoing comments may provide us with one of the major psychological differences between religion and science. Religion tends to diminish the role of wonder as the child ages for the sake of preserving the sense of communality—even when adult wonder can be identified at the basis of a founder's teachings. In Christianity, for example, we can identify the source of Jesus' teachings in statements like, "You have heard it said ... but I say to you ..." The first part of the statement indicates the inherited doctrine, the second a new one emergent from doubt and curiosity, wonder, directed at the first. Jesus is the founder of a novel community because he broke the communality of vision of the preceding one. And many in his own day were as upset with this wonder-working as they are when it occurs today. One of the great advances of Christianity, however, is that those exercising it today are no longer killed, at least not physically: an advance Freud noted in another context when he suggested that civilization begins whenever we start hurling epithets instead of stones at those who disturb us. Science, on the other hand, can continue as such only on the basis of wonder, and so in one sense can be defined as the mind's search for novelty. It is not much conducive to communality, then, except (1) as groupings occur in the search, teams utilizing common current theories and techniques, and (2) as creating a vague sense of spiritual camaraderie among scientists as those who seek ways to understand what happens in the universe without recourse either to anything outside it or to putative avenues of knowledge beyond the accurately analyzed data of sense experience. The closest this camaraderie came to anything like the communality of vision that characterizes religion in its beliefs, patterns of behavior, and worship was in Pythagoreanism, with its rituals and mystagogic approach to mathematics.

The second movement of wonder manifests itself as the emotion or excitement created by novelty, that is, anything strange or ill-fitted into accustomed sequences of thought and the expectations deriving from them. This is the characteristic of wonder that thinkers have always had difficulty describing, even those attending to it with great precision and dexterity like Schopenhauer and Hegel. In exterior experience, the kind that comes *at* you, it is usually described in terms like surprise or shock or astonishment; in interior experience, the kind that comes from *within* you in the workings of the mind, it is also described in such terms, but more specifically as insight. The physiological basis for insight shares traits similar to intuition: it appears to be the result of memory impulses that interlock neurologically to produce expressive unity in one composite thought which, precisely because it is a composite, is experienced as very powerful, in much the same way that disparate pain is experienced more powerfully when suddenly concentrated in just one part of the body. Insight occurs when disparate thoughts similarly achieve a sudden concentration. When religiously appropriated, and sometimes scientifically too, it is frequently described as revelation. In common experience this is what happens when we have been mulling over a problem, chasing down thoughts about it in seemingly endless profusion, and then suddenly become aware of its resolution, often in the most unlikely of circumstances—ones such as Camus describes while standing on a street corner waiting for a bus—but always with a conviction regarding its worthiness. As we develop from children into adults—that is, as we accumulate more experiences of the world—the more encompassing these insights can become, and the more powerful, appealing, and widely applicable as well.

2. By the child's responsiveness I do not mean the physiological but the psychological kind. This characteristic is related to wonder as the willingness to maintain receptivity to the world and its experiences as they enter life both of their own accord and as consciously sought. This last component is what particularly interests us, since it parallels the curiosity that describes the first movement of wonder. The child is enormously curious about the world in a receptivity that seeks continual novelty, even when it might be somewhat frightening. I'm not sure why this dissipates in many adults, replaced by a xenophobia of the intellect that prefers protection from new experiences, and correspondingly new insights, in a search for the reliability of sameness. I suspect, however, that it has something to do with what I call the seduction of domesticity, first analyzed in my own life by reflection on certain biblical narratives, most notably that of Lot's wife and Moses' reluctance to return to Egypt. Domesticity is the comfort of being in a rut, one in which predictability reigns and novelty is seen as a threat. Lot's wife doesn't want to leave her

home, its reliable surroundings and the circularity of disposition and deeds that consoles her. She prefers indeed to be a pillar of salt, binding and blinding her receptivity to life's experiences whenever possible and remaining spiritually inanimate. And Moses, too, is caught in his domesticity, the steady life of shepherd and husband, its frugality of worry and metronomic regularity. Only, unlike Lot's wife, enough of the child's receptivity toward novelty remained so that he could finally respond to the call of his God. But as an adult he was aware, unlike most children, that this responsiveness had within it not just the enticement of new directions but also less pleasant results: the probability of suffering and the demand of *pathos*, the willingness to sacrifice as a policy of life whose refusal the Greeks called apathy. Lot's wife is a study in apathy; Moses only plays with its deadening appeal, then finds resurrection in something new.

Domesticity is more a temptation in religion than science, at least in their institutionalized forms. Affirmed by enough people over a lengthy period of time, ways of thinking and behaving tend to become paradigms, and these in turn tend to remain in place until sufficient anomalies force their alteration. This relates to what we've already noted about the ambiguity surrounding the legitimacy of inductive reasoning, its habit of giving one or two experiences a compass of interpretation that should always be greeted as tentative but frequently is not: the way, in short, induction insists on the construction of paradigms, and the inclination to make these infallible. So too, in the opposite direction of this process, deduction, there is also ambiguity. Deduction is the method of reasoning that seeks to go from the whole to the particulars, so that together with induction we have a two-way street: the paradigms are shaped through induction, then applied to specifics through deduction. But whereas a single anomaly in the deductive process can alone spoil a child's paradigm (the playmate who lies once will have this returned a thousandfold as the reason for a continuing mistrust), sometimes a whole army of them will not disturb the paradigmatic slumber of an adult. Somewhere between the two a compromise must be sought, so that what is still of demonstrable value is retained (as in Newtonian mechanics describing the ordinary motions we perceive) while what is not gives way to something new (as this mechanics has to quantum mechanics regarding motion in atomic and subatomic microspace). And the same must occur whenever religion is aroused from its dogmatic slumber. But as with some human beings, the sleeper may be less than courteous when awakened, and seek mightily to remove the disturbance so as to sleep again.

When paradigms are offended, anger is an understandable response. There are three qualifications to this. The first is that the anger must never be of sufficient violence to cause permanent damage or death, as this offends in a radical way our primary ideal of peace and its foremost expression in the cherishing of life. Unless children have been formed in households of violence, they seem to have an inchoate sense of this restriction. Ask a little child who is in a fury at a sibling or playmate if he or she would want to kill the other (presuming the child understands what killing means, especially its permanence), and repeated tests of this situation indicate a response of either utter perplexity or spontaneous denial, typically accompanied, however, by a strong desire to hurt in unforgettable but not permanently damaging ways. The inheritance of this is lost in the lives of many adults, and the desire to kill in fury can become rampant, especially when bolstered in groups. A second qualification pertains to manipulative anger. Children are susceptible to this—many parents will say they are masters at it—and it is one of the few workable devices they have for the satisfaction and protection of their self-interests. But their various techniques are obvious to everyone-except, perhaps, those who over-indulge the child—whereas the adroitness of the same type of anger in adults frequently is not. This is the verbal bully, for example, who will wear you down no matter what with a posturing volley of shouts, threats, and insults until for the sake of peace or from sheer weariness you consent to his or her will. We need hardly add that this is also one of the more time-honored practices in diplomacy. The third qualification pertains to brooding anger, the constant rehearsal that keeps an offending remark or deed alive for years through attentive nurturing in the mind. This anger provides a prime example of the perversity into which inductive reasoning can lead: when on the basis of a single incident, or even several of them tightly or loosely allied in time, we generate a whole attitude of dislike or hatred. We see this repeatedly in individual lives as well as those of whole groups—in this latter case sometimes for centuries, as the offense, not suffered by those now alive, nonetheless remains vibrant in the memories passed down and usually embellished from one generation to the next, thereby

creating a volatile anticipation of inevitable repetition whenever the opportunity arises.

3. But there is such a phenomenon as righteous anger, our third characteristic of childlikeness. The presumption that the anger is righteous
is based on the judgment that a legitimate and fair expectation has been
offended, and that to remain silent before the offense would constitute
consent. The classic Christian illustration is Jesus driving the merchants
from the Temple courtyard and releasing the animals sold there for sacrifice. (I would offer a note pertaining to the use of this passage by those
who would cite it against pacifism at times of threat: if Jesus indeed struck
the merchants, it would have hurt; as noted earlier, though, the point is
that he produced no permanent damage, let alone death, and the hurt
wasn't habitually applied.) The offense in the Temple was twofold: both
the profanity of hawking religious wares and services reminiscent of what
occurred in the temples of Roman-Hellenistic religions, and the abomination of sacrificing animal life to please or placate God. This second
motive is an excellent illustration of the criterion I would suggest for all
obligatory expressions of righteous anger. We are all aware of how criteria can vary on this issue, how the combatants on the side of every dispute believe their anger to be righteous, and how this can especially bond
with brooding anger so as to survive for long periods of time. We are
also aware of how righteousness can easily become self-righteousness in
anger, that peculiar and sad demonstration of pride that Jesus isolated
for particular attention in his teachings. For as we've noted before, self-
righteousness presumes goodness in the person displaying it—and this
is where its sadness is rooted—with the additional factor of using this
goodness as a criterion for judging others—and this is where its peculiarity lies, in its contradiction in behavior toward others of the goodness the individual otherwise manifests. Righteousness consists not in
self-glory, a drawing of attention to one's own goodness, but in doing
the good for purposes of instruction and hope, that is, to demonstrate
confidence that providing enough evidence of right behavior through
satisfying the demands of conscience will induce others to a conversion
toward similarly good behavior. In this context anger can be a creative
act, instead of the depressing one it usually is.

As suggested, it is the freeing of the animals during the Temple incident that gives us our primary criterion for self-righteous anger, which

is the same as the primary ideal being proposed throughout this book: the honoring of peace in the cherishing of life. Little children are constantly and powerfully moved by this ideal, especially in their reactions when they have offended it—at least until they learn the tricks of casuistry to excuse the offenses. Piaget and Kohlberg both place the general age span where this ideal dominates at four to eleven years—always, of course, with broad latitude and the recognition that an abused child is almost always echoingly abusive of other, weaker life-forms. For adults these other life-forms can be much more inclusive than the obviousness of tortured and sacrificed animals, children, or other adults. Religious wars, for example, are fought on the judgment that others have abused God's existence, by denying it or demeaning it in heresy or sacrilege—though thereby ridiculing our first criterion. Wars have also been engaged for the cherishing of a nation's life—though again the first criterion is ridiculed. Cherishing life must never cause the permanent damaging or death of other life. And in cases of biblical tragedy as I described it in the last chapter (where all the choices are evil, and you must choose; in our context, where every choice will issue in permanent damage or death), the weight of consideration must always be given to an assessment of how many lives will be damaged or dead due to enacting the choice when compared to refusing it—and if such brute quantity is not an issue, then a judgment of whose continued life will most likely enhance the cherishing of life. Righteous anger is always centered on considerations like these. Yet its root always lies not so much in an assessment of actual deeds as in a contemplation of those facets of human temperament, and a rebellion against them, that make outrages against the cherishing of life possible in the first place.

4. Everyone is familiar with the persistence of the little child, especially when playing either intellectually (as with continual questions into the what and why of things) or with challenging toys. The child imagines a structure to be made from building blocks and begins its construction. The edifice reaches a certain height or complexity and falls; the child begins anew, and again it falls, and again and again. The child knows little or nothing of the variety of pieces needed, the demands of geometry, the competent training to bring the building beyond a certain point. And yet he or she persists until boredom or exhaustion intervenes and the play is stopped—but not the idea of success. Accountability for the

failures will not be self-directed but attributed to such things as a crooked or wobbling floor, the imprecision of the blocks' manufacture, the wishes of a jealous peer or sibling, the clumsiness of an angel or malice of a devil. We admire the persistence of the child, the self-confidence, and wish it were our own. But we also know of the need to instruct the child in the difference between fantasy and reality, dreamworlds and the real world, for we do not wish him or her to grow up into a stunted idealist, any more than we wish him or her to grow up as a stunted realist, incapable of imagining anything beyond the immediately perceptible and useful. We must instruct that where possibility has become impossibility, persistence has a way of becoming a stubborn willfulness that exists only for itself and its own pride.

From examining children when they are in a different frame of mind, we also discover the harbinger of that ambiguous phenomenon we usually call "giving up." Here the controlling distinction lies not between possibility and impossibility, reality and fantasy, but between ease and difficulty. Like children, adults make a category mistake here quite frequently, confusing difficulty with impossibility and concluding that because a task is more difficult to accomplish than we anticipated, it is impossible. Again, the classic error of inductive reasoning is at the root of this judgment: because we have failed once, or twice, or many times, we conclude that we will always fail. Thus, we become as concerned about a child who quits after one attempt with the building blocks (when this exemplifies a pattern found in other situations) as we do about the child who refuses to admit the clear impossibility of the task (again, as the instance of a pattern). Giving up on tasks is of course one of the easiest things we can do; it is almost as easy as denying the existence of God, which can be done while sitting in an armchair sipping a martini. Discretion must come into play here, the intelligence that makes accurate distinctions, followed by a discipline like the obedience I have described: the thorough acquaintance with oneself to determine talent *and* passion for the task, the latter deriving from a conviction shaped through critical interrogation that the task is worth pursuing. Indolence is the problem here, or what medieval divines called the capital sin of acedia, or what William James analyzed as the easygoing compared to the strenuous mood—complacency at its furthest extent, when we prefer that being awake be as close as possible to being asleep.

The Messianic Traits

As mentioned earlier, I am pursuing in this chapter the outlines of a spirituality that moves from dimensions of it that are acknowledged only intermittently (childlikeness), to ones more fully acknowledged (the messianic traits), to ones universally acknowledged by all worthy religions (the doctrine on love). So my task now is to move to the messianic traits. In doing so I will be concerned, as throughout much of the book, with religion or the religious consciousness as specifically but not exclusively Christian. This dependence on Christianity will be quite overt in the following remarks and in those on the doctrine on love in the next section. Three further preliminary comments are also needed. In Christianity, following its early creedal dependence on Judaism, there are three distinct groupings of messianic expectations: those of the king messiah, or political liberator; the priest messiah, or religious liberator; and the servant messiah, or personal liberator. I will not be discussing the first two directly, since neither Jesus himself nor anyone else has fulfilled them, but will devote myself to the third grouping, formulated above all by Second Isaiah in his exquisite Songs of the Servant. Yet this discussion of the traits pertaining to personal liberation also has profound implications for any description of political and religious liberation; for in analyzing the liberated individual we have our primary indicator of what a politically and religiously liberated humanity would also look like. A second preliminary comment is that this chapter as a whole seeks inclusion on any agenda for Christian religion in the coming millennium precisely as an outline of a *spirituality,* that is, according to our previous definition, as a delineation more of attitudes than activities. Thirdly, there are five traits of the messianic servant. Yet since I have taken up the first, obedience, in other contexts, I will not attend directly to it here, but only to the other four, with the critical proviso that without obedience and the conviction born from it, encouraging the other four can amount to little more than a sentiment of devotional piety. The four traits are: generosity, mercy, humility, and poverty. Since they interrelate so closely it makes little difference in what order they are described.

1. **Generosity.** The teaching of Jesus on generosity is very clear: we must divest ourselves of all material goods we do not need for healthy

sustenance and give them to those who do not have enough, balancing out in similarity what we and the poor now possess. There is nothing in his doctrine that condones a spirit of accumulation, the continual ingathering for your own use of wealth beyond what you need for your own well-being and that of living things dependent on you. An army of observers of human relationships over the centuries should be enough by now to convince us that discord results when glaring discrepancies exist between the haves and the have-nots. There appears to be a spirit of solidarity that exists among human beings—some scientists propose that it is inexorable, a product of genetic control within our species—that for many creates a natural repulsion toward situations that bless the over-indulgence of some with the "good things" of life while others within eyesight are dying of starvation, lack of adequate medical care, the untended pains of old age. As the refusal of a spirit of generosity, greed will always breed and sustain antagonism within human communities between those who suffer from want of basic needs and those who have more than they need and hoard it. Jesus says, "If a man asks you for your cloak, give him your tunic also." But the spirit of greed says, "Give him neither your cloak nor your tunic, but your open hostility, your indifference, or the advice that he can earn the cloak and tunic by his own labor should he decide to make the effort." There is a special type of cruelty here, a refusal to acknowledge the bounty of inheritance, education, physical and psychological health, or blunt good luck that has given wealth to one but little to another.

There is more involved in Jesus' doctrine on generosity, however, than simply the distribution of material goods. There is also the requirement to distribute one's time. What the doctrine is getting at here is the willingness to communicate among ourselves—the proposal, in other words, that a shared awareness of community is never served by silence. The steady refusal to speak to each other that can consume in hurt and hatred even the best relationships needs no argument, since its truth is as clear as the noonday sun and experienced by all of us. The self-righteousness we previously described is never quite so perverse as when it becomes a deliberate self-isolation, whether among friends or nations, a decision to gamble on one's ignorance in the other's regard. For Christian religion the contrary witness is again the example of Jesus, of whom there is no reliable record that he ever consistently refused to speak to anyone, even to those who were openly antagonistic to him during the course of his two trials, when silence might have been more soothing than debate, no words at all rather than words of defense. Wherever we are in human communities, in dwellings of home or state or church, we must take to heart this witness and learn from it. Relationships are never served, predominantly those that touch our minds with love, when language between people is struck dumb. Good relationships always tend to become bad or indifferent relationships, and bad or indifferent ones tend to become worse, whenever we refuse to give generously of our time for the sake of what each other is thinking and feeling.

2. **Mercy.** There are two meanings here. In the first the practice of mercy is directly related to that of generosity. So when the beggar cries out, "Have mercy!" he or she is calling on your willingness to relieve an underfed belly, the cold and homeless days of life. And when the leper moans, "Have mercy!" he or she is seeking aid from you in the healing of wounds. The cry for mercy in each instance is an attempt to tap your prodigality, the readiness to give of material goods and time to overcome a source of pain. It requires what the Greeks called *empathy,* the ability not only to stand side by side with those who suffer—this is sympathy—but to feel their suffering as your own, so that in healing them you are in effect healing yourself. Mercy is the empathic response of the Christ whenever he confronts the misery of the world; it is the inevitable child of the sense of solidarity we mentioned above, the feeling that we are in life not for individual but for mutual benefit. The chilling figure of Midas, the hoarder of everything that comes into his possession, everything he touches as if it were gold, is therefore an anti-Christ whom the unmerciful will always praise as a hero. When Midas sees the beggar or the leper he does not say, "Come closer and let me heal you." He screams a curse and runs away to his mansions of wealth and health and pleasure. But even his gods finally have their fill and punish him without remorse by making his lack of mercy toward others the fate he himself suffers when he needs mercy in turn. In his parable of Lazarus and the rich man, Jesus is not far from the same response, though he utilizes it only to impose seriousness, not damnation, on refusal to practice mercy.

The second meaning of mercy involves the practice of forgiveness. Here it is not the bodily needs and wants of others that draws our response, but an offense they have committed against us. How do we respond? The eternal delight of the human spirit is to respond with spite, the desire to "get even," and preferably more than even. For there circulates a feeling of fair play within us that often gets disturbed into the idea of equal retribution, so that if someone offends us we conclude to a *right* to seek satisfactory redress. The Old Testament recognizes this in its famous law of the talon—the prerogative of the one offended to take an eye for an eye, a tooth for a tooth—with which Jesus had such an uncompromising argument. In its place he wishes to assert the abdication of all rights of retribution, not just theologically in respect to how God acts, but psychologically insofar as peace is never served by escalating hostilities. It is both a discipline of the memory he is calling for, the refusal of a brooding anger that keeps the past hurt alive and vigorous, and a discipline of the imagination, the refusal to anticipate in cold-blooded reasoning or vagabond daydreams the punishment of the offender. In a demanding codicil to this teaching, even the innocent must not strike back, but through forgiveness allow the offender's hostility to wear itself out, depriving it of reason for growth. The Christ is committed to the idea that mercy is a greater virtue than justice, no matter how much hurt this might bring. Peace, and whatever is needed to secure it, always precedes causes, no matter how just they may seem, for hostility among us.

3. **Humility.** We all tend to invest our desires, the goals giving shape to our lives, with enormous importance. We like to think that what we are doing counts; the tight trap that feelings of absurdity can weave around our lives produces a boomerang effect impelling us to assert that what we do has value. This is a disposition that has occupied the creative attention of many of the most brilliant minds of all centuries—in our own we can think especially of Albert Camus—and I've no wish to contend with it. For to do so would be to contend not only with brilliant minds, but with my own experiences of life as well. The difficulty embedded in the disposition, however, arises whenever our assertion of personal value becomes unleashed and produces the manic conviction that *everything* we do possesses unqualified importance and nothing must be permitted that threatens or diminishes this judgment. Pride of self has here taken hold, and we are again on the verge of the perennial temptation offered us since the origin of consciousness: to think of ourselves as gods whose

every desire, every thought possesses sanctity and infinite worth. We begin walking the earth with our heads held as high as heaven. It is the seduction irresistibly voiced by the serpent in Eden, and it will strangle humility, the awareness of our limits, as surely as a python coiled tightly around our throats will strangle us to death. Our ancient myths tell us that when there is more than one god, each asserting the limitless worth of what he or she desires or thinks, serenity inevitably gives way to envy, rancor, and war. Olympus looks more frequently like a battlefield than a sanctuary.

We can learn something about humility by looking at its companion virtue, humor. Both appear to come from the same root, *humus,* meaning "earth" or "soil," and both require for their practice—particularly humor when self-directed—a willingness toward self-abasement. Humility is the acknowledgment of boundaries; it is bowing before the truth that our desires may not always be justifiable or capable of fulfillment; that other considerations, such as establishing and maintaining peace, can provide a brake on what we wish to do and be. Humor is the ability to smile at ourselves at the moment humility is appreciated; it is the assassination of Narcissus within us. It allows us to understand that our desires are frequently self-serving and out of proportion to their legitimate worth, and that to think otherwise can in one instance make us a figure of tragedy, like Narcissus, while in another a figure of comedy, like the clown no one likes at a circus. We develop what I call the talent of the inward smile, not at some monstrous joke played on us by failed goals—the rictus smile of despair—but at the monstrous presumption that all that finally matters in life is the singular, the I, ridiculous in its dominance over thought and feelings, and at the final tally, immensely boring—the encouraging smile of mutual need.

4. **Poverty.** In the messianic prophecies of the servant, this can arguably be interpreted as the master virtue, the one that includes within itself the fullest appreciation of the previous three. In its first meaning poverty is what incites you to divest yourself of unneeded—or at a high pitch of sanctity, needed—goods for the well-being of others. It incorporates what we said about generosity and the first meaning of mercy. It is the practice of detachment, the discipline of mind and heart that issues in a freedom from material goods, and a too concentrated attention on time for oneself, because you have learned that value does not reside

in their mere possession. Aesthetically, it is an assault on the thinking of the fool who hoards great works of art that he or she will never appreciate but whose simple ownership gives enormous satisfaction. We might argue, in fact, that the practice of poverty is much like the practice of art, when this is engaged nobly: the artist practices his or her craft for the sake of others, expending time and energy to console, excite, inspire them, to provoke but also to ease their drive toward beauty with whatever passion he or she can provide. Or differently: giving things away freely, selflessly, and without condescension is not the harsh, self-defeating, naive, or merely silly activity we often find it described as today. As practiced by the Christ it is a creative and nurturing activity that binds us close, allowing us to take not just barely but abundantly needed sustenance from each other—or what Jesus was likely getting at when, in a stunningly symbolic act, he gave himself over entirely to his disciples at his last supper. We can devote just a few brief remarks to the second meaning of poverty. It is here that poverty becomes the talent allowing you to forsake the need for complete control over your life, the antagonist of any spirit of mastery that attempts to chain destiny to a pillar and dominate it. It is the recognition that autonomous forces—people, events, for the alert religious consciousness, God—can intrude themselves into existence, and that before these forces the proper response is acceptance. Poverty, in other words, now means both an awareness of one's powerlessness and the willingness to consent to it, though not as a shabby excuse for indolence, as well as the refusal of a spirit of impetuous rebellion that can only confuse the course one's life must henceforth take, at an extreme creating a paranoid inability to distinguish between reality and fantasy. It is the consent to our limits underlying this awareness of powerlessness that was the basis for our previous remarks about the second meaning of mercy and humility. Narcissus, the stunted egoist who believes he is a dictator over life, preening on his right to do with it as he pleases without accountability to anything or anyone, is the antithesis of the Christ who gave himself over to all that came his way as the will of God, with grace, a loving passion, and an unqualified spirit of acceptance—and a conviction, too, insisting on a change of heart wherever discord and triviality prevailed. In his egoism Narcissus will always be a peace-breaker among us, a cherisher of no life but his own; in his selflessness the Christ will always be a peace-bringer, calling out his invitation to a mostly deaf world.

I would like to close this section with the following brief recapitulation, interlaced with some further reflections. Of the five attributes of the servant messiah, obedience enjoys priority of practice, not just in the prophecies, but in the life of Jesus, and indeed in the life of anyone submitting to a similar life-style. It defines the process of undistracted attentiveness whereby we shape the convictions that drive our lives. These in turn can become so powerful that the phrase Isaiah uses in his songs, *ebed Yahweh,* actually translates more correctly the "slave" rather than the "servant" of Yahweh: a designation that captures exactly the influence that convictions born from obedience exercise over the individual—one seeks an identity of will with them—and the peace of mind such submission can assist. Furthermore, it puts into sharp relief the discord that inevitably occurs whenever the individual rebels against or denies these convictions: we cannot relate to others with integrity until we first relate to ourselves that way. What this means is that while we can have no patience with the narcissism described above, the five traits of the servant must be applied in interlocking ways not just to how we treat others but how we treat ourselves. The descriptions I've offered of them thus have a self-application and other-application, which the descriptions themselves make available to the reader. In this way, such as I've judged them from my own life and the lives of others, the traits do indeed become liberating from things that would otherwise oppress us mightily. So, for example: as we must be generous in goods and time for the health of others, so we should be toward ourselves and our own health; as we must forgive others, disciplining our imaginations away from the brooding of hurts and the contemplation of punishing revenge, so we must learn to forgive ourselves; as we must learn to smile at our own failures, refusing the humorlessness that takes everything we do and think with dead seriousness, so we must practice this same smile toward others; as we acknowledge our own limits, the poverty or powerlessness that tells us we need others—and gives birth to prayer when the other is God, and to Church when the others are of our own kind—so we must acknowledge the limits of all. To be ungenerous, unforgiving, unsmiling, and remorseless in demands toward ourselves can never bring peace of mind, a liberation from the ways of self-oppression, because they tell us that we are not cherishing even our own lives.

If the fundamental task of Christians is to become Christlike, then this must be at the heart of any agenda for Christian religion in the coming millennium, as it has been from Christianity's beginning and will remain to its end. I have taken this brief journey through the terrain of messianic expectations, then, to discover something of what it means to call Jesus the "Christ," and why it is that if Christians are to become Christlike it can only mean to become like the servant. For Jesus did not acquit the deeds of the king or priest messiahs; their ancient prophecies are still lying in the folds of history, where, because of their ambiguity, it is this theologian's hope they will smother to death. The life of Jesus gives us only the deeds that justify the descriptions in Isaiah's songs. There even seems to be a conscientious attempt in the gospels to steer the disciples away from an interest in the king and priest. As to the first, for example: the pacifism of Jesus before his enemies is well enough known; as to the second: his injunctions against the self-righteous judging of others—that peculiarly sad flaw we've already described—appear repeatedly. The concentration is clearly on the qualities defining the servant, and for all time makes the gospels something that will go against the grain, an imposition precisely on that clear preference we all have for exercising power over others and self-righteously judging them.

Sometimes imagination takes an easy turn toward the idea that if Jesus came again among his disciples he would die not from bloodletting on a cross but from shock over the misapprehension that he came as a servant, not a warrior or magistrate, to provide a way of life, a cherishing of life giving peace to troubled histories and broken hearts. His life is the most effective portrait of a saint our history has ever known. There is beauty of mind here, a delicacy of heart that touches us in ways that, while many may wish to keep them secret in an odd type of embarrassment, cannot be ignored or ridiculed by any sensitive man or woman. The servant is goodness without taint, sanctity without righteousness, the praise of God without pride or fear. The servant is what we would all like to be, *if* it is holiness we desire; king messiahs and priest messiahs are too harsh, too undeniable in their power. And the servant is what Jesus was—so that to whatever extent he becomes the paradigm to his followers, a corporate personality, as Isaiah also seems to say, capturing the intent of all their lives, to that extent we begin to understand this corporateness as involving not only his own role as representative of his followers but their responsibility to become images of him. A mutual representation thus becomes the lifeblood at the heart of all Christian spirituality. There is nothing that compels an incarnate Christ of God to occur just once.

The Doctrine on Love

Let me begin these reflections on the heart of the Christian spiritual life by noting a fact about biological life. It pertains to the fourth characteristic we have been using to define this life, adaptation, and it simply acknowledges the pivotal role this characteristic plays in explaining why species survive in the world. Darwin, in fact, thought that it was *the* factor explaining species survival and considered those who were biologically most adept at it the fittest to survive. A common mistake, however, is to think that by "fittest" he meant "physically strongest," whereas adaptability clearly implies in his analysis more the ability to adjust, sometimes rapidly, than to be physically strong. Tree shrews are still around, small and biologically pliable mammals, whereas the dinosaurs have been long extinct. When strength enters the scenario of adaptation, in other words, it does so not necessarily as physical strength in adjusting to new surroundings but as a mastery of them through any one of a number of adjustments, such as camouflage, lungs for breathing on land, warm-bloodedness, and so on. The initial stage of any lasting adjustment is apparently always a hit-and-miss occurrence at the level of genetic mutation, usually happening in just one primal individual whose offspring then have advantages that others of the species do not. Furthermore, and of much greater importance to our present concern, is the fact that while this mastery is often assisted by the presence of brute physical strength and its manifestation in such attributes as size, speed, jaw and leg muscles for purposes of competitive aggression, more often than not it is achieved by a mutuality of aid among the members of a given group, a cooperation that an initial advantageous mutation, even one like enormous physical strength, would of itself not secure. This is perhaps above all true of ourselves, where increased brain size—a clear adaptational advantage—would have meant nothing without this mutuality of aid: a point that once led the great biologist T. Dobzhansky to remark that humans are thus genetically determined as "ethicizing beings." If this is true, and I think it is, then we can also say that human adaptation has at its core a degree of control based on our willingness to assist each other. In the previous section we suggested something of what this might mean in a Christian anthropology where behavioral decisions are based on the traits of the servant messiah. In this section I want to tighten this basis and discuss the doctrine on love.

For as we look down the days and down the nights, throughout all the millennia of human reflection one reality captures more than any other the longings of the human spirit. We find it breathing in our music, posing in our art, speaking in our poetry, a presence to all the muses as they seek to capture what is finest about human living. It is there, too, in all the great religions, a still point around which circulates their systems of belief, behavior, and worship, attempting to give coherence and attractiveness to them. In the serenity of the Buddha's smile, the passion of the Jains, the ecstasies of Muhammad, the prophecy of Micah, and in countless other places we find its presence seeking release into the world. Above all, in the common way he taught, in exhortation, parable, and example story, and in the way he lived, as healer, teacher, seer, and son, we find it in the person of Jesus, a revelatory impulse toward which he is always faithful—the impulse, and the reality, that we will be describing here as love. Jesus, we might say, thus represents for the Christian community a single mutative agent coming suddenly and unexpectedly into the world and requiring repetitive incarnations if his presence is to survive in his descendants. Furthermore, this repetition can be fairly described as a "natural" activity insofar as the word itself derives conceptually from the Greek *physis* and etymologically from the Latin *natura*, both of which have their roots in verbs meaning "to bring forth" and so imply a generative element in everything that is natural. Yet success has not marked the history of this repetition or regeneration particularly well. Love does not reign in our world, not powerfully as a distinguishing trait when we examine the tableau of human behavior. It has been critical, therefore, that Christianity perpetually remind itself that its survivability depends on its willingness to adapt to the world in a way that acknowledges and redeems those human inclinations and desires that amount to a refusal of the benefits brought by the mutative agent; that to do otherwise is to court extinction.

Up to this point we have traced out the way of life Jesus requires as this finds increasingly intense expression in the practice of childlikeness and the traits of the messianic servant. In turning now to the practice of love we discover the singular characteristic representing not only the most intense expression, the *essence* of this way of life—especially as it provides the ideal motive generating mutual desire to reproduce ourselves and so survive in the world—but also, according to Jesus' own claim, its fulfillment (Mark 12:28–34). This fulfillment is a critical notion. I want to suggest that what he means by it is simplification, so that when he claims that his mandate of the triple love ("Love *God* with all your heart . . . ; love your *neighbor* as you love *yourself*") fulfills all the law and prophets, he means that it captures in a succinct and lucid fashion all that went before it in a sometimes paralyzingly complex history of ethical reflection. Even more, it is to provide the basis on which all subsequent behavior is to be premised. In this his mandate functions similarly to what we often find in the equations of science. Newton's stunning laws of motion and gravity, Einstein's remarkable insights into the conversion of mass and energy, Hawking's and Penrose's intriguing analyses of black holes: all of these can be put in the most amazingly simple equations, which capture extraordinarily complex and demanding work leading up to and then succeeding them. So it is with the mandate of the triple love.

In what follows I would like to outline what specifically this love is that Jesus teaches. We may say immediately that there are actually two dimensions to it that pervade his teachings, the one called *agape* and the other called *eros* (the fact that the word *eros* does not appear in the gospels is not important; the type of love it represents is repeatedly described). To these two loves, then, I will now turn, and I will begin by characterizing agape according to the following points.

1. Agape is disinterested love. It is love for its own sake, without qualification. It goes out to all persons and does not ask whether or not the person is lovable (while Jesus thus applies this characteristic above all to intrahuman relationships, there is nothing in his teaching that excludes its application to other life-forms, most especially God). He thus teaches agape even toward those who persecute you, your enemies, people who hate and harm you—or more generally, as we suggested in another context, toward anyone or anything that for whatever reason you might find unlovable. This is the trait that must undergird all ideological constructs of Christian pacifism designed to promote nonviolent resistance, as well as the trait establishing the doctrine on love as hopelessly unworkable in the minds of many. It is obvious that in offering this first characteristic Jesus is also departing from other viewpoints, other spiritualities (like Stoicism) in which apathy or indifference, not love, is counseled as the virtuous response to what is unlovable, or (like Epicureanism) in which pleasure gratifi-

cation terminates personal investment in the well-being of anything else. In these viewpoints you are to acknowledge the unlovable without anger or malice, so as not to perturb your indifference or pleasure, but also without any obligation to love it.

2. Agape takes no account of the response that others make toward your love. It does not ask whether they will appreciate your love or love you in return. It is a completely active love; it gives without expecting to receive. Consequently it will always be a stranger in any relationship based solely on a *quid pro quo* mentality, the frame of mind captured in the statement, "If I do this, you will do that." Or differently: it will always be a bit uncomfortable with any ethic whose guiding norm is justice. This will immediately set it at odds with the controlling viewpoint of Jesus' own religious tradition, and the majority tradition of the one based on him, as well as every system of civil jurisprudence with which I am familiar.

3. Agape is asexual. It is unaffected by the question of gender and forswears all concern for body pleasure in its description. In his teachings, therefore, Jesus develops no interest in delineating a sexual morality except as sexual behavior may function as an offense against what does interest him, such as the practice of generosity, or as an offense against the cherishing of life, as in all forms of abusive aggression. Agape is what allows us to say without sexual considerations to any man, woman, or child, "I love you," though we should also note that trying to maintain fidelity to this third characteristic has frequently had the curious rebound effect in Christian religion of emphasizing these very same considerations. The community has developed an overindulged concern for sexual morality, in other words, which obscures if not ignores the ideal that it is in fact attempting to serve. Critics of Christianity have of course pointed this out time and time again, often with considerable contempt. But the criticism is basically correct, and it provides a continual reminder that sexual behavior is not a final interest of Christian religion but one of subsidiary importance to the love Jesus teaches as the criterion for *all* behavior.

4. Agape is the unrestricted and unquestioning love of the ideal father toward his child, and reestablishes the childlikeness discussed in a previous section as again pertinent. Hence Jesus' consistent use of this title, "Father," to describe God: a description whose meaning perhaps nowhere in his teachings reaches clearer expression than in the par-

able of the prodigal son—and whose primary context should not dissuade feminist concerns, since the childlikeness Jesus encourages in adult behavior is that of the little human being (as with the previous trait of agape) before gender distinctions are made or become prominent in behavior. Agape forgives without retribution. It carries no grudges, does not demand fair play (like the older son in the parable), and knows no spite. For the healed wounds of the past it shows only gratitude, with no shadows of hurt. This trait thus demonstrates again the initially unnerving preference in Jesus' teaching for the superiority of mercy over justice. And this in its own turn receives perhaps no clearer presentation than in the parable of the eleventh-hour workers, which we tend to admire when we are the ones who have labored the one hour yet are paid the same as those who have labored twelve, yet whose admiration sours when the situation is reversed. Since the obvious intent of the parable is to present the landowner as a metaphor for God, this fourth trait provides the stunning suggestion that doctrines on divine punishment, particularly the abomination of doctrines on hell, have no place in Christian religion since they represent an insult to God's encompassing and unqualified love.

5. Agape, therefore, is an ideal love. It is love as God loves, so that no human being can ever completely express it. It is the framework, the rubric if you will, against which we judge the way we in fact love. It is the imaginable goal toward which we strive in love. And hence the insistence throughout the finest traditions of Christian spirituality on the idea that being a Christian is always an *approximation-process* (to use Kierkegaard's descriptive term). In other words, the individual never reaches a point where he or she can say, "There, it is finished; I am finally a Christian." For that point has been reached only once, in the person of Jesus, and it is unrepeatable. For the rest of us our love requires constant refinement and rehearsal as it seeks, but never fully gains, the characteristics of agape. We should also note historically that in this approximation-process toward agape, Christianity has at times taken some peculiar, even contrary turns in its spirituality. We can find evidence of this in Neoplatonism and millennarianism, the "imitation of Christ" manuals, certain forms of courtly love, and just generally in an enduring suspicion of the flesh and contempt for the world, neither of which Jesus practiced or recommended.

6. Agape in itself is not a uniquely Christian understanding of love. You

find its characteristics in various strands of Greek, Hebrew, Hindu, Buddhist, and Muslim spirituality, as well as in many other though less familiar traditions. A contribution that Christianity does offer, however, may be found in its repeated and unqualified insistence that this type of love is to be identified with the very activity of God. God is love; God is agape (1 John 4:8). Yet even in this contribution we cannot say that Christianity is *unique*. Out of the Hasidic tradition of eighteenth- and nineteenth-century Judaism, for example, Martin Buber offers a profound analysis of this identification (and in the process, we may add, a sensitive appreciation of Johannine Christology) in his popular book, *I and Thou*. The consequences of this identity are twofold. First, it sanctifies agapaic love, since it is what describes God's own activity. Agape is holy, blessed; and to the extent that we approximate it in our lives we become holy and blessed ourselves. On the other hand, though, the identification also implies that to the extent we do not approximate it in our lives we are unholy, unblessed. Yet since agape is fully characteristic only of God's activity, the result must be our willing acknowledgment that to some extent we always remain unblessed. It is this same idea, more harshly cast, that I think St. John is also expressing in his statement, "If we say that we have no sin (that we are not to some extent unblessed, unlike God), we deceive ourselves and the truth is not within us" (1 John 1:8).

We can see easily enough where the difficulty with agape primarily lies. *We desire to love as the Father does, but we do not; we are in conflict with our ideals.* We do not tend to love the unlovable; we tend to dislike it. We do not tend to remain without expectations when we love someone or something; we tend to expect certain responses in return. And when these responses are not forthcoming we find our love easily turning into something else, into bitterness or indifference or contempt. We look around ourselves, for example, and wish to love our own kind. But how difficult it is to love the egomaniac, the chronic complainer, the lazy and self-indulgent among those we see. And when we offer our love how difficult it is to keep offering it when the other responds with apathy, scorn, suspicion. There is conflict here, and we find that agape, with the standards of love it sets before us, is much more difficult than we may have first thought. For we know that our love is often not costless; that we put a price tag on it; that we pay and expect to receive. And we begin to realize that Jesus' simplification of the old law into the new law of the triple love of God, others, and self does not mean that fidelity to the law is now easy. We learn instead that it is hard, very hard, that we regularly fail, and that a religion shaped on different bases—such as the mere acquittal of cultic requirements, or theories of predestination that settle no hard obligations on us—are far easier. But we also know that we must continue to strive. For unless we were misguided in previous remarks, this is exactly what is required of us by the beauty we affirm in the witness of Jesus and the obedience we exercise toward this witness.

A final, critically important comment must also be made. It pertains to what I would suggest is the fundamental inquiry we should raise whenever we are confronted by an experience or proposition (or interpretation of either) that we wish to assess theologically. The inquiry reads, "What does it require me to say about God?" with the inherent assumption that if the assessment requires me to say something I do not wish to say, I must alter it. And to the further question, then, "Where do I discover what I want to say about God?" the Christian response can only be: in the teachings of Jesus. In this section I have been proposing that the heart of this teaching is found in the doctrine on agapaic love, with appropriate embellishments in what I previously said about the traits of messianic servanthood and childlikeness (such embellishments being a commonplace throughout Christian history in the work of imaginative and conscientious interpreters of the traits). In all of these descriptions, of course, we are utilizing the language of metaphor rather than metaphysics, though as I will draw the distinction between the two in the next chapter, this certainly does not gainsay the importance of metaphor in religious discourse, or any other kind, as competent in capturing reality. I might also add by way of example that it is the employment of the above inquiry that provides my reason throughout these pages for interpreting references to hell/eternal punishment in Jesus' teachings as a technique to indicate the seriousness of what is being said and not a description of a possible destiny subsequent to death.

Let us now look at eros for a moment, and as with agape characterize it according to its major traits, with the brief preliminary remark—since it represents a very common misunderstanding—that while a typical expression of eros may indeed be the passion of sexual desire, confining its meaning solely or even primarily to this expression represents a mistaken narrowing of the word, one found frequently among us, including those as otherwise perceptive, say, as Denis de Rougement in his *Love in the Western World* and José Ortega y Gasset in his *On Love.*

1. Eros is always a specified love. By this I mean that it is an interested, directed love attached to a given object. This object can be God; it can be poetry, politics, or nature. It can be any one of countless items capable of gaining and holding an individual's attention. Most usually it is another human being, and for the Christian within the specialized context of his or her faith, it is Jesus. The immediate desire toward all objects of eros is to spend time with them, much time, in order to experience, know, and appraise them as fully as possible. When applied to Jesus this includes not just the general satisfaction of the desire in a growing appropriation of the gospel witness to him in prayer and meditation, but also the specific satisfaction of scholarship seeking to discover through archeology and textual studies as much as possible of first century Palestine and its cultural environs. The pursuit of this scholarship should be encouraged, like prayer and meditation always have been, in more thoroughgoing ways among Christian churches in the coming millennium, both financially and in gratitude for publicized results. And should any of the results be finally judged erroneous, the example of science can teach theology a lesson the latter has found difficult to learn: that gratitude should still occur because even erroneous results provide us with increased knowledge.

2. Eros cannot love indiscriminately as agape does. *Its object must be perceived by the lover as lovable.* You cannot have eros toward an enemy, therefore, someone or something you perceive as threatening diminishment, destruction, or indifference toward what you desire or need in pursuit of a happy, purposeful life. What this means is that the considerations creating and sustaining eros are preponderantly subjective—what one person finds lovable or unlovable another might not. Pitirim Sorokin's analysis of criteria for evaluating these subjective considerations is more intriguing than most, and can be synopsized as follows: the intensity of the emotion involved, its extensity, duration, purity from deflecting interest, and the adequacy of its objective manifestation in overt actions and material vehicles in relation to its subjective purpose (it is within these criteria that Sorokin also attempts to describe the relationship between eros and agape, principally on a quantitative basis: Agape meets each of the criteria more thoroughly,

with a greater precision and fidelity of application, than does eros). This second trait means that the motives shaping these considerations, like the objects of eros themselves, are countless. In intrahuman relationships these motives are sometimes severely maladjusted, as in cases of untempered sadism or masochism, the driving need to hurt or be hurt by the loved one. Sometimes they are just inappropriate, as when an individual sets standards of loyalty or benevolence or humor for the beloved that no human being could adequately meet. Sometimes, however, they are noble and praiseworthy, as when an individual engages art to express homage to God.

3. Erotic love is specific, then, detailed and demanding. Agapaic love is all these things too. But the specific demands that agape places on the lover, it does not place on the beloved. That is why we called it undiscriminating. With eros, however, the demands are placed on both, so that whether or not the beloved retains our love depends on whether or not these demands are met. What agape understands, in other words, and eros does not, is that love must not only be received freely, without conditions; it must also be given freely, without conditions. Religiously applied we may say that agape, unlike eros, is aware that just as God bestows love unreservedly on us, so we must bestow our own love unreservedly on others. Biblically this idea is expressed in a whole variety of ways. The one Matthew uses is especially striking: "But I say to you, love your enemies, do good to those who hate you, and pray for those who persecute and defame you, so that you may be children of your Father in heaven, who makes his sun to rise on the good *and* the evil, and sends his rain on the just *and* the unjust alike" (5:44-45).

4. It is easy for us to gain eros, and all of us love erotically. In fact, for many people eros defines entirely what love is: it is loving your spouse, your children, your friends, your work. Eros is an easily accessible love for us in these situations because we are so directly involved with its object, and we have found this object loving toward us. Nothing is easier, after all, than to love a loving spouse or a loving friend or a satisfying job. Jesus himself said as much when noting that even sinners love those who love them (Luke 6:31). Eros is easy here because it is so rewarding. It brings with it a feeling of contentment, a sense of well-being and belonging that continually encourages us to gain and maintain it. Something of this same idea may even underlie the intent of the parable of the Good Samaritan. The reader may recall that the

question initiating the parable is, "Who is my neighbor?" It is safe to presume that it is asked in order to identify the specific object of Jesus' mandate, "Love your neighbor as yourself." He then tells his story and ends it with a question of his own, "Who, then, proved himself a neighbor to the wounded man?" The answer is obvious: the one who helped him in his need, the one who showed him love. What Jesus implies by accepting this answer, I would say, is that in its most reduced form eros requires at least this much: that we show love toward those who have shown us love. But this requirement is surely an undemanding one; as we said, it is not difficult to love someone who loves us. In such situations eros is comfortably born and kept alive because it results from an easy inclination toward those who have pleasingly endowed us.

5. But there is another side to the coin of eros, and it describes our final characteristic. It is exactly because eros exists on the basis of the lovableness of its object, and because the individual is so closely invested in this object, that eros can also be the "place" where love is experienced as an agony—and that this agony is akin to a death experience, a dying from broken hopes, as Plato suggests in *The Symposium*. This occurs whenever the individual's expectations of the beloved, or of his or her own character or behavior, have not been met, or are no longer met, and yet he or she is unable to renounce the involvement. It is this dimension of eros that occupies so large a space in our literature of love, from the beloved lady of Shakespeare's sonnets, Dante's Beatrice, and Quixote's Dulcinea, to the beloved God of John of the Cross' dark night. The reciprocity we expect in love is absent, the responsiveness is not there, and yet we are unable to kill the love.

We all need eros. For our specific concerns here the fact that Christians are members of a particular religious community—in the privileged Pauline metaphor, the Body of Christ—and the presumption that they love this community, its spirituality, its works, its opportunities for serving the witness of Jesus in the world: this fact and this presumption are both the results of eros. Yet this same eros that Christians must possess toward their community must also grow, mature, expand outward toward an ever closer appreciation of agape, so that it breaks the confines of the community and becomes loyalty in expressing the witness of Jesus not just to the members of a particular group but to everyone we meet.

The logic of this move is grounded in the founder himself. For to the extent that the primary object of Christian eros is Jesus, and to the extent that eros demands time with its beloved—much time for purposes of knowledge, intimacy, and communion—then to the same extent the Christian learns that to continue loving Jesus means a learning how to love as he did, establishing an identity of wills as the servant Christ had with God. This is the transfer point between eros and agape.

Still, a rankling can settle in our minds, and no agenda for Christian religion in the coming millennium can ignore it. We have been proposing in the previous three sections a spirituality moving from the specifics of childlikeness to those of the messianic servant to those of the doctrine on love as discoverable in the teachings of Jesus—and as we moved through these stages the characteristics became increasingly inclusive of other religious visions. This approach had some degree of chance to it, since much of what I've said has been said before and I risked the similarity as potentially uninteresting to the reader—though I think casting it in my own terms, plus adding some fresh interpretations, may have assuaged the risk sufficiently to make the effort worthwhile. So this is not where the rankling occurs. It is found, rather, in a feeling that recommending such a spirituality is really quite useless, that it has always been useless as a proposal for humanity as a whole, since it seems to touch the mind and encourage the deeds of very few in any serious or pervasively effective way, and thus is a failed effort from the very start. I am sympathetic to this view, enormously so, and to it I would now like to turn as the focal point in our concluding section to this chapter. Yet while the sympathy might remain, it will also be amended somewhat as this final section moves us closer to our fifth chapter and its attempt to construct an understanding of God appropriate to an agenda for Christian religion—because an understanding of God is the heart of any religion—at the turn of the millennium.

A Failed Experiment

In any religious vision based on a doctrine of love such as the one provided in the previous section, the doctrine simultaneously becomes the heart of any agenda being proposed for considering the religion, both in its ethical demands and its metaphors of God. Since the latter concern will occupy us throughout the following chapter, I'd like to devote the final section of this one to further remarks on the former concern: the ethical demands of the vision. The doctrine insists that the love described is an ideal, that it can never be achieved or possessed fully as one might a commodity, and that therefore the proper context for judging its demands centers on the question of striving. This in turn involves us in the question of ascesis, or how willingly we discipline ourselves toward the passion or intensity of the striving (I've noted already that the word "ascesis" derives from athletics as the regimen undergone in seeking victory in competition, but that its basic meaning is not so much the victory itself as the commitment of the athlete to prepare to compete as best he or she can). Likewise, it involves us in pathos, or the specific element in ascetic discipline that requires self-sacrifice. As we engage both commitment and pathos in the striving for agape, each becomes stronger the more attentive we are to the opportunities provided them in daily experience, just as each becomes weaker the more we do not. I've suggested that these two qualities, strength and opportunity, are also the defining traits of the Pauline understanding of grace. When we look at humanity as a whole, we must not be seduced into the conclusion that those who have striven mightily have somehow become the personifications of the whole species and thus the paradigms within which we judge the behavior of all as somehow alike in worthiness to the behavior of a few. This is to commit the same paradigm mistake we sometimes find in the history of science when the importance of anomalies is diminished or dismissed in the presumption that they meet the demands of the paradigm, but in currently undiscovered ways. Now and then this is the case. When the science is being done well, however, it is never the case for very long.

But in the context of agape as the fundamental paradigm of ethical behavior, we have had a very long time to observe anomalies in its regard, almost as long as recorded human consciousness, so that any claim that these anomalies bear undiscovered affinities to agapaic love becomes ludicrous. Science in this situation, when the anomalies are serious or consistent enough, seeks a new paradigm. Ethics must do the same. My judgment here is quite harsh, and many will rebel against it as alarmist or misanthropic, preferring to maintain that the paradigm is still workable according to the fallacy noted above: that the few can stand for the entirety when the latter are appraised. But what actually appears to be happening here is the unreflected and perhaps unwitting admission that another paradigm prevails over human behavior, and those seeking agape are in fact the anomalies. This is my own assessment when I scan the story of human deeds. It is the question of weight that again comes to the fore, and whether or not it is sufficient to guarantee that peace as the fundamental ideal making our survival possible, and the cherishing of life as its basic demonstration, are demonstrated in deeds of love acknowledging them. My own resolution to this question is that it is not; that the weight of our behavior indicates far more an inclination toward violence than peace, the damaging of life than its cherishing, self-infatuation than love. I am not alone in this estimate, but whereas some still see hope for conversion experiences of sufficient power to alter the weight of the judgment by their successors, I am with those who do not. And I do not experience this hope for both a scientific and a religious reason.

The scientific reason derives from the huge percentage of extinctions of species. This is a statistical motive based on the uncontrollability of environment and the potential ability of as yet unknown life-forms, or of mutated ones, to invade our bodies and kill us, especially of viral or bacterial forms. The first portion of the motive, the environmental factor, can be largely ignored for earth-generated cataclysms. Our species is too populous and too widely settled over the planet to permit even a large series of such cataclysms to cause our extinction, particularly with the increasing development of predictive and protective technologies against them. The planet, however, is susceptible not just to internal catastrophic destruction, but to external types as well. I've already mentioned the disintegration of the earth when the sun expands into its red-giant phase—and our extinction unless we have learned to live and breed elsewhere (a not unlikely prospect, should our destruction not come sooner from other sources, given the time involved to develop it). Of considerably more immediate concern are the nemesis comets and asteroids. It is a fact that there is a comet in orbit within our solar system called Swift-Tuttle after its co-discoverers in 1862. It is also a fact that it is about five miles wide at its solid core (the estimated size of the one that collided with the earth at the Cretaceous-Tertiary boundary when the dinosaur species went extinct) and that it will barely miss collision with the earth in late summer of 2126, but will be a definite threat in 3044 (or about one half the time that now separates us from Jesus). Many scientists tell us that it will seriously diminish the human species, and some that it will obliterate us unless a deployable technology can prevent it. And this is just one of a countless army of comets and asteroids in or entering our solar system in just one very small arc of its orbit around the galactic center.

The theological reason centers on how we evaluate ourselves in the light of God's love. Far more often than not Christians seem to understand this love as erotic in the effective devotional pieties that sustain their faith. God loves us, their pieties say, in ways that God loves nothing else, and thus God will prohibit our self-infatuation from running amok as we extinguish ourselves (the causative agent of extinction now being self-inflicted). This is certainly a soothing thought, a pleasant foray into God's kindly power—and the bane of all self-imposed moral advancement theologically anchored. But if our previous analysis of agape was correct, our understanding of God's love must extend beyond the confines of distinguishable groupings to include the whole of creation, and the cherishing of life within *this* context. There is nothing, in other words, that sets us apart for a special care not shared with all, nor, as God seeks to persuade a more intense cherishing of life from the universe, that we can consider ourselves theologically the inextinguishable fulfillment of this process. What I am saying is that our theology cannot demand the impossibility of our being superseded by life-forms more faithful than we to the cherishing of life, either eventually on this planet, perhaps as a successor species to ourselves (though likely not, unless we, along with our violence, are absent), or elsewhere in the universe. For me this is the truth implied in all religious, specifically Christian doctrines of our corruptibility and sin, that any salvation from this situation can be freely denied, that this denial is the overwhelming mark of our behavior, and that a sudden or gradual apocalypse removing our species from the universe is the result. The critical addendum I am offering to this is that successor life-forms, possibly ones already existing elsewhere than on earth, will perhaps choose differently than we and so prove themselves more manifest of God's own love.

I've no interest in providing here an inventory of our malice that points to this assessment of ourselves, this judgment that we are a failed experiment in evolution. I've provided enough of a sense of what this inventory would include throughout these pages. Our tendency toward destructiveness is the one parent of this malice that we see gather all around us whenever we cast a cold eye on our history, the other parent being our tremendous attraction toward triviality and its heart of discord. And the pity of it all, the crushing and tear-soaked sadness, is that we have not been fated to this story of our stay in the universe. For staring us straight in the face denying such a fate are those like Gautama and Jesus, St. Francis and Gandhi. Should it not occur from some source outside ourselves, our story will end from within ourselves as a destiny, the result of choices that have become not a fate but a way of life. It is not that we can reach a stage where we never destroy; this is utopian fantasy unaware of biblical tragedy. It is that so much, so overwhelmingly much of our destructiveness is malfeasant, acts of infidelity to what the above people demonstrate as the realizable potential of our striving toward love. I have no more use for reductionists who say that we cannot help but destroy ourselves than I do for those who insist that we cannot help but perfect ourselves. Both stances ignore the will and its freedom, or reduce them to an excrescent fantasy of a brain seeking a self-serving explanation of an inevitability. The inevitability lies in the freedom of the will and how it has been trained: it lies in the willfulness that has created nuclear and chemical weapons; it lies in the freedom of megalomaniacal tyrants; it lies in the chosen indolence of silence and inactivity; it lies in nostalgia for the *tohu-wa-bohu*, that primal incoherence, the diabolism and discord from which Genesis says all creation was shaped; it lies in the weight of all these things, and many others, as they slowly assassinate another destiny that could have been ours. In Buddhism there is a central doctrine called *dukkha*, which literally means "a wheel that grinds on its axle." The doctrine is saying that there is something out of order in the world, there is something wrong with existence. We are what is wrong; we are the grinding wheel.

My judgment, therefore, does not itself express a fate; the inevitability it describes is not a programmed itinerary that tolerates no contradiction. For I am just a single analyst here, and though I am in a large company of sympathizers, there is another large company that would decline my judgment. Fate means a metaphysical inevitability, something built into our very being, like death; destiny means an ethical proclivity, something built into the preferences of our choices, like pride. Fate cannot be altered for anyone; destiny can for individuals within the species, though for the species as a whole, at least regarding the cherishing of life, I believe we have no compelling evidence that it will. Our mere survival so far certainly does not provide such evidence, since as a species we've existed for only a short period of time. And the panorama of our behavioral history is a long nightmare of slow wars of attrition against ourselves, and many other life-forms, periodically building to crescendos of unspeakable violence and death. We are not a species comfortable with our own kind, nor satisfied with only ritual displays of self-assertion. We are locked into a track of absurdly destructive behavior that makes us the foremost parasitical life-form on the planet. We think of the universe as a magnificent cloak giving glory to ourselves, of the earth as a brothel for our pleasures, of the plants and animals as expediences for our food, clothing, and entertainment, of ourselves as a threat to our individual and group self-satisfactions. The good ones can cry out that all this must cease; the din of the wicked will drown out this cry every time, just as the indifference of the sometimes good, sometimes evil, those proclaiming "we're only human" as a universal justification for ethical indolence, will turn a deaf ear to it.

To choose ignorance as bliss is always to choose intellectual blindness. We don't like this in the tight world of our personal relationships and insist on as rich a knowledge as possible—at least in what we demand that the other offer us, even if we are reluctant to offer it of ourselves. But we often prefer not having knowledge that will impede our plans for the future, proposals of possible disruption or greater difficulty in carrying them out. I rediscover this fact every time I teach a class and offer the foregoing description of the evolutionary failure of our species. The very large majority of my students prefer to hear only of success, one that concentrates on the march of technology into a betterment of life in which they will share, of communal amorality as the seedbed of their individual freedom, of religion convenient for consolation but having no serious role as challenge, of a universe, a planet, other life-forms as tickling curiosity but put to sleep when decisions of self-interest must be made. Yet my students are not evil, not outrageously so; their evil, like mine, tends to be banal, the kind that becomes tolerated, even expected, and any criticism of which is judged as sour grapes. And this is not just an acculturated phenomenon, something to be dismissed as a local disgrace in the United States at the turn of the millennium. It is worldwide and respects no length or uniqueness in the histories of human groups. But now and then a student emerges who gives the lie to this analysis, just as similar individuals have emerged on the world scene. But his or her presence does not obscure the validity of the panoramic appraisal, not for me at any rate, but only makes it the more poignant. These people arise among us, but there are not enough of them. The holy one is a freak.

Though we haven't yet survived very long as a species, we have done so long enough that an attitude of "we'll get by" can indeed set in, somewhat like putty on a wall when one is trying to camouflage an ugly gouge. It is not a particularly energetic or positive attitude, but it possesses the eternal appeal of the status quo. The attraction here is undeniable in the context of the assessment I've offered. For it produces an ethical drudgery that at least maintains attempts to live in virtue while convinced that no overwhelming advance will be made. Metaphors employed to describe humanity are commonly of illness or senectitude, neither one of which is killing but only cramping on our ability to perform tasks. Sometimes images of economic or psychological depression are also used, a "carrying on" that acknowledges drastic limits to what we can afford to do for the sake of cherishing life, but within them endures with resigned determination. This is a version of the apathy I've described before, and we can now see its appeal in many visions of human living, the implicit virtue it possesses by neither giving in to the brute pursuit of immediate pleasure nor giving up by a withdrawal from life in either biological suicide or the spiritual/psychological kind that kills self-reality to bring self-fantasy to birth. It is similar to the life of quiet desperation that Thoreau lamented as the destiny of most people; the humdrum stasis analyzed by existential psychiatry; the monotony of predictable discourse, music, and art; and the lukewarmness vilified in the book of Revelations. We are getting close here to the condition of Lot's wife after she has been turned into a pillar of salt. She endures, but the life has gone out of her, and the future is bleak in its sameness.

Acceptance of situations when there is nothing one can do to alter them is universally held to be a sign of maturity, and eventually, when the acceptance turns into comprehension, of wisdom. I am in accord with this judgment, and find its personification now and then in elderly men and women, especially when the acceptance has been hard-won and not the easy child of indifference. You can walk a far distance along the road of human betterment, but eventually a roadblock is reached. Whispers of despair can creep into the mind, raising horrendous questions of

effort expended for dead-end purposes. The journals of countless saints are filled with such lamentations: that our history is diabolic and not symbolic, a tale of divisiveness and anger and arrogance, with too little of the generosity, mercy, humility, and poverty that can make us one. There is scant beauty in this history; the whole does not come together in that strangeness of proportion that Francis Bacon says defines beauty. Instead, the history remains fragmented, unkempt, disarrayed, and displeasing; it is ugly in the old meaning of that word as something producing vomit. But in the wisdom of true saints, as in the wisdom of the very old, there is a blessing on all that must be accepted because there is a sense that the roadblock can be breached—but not by us. This breaching will be a major theme of our next chapter.

For now, however, the roadblock remains, and the question becomes what we should do when confronting it. The option of paralysis, of Lot's wife as a pillar of salt, is a common one. We stay still and secure, reducing our life down to the immediacy of its close environment and not giving a damn about anything else. The projection of magnificent messiahs is also popular, the single individual who will crack the roadblock's stone and send us on our way into harmony.

Reversion to the past can likewise be appealing, the romantic sentiment that obscures the savagery and vice of some former time where we discover utopias because weariness with current evil produces nostalgic daydreams that we want desperately to be real and to become real again. Escapism through intoxicants is also an option, seeking in drugged or drunk consciousness a confidence of imagined strength and virtue and victory that makes a diagnosis like mine seem ridiculous, misanthropic, and personally insulting. And there is the crushing weight we willingly lay on our own children, the soft or petulant demand that they be better than we are, that progress in this is at their fingertips, that they not make our mistakes, that they make us proud of them—all the while knowing in our hearts that this will not occur, but not admitting it because to do so seems like a defamation of our own flesh and blood. We mouth by rote the demands and encouragements of every generation upon the next because the saints are there in our history, we can point to them, and because we have a compulsion to require of others, even our own children, what we have not required of ourselves. These saints, therefore function in our spiritual life in the same way "imaginal disks" do in our bio-

logical life ("imago" being the taxonomic term for mature adult): they hold out the possibility of a higher reality lurking within present imperfection that can be either suppressed or incited by circumstances—when applied to the spiritual life, the circumstances of our choices.

I have been asked why I have devoted myself to the task of this book, but also to my other writings and my tasks as a teacher and priest, given my assessment of our failure as an experiment in evolution. It is a hard yet worthy and familiar question, and in beginning to answer it many years ago I kept reverting back to the messianic trait of forgiveness I discussed earlier. I had found that it was something I longed for in my own life, particularly the "as if" component generated by imagination: to act as if I had not been offended by someone else, or by myself. I knew, of course, as all of us do, that the "as if" did not imply a literal forgetfulness. Harsh wrongs against oneself are never entirely forgotten; at best they are always on the verge of awareness, and the slightest provocation can push them into it. Yet I knew that an effort was needed to push the memory back if decent and humane, let alone loving behavior was to characterize my life. Herein, I think, also lies my response to the above question, and I would recommend it for any religious agenda concerned with the spirituality of a vision of humanity like mine. We must act as if our efforts at betterment have a chance at succeeding, as if the saints among us prove the possibility for enough of us to shift our species destiny from vice to virtue, as if enough are capable of gracing all with the cherishing of life, as if each of us can and will strive mightily for the love that is agape, and of which we now know at least these three things: it is an art; it is a risk; it involves humor. But these characteristics also parallel the implicit description we have been giving to faith in God throughout the book, so that the faith and love we direct toward God are now to be understood not as diverse but as similar activities. In each case, faith and love, we perceive what we are doing as: (1) something to which we must attend carefully, drawing on all our experiences and refusing to compromise our willingness to pursue it; it is an art; (2) something that is not inerrantly successful, always satisfying, joyful, and passionate; it is a risk; (3) something requiring our acceptance of personal ignorance, the willingness to recognize our mistakes and learn from them; it requires humor. Each of these characteristics contributes to the awareness wherein we relate to God in faith and love; without them the faith and love inevitably go awry,

attempting to relate to God (1) incompletely, (2) naively, or (3) despairingly. And this relationship to God, I will now say, is of ineluctable importance to our well-being. For when we confront the roadblock befuddling all hope that of our own account we can redeem ourselves from the weight of the evil cloaking our history, we must break the circle of our humanity, which is a vicious circle. That breakage is the faith in God I've just briefly described and to which I must now turn more thoroughly—not, however, with the lack of appeal accompanying the turn to ourselves in this chapter, but with the hope of a theologian working his craft, and knowing what impels him so.

Chapter five

GOD

As far back as we can identify the tracings of human consciousness there has been a belief in entities more powerful than we who are not obliged to manifest themselves. No rituals can compel their presence, and science can neither openly nor surreptitiously uncover it. These are the deities. Communication is possible with them, though it is typically successful only in certain locales when accompanied by the proper formulas and an appropriate frame of mind. With others, however—ones more gently disposed toward humanity—communication occurs whenever it is wished. This is especially true for select individuals who for whatever reasons share deeper sympathy with the deities, or a select group of them, or even just one of them. From the beginning of the tracings we also discover a thorough anthropomorphism, not just in the need to assign the deities familiar mechanisms for communication (hearing and speech) but a comfortable and pervasive accessibility to the senses. And so we find deities easily described in the usualness of such experiences as the human body, animals, plants, wind, rain, the land, and of course the Sun. Immediately upon examining religions, in other words, we notice intense and often intimate linkages between human experience and the experience of the divine. This is going to be of tremendous importance to us, since it will provide the basic criterion for assessing the relevance of religion to the lives we lead, or more fundamentally still, to how life itself, when experience leads to reliable knowledge, is constituted. Religion comes alive not because of a historical record in which we assert a privileged contact with deity, but because deity is experienced in what we are. This must be the primary *theological* item on any agenda for Christian religion in the coming millennium.

From our earliest records there likewise emerges an extremely tight identity between deity and power. The original reflection here may have centered on observations of the sun, moon, stars, land, and seas (theology as the disciplined reflection on the concerns of religion appears to have been in its initial stirrings natural theology) and the awareness that neither human authority nor that of any other observed life-form on Earth brought them about. Hence the source must reside in entities more powerful than ones we experience in the confines of biological life, and these entities must reside in some different environment, or as we familiarly name it, heaven. This linkage between deity and power cannot be underestimated. To this day it still provides the underlying rationale in polytheists, or among disputing claims between monotheisms, for asserting the intelligence of devotion to one deity over others, or one understanding of a single God over other understandings. It also underlies the sociological phenomenon we discover everywhere in human history of paralleling the possession of political or religious power with attributes of divinity, willingly admitted or not. When Elijah and the priests of Jezebel come into conflict over which of them represented true divinity, they did not resolve it by intellectual persuasion or the ethical appeal of their respective behavior or the beauty of aesthetic or mystical insight. They did it through displays of power on Carmel, in the same fashion Moses did against the priests and pharaoh of Egypt, the seers of Zeus or Marduk against their competitors, Muhammad against the tribal deities of his homeland, and so on. Jesus, we might note, never took this tack, at least not directly or coercively, and preferred to isolate qualities other than competing power that pointed to the singular worth of submission to his God.

In the myths of these natural theologies, therefore, we find an obvious predilection for those very images of deity that seem best to indicate power. And so there is a tendency to revert back to those same observations and experiences that likely initiated religious reflection in the first place and think of deity in terms of the awesomeness that land, water, and wind can have, of mighty animals and seemingly ubiquitous and deathless plant growth, the sun as source of potent heat and light. In a previous chapter we noted the old Hebrew preference for mountains as signifying power (their tribal god as el Shaddai) and Yahweh's epiphanies in fire. Zeus's dominance was in his wielding of the thunderbolt, and an angry Osiris could bring drought and famine. The list could go on, but eventually it would have to include as a turn away from these images of essentially violent power the preference of Jesus, among others, for images of compassionate power. These two understandings of the expressiveness of divine authority will in fact provide us with our primary rubric when offering our own understanding of divine presence in the universe later in the chapter. For now we need only rehearse a point we've made repeatedly but obliquely throughout these pages, namely, that how we understand the final authority in the universe—which I will designate by common custom as God—determines inevitably the basis for behaving in sympathy, rebellion, or indifference toward it. This is what Einstein was getting at when he said that the most important question we could ask was whether or not the universe is friendly. He knew the answer provided a critical juncture whenever we are in the process of determining how we evaluate our own and other lives. And as he observed human behavior the great scientist concluded that far too many choose to answer the question negatively, and toward the universe—at least that part of it they can influence—are themselves unfriendly. It is abundantly clear by now that his conclusion is one that I share.

The Pursuit of Natural Theology

I have been recommending in this book that in the coming millennium Christianity return to the practice of natural theology, not only because it is there that the very oldest roots of religion lie but because this return would also be deeply amenable to the marriage I've been proposing between Christianity and science. But this is not meant to devalue the needs of the human heart, nor the fact that for countless people caught up in these needs this is where religion is effectively lived. Suffering and death are primal experiences here, often raising the question of God *against* the assertions of natural theology. The lamentation coursing throughout this inquiry is heartbreaking: if God could create the heavens and the Earth, why has my beloved died? Why is the life so mindlessly torn out of living things? These are the questions of theodicy, and the suffering cloaking them is so poignant because from a distant observation we see that it has even obscured the distinction between having power and exercising it, or the distinction between coercive and persuasive power, and has presumed that God's exercise of power will always abide by our criteria of goodness in an absolute fidelity. We have moved here into monotheistic religions, since in polytheisms theodicy does not arise except as petulance: in every polytheism I know of there are evil deities who have won the day and done these things, against the benevolence of one's personal or family deity. Heaven and hell are like bellicose nations in which war has become a way of life and never ends. This is an attractive resolution to the above inquiries, and formal monotheisms have often adopted it indirectly in the power given demonic wills over the divine will. But orthodox formulas insisting in this context that God's will is still absolutely powerful, but that God gives the demons freedom to disobey, are often greeted by many with a wink—because they perceive that the orthodoxy has merely altered the terms but not the intent of the questions into a further inquiry: Then why doesn't God overcome or rescind this power? We will take up this matter at greater length later in the chapter.

I've noted before that from the standpoint of religious psychology polytheism has an appeal in at least two areas where monotheism tends to be weaker. I want to expand on them now. The first pertains to the affective dimension of feelings of possessiveness and a subsequent loyalty. Here the personal, family, or small group god or goddess need not be shared as with a single God of all creation. Through proper devotion and acts of fidelity on the human part, linked to perceived blessings and protectiveness on the deity's part, a mutual possessiveness along with proprietary rights occurs that is psychologically satisfying in its intimacy. Secret rituals known only to the individual, family, or group frequently accompany this so as to exclude unwanted intrusions into the relationship by others. The psychology also produces manageable responsibilities pertinent to the immediacy of the concerns of the devotees, a greater sense that the deity is concerned with what is happening here and now in the devotees' lives, and a confidence that in a conflict with other superhuman powers he or she will come to their defense. What occurs, in short, is a more effective personalization of the divine/human relationship than is perhaps usually the case in a monotheism where the relationship, precisely because it is universal, is looser, less accommodating or attentive to the particularities of need or desire of any individual or select group. Loyalty then inclines toward greater intensity as the manageable responsibilities are mutually met, but also toward a greater fury when they are not. The sociological dimension of the psychology is obvious and irrefutable: you expect your beloved to be more loyal to you than to others; the family expects the same of its father; and the nation the same of its monarch or president. But you personally cannot expect your monarch or president to be more loyal than your family or friend; his or her loyalty is too widely dispersed among the much larger group to be so individually adjustable, and from concern for this group may in fact sometimes act in ways quite disloyal, indifferent, or antagonistic to you personally. A generosity of understanding or forgiveness may occur intermittently in this situation, but if called upon too often will in its own turn tend to metamorphose into disloyalty, indifference, or antagonism.

The second area where polytheism inclines toward greater appeal than monotheism is ecology. This is particularly true of so-called nature religions in which reflection circulates easily around the concerns of natural theology. Here polytheism invests all inhabitants of creation with characteristics of divinity appropriate to them, and then typically personifies them. The river, therefore, is never just a body of flowing water, but a goddess; the tree never just a composite of wood and leaves, but a god; and so on. This produces a reverence for the river or tree deserved in its own right, and not, where it exists at all in monotheistic theologies, imposed on them by reverence for the Creator (by and large, for example, Christianity will be comfortable with the image of the universe as God's body, but only as it expresses the intentions, certainly not the "parts" of God). However, this imposed reverence has a way of gradually distancing itself from that given the Creator because it is considered inappropriate that the same reverence be given both. And this almost inevitably results in such a great distance that proper reverence now becomes the exclusive prerogative of God, which, if shared, is now considered idolatry. One of the reasons, then, why a monotheistic religion like Christianity took such a dislike toward paganism—as the very word itself indicates: *pagan* originally meant "country folk"—is that people whose livelihood was closely attached to the benevolence of the land, water, plants, and animals, who worked with these each day and refused to tempt this benevolence by religious indifference, criticism, or mockery toward it, maintained a sense of the divinity in these things that the formal theologies had distanced all the way to heaven. The urban population, especially the educated among them, became fond of considering the pagan badly ignorant, superstitious, and dirty, at an extreme debauched and damned, and any religion attached too closely to them a diminution or sullying, a sacrilege against the dignity of God. If my suggestion is worthy that a Christian religion weak in natural theology needs to heal this, then the healing need also involve in the coming millennium a new paganism, as the basic meaning of this word has been described.

It is when monotheism deprives individuals of the personalism they seek in religion by abstracting divine presence into unreachable times and places, or by teaching an immanence of this presence in the world that is yet so hidden as to be itself unreachable, that people develop surrogates for God that in effect reintroduce both polytheism and paganism. In Catholicism, for example, this occurred in the cult of the saints, those whose stories touched people in the "natural" ways of their lives: the security of decent food, water, shelter, protection against enemies, illness, accident. And while these saints were of course never divinized, in devotional piety they were nonetheless the major focus in place of a too distant or too hidden God. There was a liveliness of intimacy with them that could not be achieved with God: the difference between a loving respect and an adoring respect. In other, more profane contexts this same phenomenon occurs in the deification of political causes, the pursuit of power, wealth, fame, health, pleasure, and so on. These become the multiple deities worshipped intimately that relate to the everyday concerns, the "natural" ones of human desire that populate people's lives in countless ways and degrees. And the worship has its own stylized rubrics to guarantee special favor, and typically texts for revelatory advice as well: the plans, procedures, and moral codes that will guide the individual to the desired sanctity of sharing in the deified object. This is what we mean when we say of someone, "Money (or fame or power or health) is his/her god." And we have an intuitive sense that the attempt to deify these things is as ill-advised as the attempt to personalize a God too removed from our experiences to be natural to us, that is, a part of our nature. A natural theology, therefore, would have to attend not just to nature as the world around us but to nature as the world within us. In the coming millennium it would need to be both profoundly ecological as well as psychological.

While I am recommending a new polytheism and new paganism (again: as I am describing them), I am not recommending a new tribalism. By tribalism I am referring to any gathering of human beings marked by two dominant descriptive traits. The gathering can be of any size, from a group of two to whole nation-states or worldwide religious organizations—though the larger the group, the more these traits tend to dissipate because of the greater "mutation" rate of rebels and heretics. This last phrase provides a clue to the first trait. Tribalism produces an extraordinarily tight binding among the participants centering on the three characteristics we have already used to describe religions, but could be used just as legitimately to describe any community of people that is composed by more than mere juxtaposition. first, there is a creed, or system of belief, which is almost always accompanied by an apologetics or polemics explaining and justifying it. Secondly, there is a code, or system of behavior, which is almost always accompanied by promises of reward and punishment. Thirdly, there is a cult, or system of worship, which is almost always accompanied by rubrics detailing proper recognition of the power and role of deity within the group. Tribalism occurs whenever these characteristics become hardened into a dogmatism that tolerates no opposition, refinement, or creative transformation. It premises this intolerance on claims to absoluteness that have been historically, charismatically, or ideologically produced, and which are frequently set within the structure of a sacred or secular myth or series of myths simply stated and usually memorizable, at least in general outline. Most fundamentalist Christian groups, for example, are tribalistic, as are their nonreligious counterparts in some schools of psychology, political theory, and science. It is usually conversation that is the first clue to a tribalistic mentality: a refusal to permit leeway to alternative viewpoints prevails.

The second trait is a distinctly theological one. In tribalism the participants transfer themselves into divinity rather than the other way around. What we note when examining the creed, code, and cult is an immediate, only sometimes subtle parallel between the image of God that emerges and the image the tribal members have of themselves. The most telling analysis of this phenomenon still belongs to Ludwig Feuerbach, with a far more popular but much less profound repetition in the theological commentaries of Sigmund Freud. Patriarchalism as the dominance of acculturated traits of masculinity in a group is possibly the most ancient of tribalisms, with the image of God affected accordingly. Today in Euro-American Christianity one is likely to find a similar tribalism among some feminist theologies, counterposed to (and often quite antagonistic toward) the previous or still presiding patriarchalism. A tribalistic attitude can also be found among the holders of specific offices in some religions, most notably their respective priesthoods or vowed religious communities. But one can also discover it among secular groupings such as politicians, lawyers, and above all physicians: a divinizing of their own interests, perspectives, and ethics either nonpersonally (there is no actual transference of these to the preferences of a deity, only an assertion of their ultimate importance) or personally (there is such a transference as the substantiating rationale for this importance). What distinguishes this process from polytheism *per se* is that tribalism as a form of polytheism (i.e., when the groups are considered together) is always prepared for intellectual and/or physical violence to defend its exclusivist claims. While fidelity to our primary ideal of peace as the cherishing of life is not, therefore, offended by polytheism as such, it is by tribalism, whether it exists in fact or as a chronic potentiality. Any agenda for Christian religion in the coming millennium must seek to diminish this offense, especially, as we suggested in chapter 2, if the world as a global village is becoming more obvious in our communication technologies and so must become more pertinent in our thinking and behavior.

I would now like to follow Whitehead's analysis that when we take an overview on all the different ways that deity has been described ("deity" as the nature of God or gods in the most commonplace description, or the Absolute in a more metaphysical one, or the object of ultimate concern in Tillich's terminology) there emerge three dominant ones, the first two of which clearly align with ancient preferences for power as the foremost divine attribute, the third more subtly so. The first is that of God as monarch, a sociopolitical designation born from the earliest structures of human organization in patriarchal families, subsequently extended to the highest office in despotic clans, tribes, and nation-states. The will of this God is contestable but supreme, and there is no court of appeal—though precisely because of this there is usually a corresponding concern for divine fidelity to the requirements of justice understood on the model of a contract or covenant relationship in which submission to the requirements or laws laid down in the contract issue in reward, rebellion in punishment. We've already noted that when the problem of theodicy becomes bothersome in this scheme, and justice has manifestly not been served during life, the notions of heaven and hell enter the piety and theology to guarantee the divine justice. But in all the illustrations known to me where this occurs, there lurks here and there—though its presence rarely comes starkly forward—the uncertainty whether God in the absoluteness of his will as despotic king can be obliged to this justice, or whether, as with human despots, we can anticipate lapses into amoral tyranny, without, however, the options of exiling or assassinating him.

We should also note again that the tribalism of any conquering group typically understands victory as an expression of the more thorough power, the more inclusive absolutism of their God(s) over that of their opponents, and then either demands the destruction of the offending creed, code, and cult, or its diminution to vassalage under suzerainty of the new, imposed God(s).

A second way that God has been understood is that of absolute moral agent. This is usually linked to the first image insofar as God as monarch has the power to determine issues of who will live and die, whereas God as moral agent determines *how* one will live and, where belief in it exists, what the disposition of one's afterlife will be. It is within this image that there arises, then, not just the notion of contract or covenant as the safeguard for justice in the previous image, but also the notion of revelation. The idea of God as monarch, after all, does not in itself require a belief that God's will has been ascertained: a conclusion that is the seedbed of all concepts of predestination, even sophisticated ones like that centering on *moira* (fate) in ancient Greece or that of Calvin in his *Institutes*. But the image of God as moral agent has embedded within it the idea that the deity you are dealing with is not some aloof Olympian isolated on the island of heaven and unconcerned about creation once it is originated—the God of most forms of deism, and the one many scientists are still the most comfortable with in the working of their craft—but one actively involved in the creation and regularly intruding into it to express the divine will. The further doctrine of providence is also involved in this image, though again not as predestination but as a goal that can be thwarted by creation's striving to the contrary. For without this freedom the revelation becomes superfluous, or, as in some viewpoints, solely an act of divine self-glorification. These revelations are generally offered to the entire believing community as describing requirements for behavior, though all religions recognize the possibility of private revelations influencing only the receptor's individual life, and some, like that of the Crow Indians of the American plains, recognize these private revelations as the only kind.

The third way that God has been understood is that of the Unmoved Mover. The term itself is from Greek metaphysics, particularly as represented by Aristotle, though you can find its analogue in other theological traditions, as in some schools of Taoism, Buddhism, and Hinduism. In this image God is often presented as Being itself, the ground of everything that is, and any divine power exercised is done almost exclusively through secondary causes, that is, through the specific determinants or ontic components comprising how it is that particular beings act, or in a favorite terminology, how their essence is expressed in their existence. Despite some heroic efforts throughout its history, this image does not lend itself to personalization, certainly not as obviously as the images of monarch and moral agent, and so has remained obscure in devotional pieties and most spiritualities. Yet of the three it is the one closest to the image or understanding I will be recommending, with several major provisos and one radical departure regarding the motive of God's activity when this activity is understood as *expressive* Being. The power that God exercises, or in the tight terminology of adherents of this image, the power that God is, will not be coercive but persuasive through the working of the secondary causes (such as you and I and the rose outside my window). And the need in human hearts for divine personalism, along with the need to identify God's expressive Being in terms drawn from our common experiences (which we set as our guiding rubric at the beginning of this chapter), will both be addressed by honoring the uses of metaphor in theology—though not those of the first two images.

Whitehead himself is critical of all three of these images, and in my judgment the criticism—when the third image does not have the alterations I am going to attach to it—is valid. He is being influenced here by his Christianity, or more exactly, his understanding of the teachings of Jesus, especially those on divine and human behavior, and his criticism is correctly built on the very heart of these teachings. For Whitehead writes toward the end of his masterwork, *Process and Reality,* that "love neither rules nor is it unmoved; also it is a little oblivious as to morals." In my view this statement captures the most telling criteria for appraising religions that we possess, especially when these religions, as Christianity does, have claimed that the practice of love is the heart of their theological as well as ethical identity. In the last chapter I proposed a series of defining traits this love involves, and I will not repeat them here. What I will do instead is suggest a clarifying addendum to Whitehead's statement, which is loosely present in his writings but which he never captures with the precision of the above statement. As it reads, the statement applies exclusively to the lover's attitude toward the beloved, and is cast in a series of denials; in theological jargon, it is an apophatic description. But when it is directed not to the beloved but to the lover, the denials must themselves be denied; the description, again in theological jargon, must become kataphatic. For the love that the lover experiences does indeed rule, as absolutely as the most despotic monarch; and it does remain unmoved, as the unalterable bedrock of thought and behavior; and it is not at all oblivious to morals, if the defining characteristic of these is the cherishing of life. In love how one assesses the beloved and how one assesses oneself are qualitatively different judgments, born from the continuation of individuality even after the sense of mutual identity—the rightness of thinking of the beloved and ourselves as "we"—is achieved.

Conceptual Tools

The doctrine on love will occupy us again in this chapter, when I offer it as not just an ethical but a metaphysical context toward an understanding of God. For now, though, I wish to return to a general description of religion so as to set for our agenda a series of conceptual tools that I would suggest are requisite to any adequate approach to the working out of a religious vision, particularly one, like that of Christianity, linked irreversibly to privileged or sacred writings. There are seven of these tools, and delineating them will occupy the rest of this section. As I proceed the reader will see how one, then another has been presumed at various points on previous pages and controlled the analysis of issues. While I would never claim that this list is exhaustive, from my perspective the seven are essential, not just in the activity of religion in my own life, but as I have attempted over many years to describe and seduce a religious consciousness from my students. Many have found them not only useful in developing their own overviews of religion itself as a human phenomenon, but in their personal wrestling with the creeds, codes, and cults of specific religions where these are thought to originate in a collection of holy writings, or scriptures. However, it must be clear that what I am offering is not a *method*—much work has been done in this area in the last thirty to forty years, and in another book I have described my own contribution to this labor, which I call theological realism—but a series of characteristics that, as they imbue religion itself as attentiveness to God, or more specifically, to the word of God, would also imbue any method designed to hone or channel this attentiveness in a particular direction.

1. The first conceptual tool is the notion of *bias*. I mentioned in chapter 1 that this word is from the Greek, meaning "slant" or "angle," and was used originally to describe methods of planting on a hillside—at a slant so that neither too much nor too little rain water irrigates the seedlings—and that later it came to describe the cognitive or emotional slant at which we receive new experiences: the prejudgment or bias we already possess regarding what the experience will mean. The Greeks argued that knowing one's biases was therefore the first step to wisdom; or somewhat differently, that any claim to a completely open mind is a self-deception or a deliberate fiction. Religion, of course, represents heavily biased experiences, ones being constantly sifted through the creed, code, and cult one affirms. Sometimes the religious consciousness does not survive this process: the experiences will no longer tolerate with integrity what the creed, code, or cult of a particular religion claims, and the individual is left seeking a new religious vision or some satisfying surrogate. But often it does: there is a match between the biases of the religion and the experiences one is having such that loyalty to the religion remains intact. In both instances, in other words, what we are witnessing is a double movement: the biases of the religion itself in its creed, code, and cult, and the biases of the individual in assessing the legitimacy of these in light of his or her experiences in life. It is this second movement that now interests us—the biases or prejudgments an individual brings to considerations of religion. Of the many these might include, however, there have been six that have surfaced consistently in those I read, those I teach, and in my own thinking too. I would like to devote each of the next six paragraphs to one of these biases, thereby giving scant justice to them but at least initiating an understanding that will perhaps allow the reader to assess the bias or biases controlling his or her own reception of the creed, code, and cult of a particular religion—for our purposes, Christianity—or of his or her own religious experiences or someone else's independent of it.

a. The bias of past history. This has been a particularly controversial one during the last two centuries in Christianity, though it can be found when studying any religion. Here your prejudgment pertains to the oral or written tradition that presides over the beginning of the religion and influences its succeeding doctrines. You go to these traditions for the purposes of good history, to trace out in a reliable fashion the sequence of deeds, words, and events that played the foundational role in the religion. But after the examination begins, you find that the traditions are quite unreliable, that there are contradictions and discrepancies that can't be resolved, and that your search for origins is frustrated from the start. It becomes plain that the authors of the stories or text had only intermittent interest in providing a chronicle of objective data. Instead, they were dominated by their faith claims about the data and felt free to revise or reform it accordingly. You learn, for example, that roughly until the Enlightenment an author writing of a man's conception, birth, infancy, and childhood, when there were no available and reliable witnesses to these, would feel free to construct such narratives on the basis of what he or she wished to say about the adult man. And so you become disappointed, let's say, about the opening chapters of Matthew's and Luke's gospels. This can leave you distressed and perplexed, or it can issue in a condescending judgment: the authors were very poor historians, and the texts not worth studying. Most educated people today are aware of the flaw in this bias—that it is unfair to impose on an author criteria that either never or only here and there controlled the composition of the narrative—and avoid it. For many others, however, the narrative's truth is judged precisely as a correspondence to the historical objectivity of what is described, so that the bias now insists that the criteria of today's professional historiography do not apply, that lurking in the record is the presence of God, and that any contradictions or discrepancies are thus the result of a flaw in our perception and not in the record itself. Sometimes an attempt to resolve this putative flaw is made via the uses of allegory or analogy when interpreting the text, sometimes on the basis that further data about the literary methods and preferences of the authors, such as their application of metaphors and similes, will disclose the objective reliability of the narratives. These efforts can certainly be worthwhile, but more for enriching the narrative's meaning than substantiating their literal inerrancy. But to pursue the Christian example: the fact is that Matthew, Mark, and Luke record a public ministry of one year and John of three years. All four cannot be correct, and the reader is well advised that the early Christians were as aware of this as we are, considered it unimportant, and were concerned instead with what happened during the public ministry rather than with a triviality such as how long it lasted. In fact, to make this point very clear the discrepancy may have been intentionally retained, much like the author of Genesis intentionally had the plants created before the sun to concentrate attention on the dependence of all things on God and not on the scheduling of events.

b. The aesthetic bias. This is a nearly universal bias, shaped on a pre-judgment of the affective or emotional appeal a religion's written or oral traditions must possess if they are to remain lively and be rehearsed by most people. It is markedly subjective, though some stories and narratives seem to have an enormously inclusive attraction, such as the book of Job or the Sermon on the Mount. These aesthetically attractive passages are turned to repeatedly for consolation, challenge, the delights of spiritual pleasure, assistance in decision making, and so on. They meet the reader's or listener's expectations, often on the first experience, of what constitutes beauty in the use of words: what "touches" or "moves" them in ways that most narratives rarely do. The difficulty with this second bias, therefore, is that it can lead to a selectivity that abjures interest in other portions of the tradition, no matter how ancient or contemporary, and so can lead easily to a restricted, distorted understanding of the religion. The Buddhist who only reads repetitively and with interest the fire Sermon will scarcely understand Buddhism, just as the Christian who does the same with the Sermon on the Mount will scarcely understand Christianity. Or perhaps better said: the understandings in each case will not be as rich and sympathetic as they would otherwise be if the compass of the repetition and interest were extended more widely, including as a final stage commentaries on the written or oral tradition by competent scholars or the exceptionally devout and insightful believer.

c. The bias of scientism. This bias has emerged very powerfully since the Enlightenment and affects all religions except the most isolated or dogmatic ones. It is born from the demand for explanations of events that are empirically based in a cause-and-effect sequence in which God as the causal element has increasingly diminished. In many ways it has been a very healthy bias serving various dimensions of human autonomy; medicine and agriculture come immediately to mind. If your field becomes barren, you are acting religiously foolish if your only response is attendance on God—even though for hundreds of human generations this was the sole option for imposing external assistance toward restoring fertility. Instead, you should seek professional help in identifying needed nutrients or counteragents to pollution to address the problem. *Then* you might turn to attendance on God, not in petition, though, but in gratitude for human ingenuity. Or if your child becomes ill, you are acting religiously negligent if you first run to a church instead of a clinic; and so on. In each case, and in the formal vocabulary of our third image of God as Unmoved Mover, you are denying your own responsibility as an agent of secondary causation. As with the first two, the difficulty with this current bias also lies in the extremes to which it can be taken, though an alert religious consciousness would never adopt Laplace's superficial arrogance when asked by Napoleon of God's role in celestial mechanics: I have no need of that hypothesis. This represents the final development of the bias of scientism, and the way most scientists who are yet religiously oriented avoid it is to bifurcate their thinking into two realms, adopting Laplace's attitude when doing their science, but denying it in other dimensions of their lives. This cognitional divisiveness is unhealthy and breeds enormous inconsistency in our overall pattern of thinking about our experiences. Among others, Whitehead clearly saw this problem, and later we will make our own a somewhat amended version of his resolution to it.

d. The bias of moral outrage. This occurs in conjunction with reflection on innocent suffering, or suffering judged beyond the limits of fair retribution or punishment, and appears specifically as the problem of theodicy. It is fairly common as a bias, and is premised on acceptance of three attributes of God—power, justice, and goodness—each of which is understood as absolute. When faced with innocent or excessive suffering, one sees the juggling of these three issues in notorious if-then statements: because such suffering exists, if God is all-powerful, then God is not all-good or all-just; if God is all-good and all-just, then God is not all-powerful. There is no way out of these conundrums as long as all three traits remain absolute. Even the approach noted in chapter 3—that if we could see the whole panorama of creation as God does, we would understand that any localized suffering is needed to contribute to the goodness and justice (meaning here, the right measure) of the whole—begs the question since it does not resolve why God's power was not exercised differently to gain this goodness and justice. The only workable way out of the theodicy problem, therefore, resides in an examination of the imposed attributes. And since in a monotheism if the goodness of God is in any way qualified or limited it is difficult to imagine why the religion would endure, save in the dissipations of sorcery and black magic or psychological adjustments to permanent fear or indifference, we must do some pruning in our understanding of God's power and justice, especially in the subsidiary assertions of God's power as intercessory and coercive and in the ranking of justice as a motive of divine activity. We will return to these matters later in the chapter.

e. The bias of bigotry. This too is a fairly common bias, reflecting particularly the spirit of possessiveness we noted in polytheists, that is, the claim to social superiority because of the claim to religious superiority of one's own God(s) over others. This leads to an immediate dismissal of the truth or worth of the opponents' written and oral traditions without the fair-minded study of them that would help diminish the blind tyranny of the prejudgment (an utter absence of prejudgment or bias, as we said earlier, doesn't appear possible; also: we are clearly describing here something much different from disagreement legitimately achieved through educated information about the conflicting tradition). Far more commonly, however, bigotry does not emerge directly from religious disputes but from other sources to which judgment on the religion is then attached; racial and ethnic biases are the most usual of these sources. An example of the attitude that results might read something like this: I hate the Jews, therefore I hate everything about them, including their religious traditions, that contributes to their identity. The Jewish understanding of God, despite its subtlety and ethical high-mindedness, is consequently excoriated in the most blasphemous ways, flagrantly among the ignorant, with greater sophistication and usually calmness among the educated. And I've heard this done not just toward Jews by Muslims and Christians, but by all three toward Navajos, Hopis, and Apaches of the American Southwest. The wonderful grace in the religions of these Indians is swallowed up in ludicrous and deceptive condemnations that have no pertinence at all to the truth of these peoples' lives. Bigotry is without doubt the most stupid and useless of all the biases, and when well-set in someone's mind is almost impossible to dissolve.

f. The sixth bias—personalism. I am using the word "personalism" very broadly to designate any attitude that approaches the traditions of a religion with the expectation that there is something within them to teach us of ourselves, the world in which we live, and, for the religiously alert consciousness, God. Partly this bias arises from the brute observation that religion has functioned in this way from our origin as self-reflective beings, certainly by the time this self-reflectiveness begins to be recorded. Partly it is due to what the describing term itself indicates: that religion is capable of personal engagement without a trained or professional competence. And partly it is due to a longing to achieve as much intel-lectual/emotional or spiritual richness in life as possible—and that part of this richness pertains to the continuation of its possibility after death. I have already suggested that religion as the affirmation and establish-ment of a relationship with God likely appeared with reflection on the sky and the Earth, and questions of creative and ordering power. But there is a strong recommendation by many others that it appeared as a way of addressing the fact of death, and archeological findings of preliterate humans, such as those found in a Neanderthal grave, lend support to this: some Power cherishes life beyond death. Whatever the ini-tial prompting, however, whether in a very ancient line or relatively new, instigating individual or communal interest, encouraging this sixth bias, even as it may intermix with one or more of the others, should be para-mount on any agenda for Christian religion in the coming millennium. For in its absence among believers religion will surely fade from human consciousness in a slow walk toward irrelevance.

2. Our second conceptual tool is myth. In Christianity especially there has been a great deal of controversy surrounding the word, and a variety of definitions have been offered. There is no disagreement in theological scholarship that it is a critical concept for understanding the oral and written traditions of any religion, yet also that in this context the word cannot be used in its common parlance as a synonym for fable, fiction, or fairy tale. I described earlier in the book how I use the word, and I'd like to repeat that description here: a myth is a conceptual framework for understanding experiences. The framework is used first to articulate experiences in light of a familiar language and its forms of expression (in religious myths, analogy and metaphor tend to predominate here), and secondly to give some cohesion to the experiences. In this sense all of us are mythmakers. And when we share myths with others having similar experiences, and one of them is perceived as superior in expressive and cohesive ability, it becomes public. Often this solidifies it so thoroughly in the consciousness of a group that it is repeated and defended even when its explanatory talent has become useless in the advance of knowl-edge or a change in psychological climate. The resulting need to replace the old myths with new ones can create a group crisis, which is frequently resolved only through the lingering but inevitable demise of the previ-ous myths, and at first perhaps a sullen but later a more congenial accep-

tance of the new ones. At all such times I would insist that a general guideline already implied must prevail—namely, that it is experience that should control thinking, not vice versa, and that experience is adequately assessed only when the assessment is sufficiently informed by data pertinent to it—and, as a particularly important element in this, the psychological gestalt of the receptors of the experiences. Needless to say, religion must be responsive to this whole process, especially regarding myths about experiences of God, if for no other reason than to encourage the sixth bias described above.

3. The distinction between objective and subjective history is our third conceptual tool. We may describe this briefly in the example of keeping two diaries, the one recording a mere chronicle of events or experiences, the other recording the meaning you've given them. The first bias we described a few paragraphs ago, that of past history, would emphasize objective history as its interest, the sixth bias, personalism, would emphasize subjective history. These different perspectives are obviously determined by how thoroughly you want the author of the narrative to be involved in interpreting the events or experiences being recorded. In the primary narratives of all religions, subjective history predominates, though if the religion is a historical one (integrally attached to the actual occurrences in an individual's or community's life) some security regarding the objective reliability of the record is needed—or the religion becomes a high mythology. I do not mean this to be a disparaging description, as is clear from the presentation of our second conceptual tool. But while high mythologies can be exquisitely crafted to provide a framework for understanding events or experiences, they make no claim to be anchored in objective history. My correlate to this is therefore "low" mythology, which does make such a claim. My own impression is that there is no religion, with the possible exception of Judaism and the dependence of its self-understanding on an actual Exodus, that is more reliant on objective historical data than Christianity. For right at the point of its central claim we need to establish a low mythology—that is, that the descriptions of the raised Jesus have objective historical anchorage in *Jesus himself,* and are not merely accounts of a resurrection into the memories and preaching of the disciples, or of their passionate hallucinations. It strikes me as correct, in other words, when Whitehead contrasts Christianity with a tradition like Buddhism and says that the

latter is a metaphysics in search of a religion (in order to give its origins objective historical reality that will strengthen its vision of life in the actual deeds and sayings of a man, Gautama, as well as to trace a more persuasive understanding of the intent and purposes of the whole of history as it has been actually lived by human beings), whereas the former is a religion in search of a metaphysics (in order to make the sayings and deeds, the destiny of Jesus, along with the vision of history they have engendered, as persuasive as possible intellectually).

4. Another distinction, that between problem and mystery, is our fourth conceptual tool. Since I know of no analysis of this distinction more lucid or convincing than Gabriel Marcel's, I will follow his. A problem is something that lies outside us, that we can analyze and resolve as an objective observer. Once resolved, the knowledge for doing so is stored in memory so that should the same or a similar problem arise again, the resolution can be quicker and more adept. Once a problem has been resolved, there is no further need to continue at the attempt. A mystery, on the other hand, is something of which I am an integral part. I cannot step outside it, as with a problem, and by employing the proper skills of logic and/or technologies resolve it. I am interwoven with the experiences in ways from which I cannot extricate myself, so that to attempt to do so—to transform the mysterious into the problematic, as is the inclination particularly among scientists—always produces frustrating inexactitude since I am insisting that one of the defining components of the mystery, myself, can be fully scrutinized the way one might a theorem in geometry or a piece of tissue under a microscope or the diet that might cure my child of a cold. But this is exactly what the mysterious prohibits. Thus we may agree, for example, with ancient descriptions of love as a mystery, or faith in God. Try as I might to capture the meaning of this love or faith fully, no matter how eloquent or detailed I might be, there will always be an intuitive awareness, frequently quite aggravating, that something is still missing. This something is I myself, and this is the mystery. Christian religion must always keep the awareness of this distinction in mind, so that in the new millennium it can avoid the wasted attempts, like many that have percolated throughout the past two millennia of its history, to metamorphose the mystery of God into the problem of God. This is all the more urgent since in my view science and its

dominion over human thought—the success of its resolving power over problems, its justified pride in pointing out that much that was previously judged mysterious wasn't so at all—is going to increase enormously over how we approach the universe and our role and God's within it. What I call "the seduction of the extreme" lies in wait here: specifically, the temptation to think that if God or any other claims about existence cannot be reduced to the parameters of a problem, then they are properly fantasies and not realities.

It is the above understanding of mystery that also prohibits the accomplishment of the so-called Theory of Everything that has mesmerized a number of contemporary theoretical physicists, though it has likewise met with telling criticisms by others like R. Stannard and J. Barrow. The former especially notes the element of mystery when describing our investment in establishing the axioms of such a theory (we cannot separate the choices for these axioms—we cannot justify them beyond our choosing them—from the theory they produce). Or in Barrow's similar judgment: no Theory of Everything can provide total insight, since to understand everything excludes ourselves as the critical factor in the understanding, and so would be to understand nothing. Such a theory, in other words, would require the elimination of contingency from the universe, above all the contingency—or we could now say, in this context, the mystery—that is ourselves and our thinking, and require the universe to be as it is (again including ourselves) as a necessity. Thomas Torrance is especially precise in criticizing this position, as are Ian Barbour, Paul Davies, and others: All of them insist that what we actually experience of the universe in our science as well as our everyday lives is neither pure necessity nor pure contingency, but *ordered* contingency that allows the analysis of our experiences, and our science, to be reliable, in fact enormously reliable (we are indeed successful problem solvers), but never complete so as to need no further refinement. By inhabiting the universe, we are also the inhabitants of mystery.

5. The fifth conceptual tool pertains to a variety of literary approaches. There are three of these I wish to isolate, the first being literalism. This approach is governed by the maxim: the truth is in the words. There is no doubt that in the foundational narratives of all religions there are passages where literalism is appropriate. When Jesus is asked, for example,

how often we must forgive an offender, and replies with a cultic number (70 times 7), meaning "always," the passage is to be taken as is and needs no interpretation. The difficulty with literalism therefore arises when it is made to apply clear across the board, as in our previous illustration of the Genesis account of the creation of plants before the Sun. All such indiscreet literalism must ultimately rely on the power of God as the clarifying device for its triumph over easily accessible data to the contrary, such as that plants cannot live without the Sun. Many people in all religions find deeply satisfying security in literalism, and some religions, like Islam and Mormonism, have made it the exclusive approach. But for others not easily soothed by a tradition's contradictions—again, most pointedly in its foundational narratives—nor willing to invoke the power of God when they arise, the other two of our three approaches become options. The first of these is creedalism, and its guiding maxim is that the truth is *in* the words and must be coaxed out. Joined to this, however, is the further awareness that this task requires a trained competence, or, less frequently, a charismatic endowment, that most people have neither the talent nor time nor detailed interest to engage. A priesthood or some analogue to it is thus established to gain this expertise, and then to preach and teach viable interpretations of the narratives. But just as the potential difficulty of the first approach is the reduction of thinking to stupidity, the potential difficulty of this second one is the reduction of the preaching/teaching office to tyranny: The priests or their analogues become the only interpreters, and no other claimants are tolerated. For good or ill, this is usually the context in which dogmas emerge, and the formal authorities in any structured or hierarchical religion must remain constantly wary about encouraging its occurrence. The third approach I call the existential, and it is identical to the bias of personalism, with this qualification: The individual is interested enough in religious concerns to pursue as much as possible education in them, both under the tutelage of teachers (so recognizing the validity the second approach does possess) and autodidactically when meanings need application more than interpretation (so recognizing the validity the first approach possesses). This third, blending approach is the one I personally recommend and would wish to see encouraged in the coming millennium. As already noted in chapter 3, the availability of an education that develops a respectful yet analytic and critical spirit toward its contents is a perennial need on any proposed agenda for Christian religion.

6. The notion of inspiration provides our sixth conceptual tool. It has had a somewhat ambiguous history in most religions, and because of this is generally disregarded by academic theologians. The primary reason appears to be that throughout this history inspiration has been typically linked with revelation, our next conceptual tool, as the mechanism of its delivery. And these mechanisms strike many as unnervingly close to the devices of talismanic and incantatory magic—as in oracles, epiphanies, dreams, and seizures—as well as too indifferent to the influence of the receptor on what is being received. I wish to propose a description of inspiration that bypasses this whole situation by understanding it not in terms of mechanism but of the character of what is claimed as inspired. For this purpose, therefore, I would suggest that to identify an oral or written tradition as inspired is to do no more than claim that no accusations against the authors as engaging in deliberate deceit can be justified. This is an intentionally loose description, deliberately meant to apply to many contexts other than religion so as to spare its religious use from the above observations, and more importantly to provide the inspired individual with a determinative role in what is being told or recorded. The primary conclusion we can then draw is that while the notion of inspiration is recognizing that the author did not lie, it is not a comment on whether or not the author was mistaken, since between the two judgments there is a clear qualitative difference.

7. The above understanding of inspiration immediately affects the meaning of our seventh conceptual tool, revelation. Of the seven, this is the only one that is strictly theological—that is, it requires us to make at least the following three statements: (1) that there is a God; (2) that this God intrudes into the course of history (of the universe, the world, and humanity) to express God's will; (3) that these intrusions occur because they are integral to any adequate image of divine creativity: that God creates not as a technician merely for purposes of utility or pleasure, but as an artist with whose works there is the possibility of communication, or differently, the purpose of whose art is communion. These intrusions are what we call revelation, and the detection of their primary expressions, according to our second statement, belongs to cosmology, ecology, and anthropology. It is the last of these that has occupied by far the greatest and most consistent attention in religions, though the first two are currently emerging into greater consciousness throughout the world.

The first criterion for determining whether an experience is revelatory is that we have no warrants for believing the experience is deceiving us; this is the criterion of inspiration. The second one is that the revelation does not contradict in essential ways some previous revelatory experience (by "essential" I mean that deception in the one causes deception in the other); this is the criterion of consistency. The third criterion is that the revelation addresses the world in which its receptor lives (the values, crises, etc., of his or her culture); this is the criterion of relevance. The fourth one is that the revelation provides novelty in patterns of thought and feeling, a new insight or aesthetic consolation or challenge; this is the criterion of illuminating power. The fifth and final one is that the origin of the first four, or at least a contributing partner in them, is in some fashion understood as God; this is the intuitive criterion, or as some might prefer, the faith criterion.

The foregoing remarks on revelation will terminate this section of the chapter. But they do so only as the prologue to the next. For while at the heart of all religions is the affirmation of God's existence, this is only half of what is there. The religious consciousness cannot issue from the mere assertion of divine existence, any more than love can from its mere assertion, but requires that this existence also be communicative. A completely silent God is an idol that can gather around it only silence in return—the God of all mysticisms gone awry—or hope and fancies that only serve an easy conceit—the God of all narcissists gone blind by looking too steadily at themselves. Let us move more closely, then, and seek a tighter embrace of the concept of revelation.

Revelation

In the last chapter we discussed the meaning of messianic poverty and suggested that it is born from an awareness that we cannot go it alone in life, and that in religion this gives rise to the need for church and petitionary prayer. I would now add to those comments that this last need is most adequately understood in the context of revelation: (1) that petitionary prayer, undoubtedly the most common form of prayer, presumes the bias that God can disclose divine presence in the world; (2) that this presence is communicative; (3) that it can enact novelty in the world through secondary (mediated) causation pertinent to the need requested; (4) that there is an overwhelming consistency throughout history in witness to the efficacy of this prayer; and (5) that the mere petitioning illuminates the call-response dialectic that is at the heart of any personal relationship. Yet the dependence this prayer demonstrates in our lives is also guaranteed its truth independently of religion; or perhaps better, its presence in religion is an extension of a brute biological fact of our individual beginnings, namely, that for a lengthy time after birth, even when internal systems of the body are performing autonomously, the continuation of our life is completely dependent on the cherishing of that life by others. Unlike the glib and annoying habit of some psychologists who use this fact of early childhood to explain what they insist is its later transference to a wish-fulfilling and unreal God-fantasy, we have preferred to view both the childhood fact and belief in God as distinct manifestations of the single truth that we are by nature, or by fate, completely dependent on others in various ways for our distinct form of existence, and that this is true of all things in the relationships needed to construct our universe. Even a quark manifests this truth, since without its relationships of dependence it too would not exist. A little later I will be proposing that underlying this truth, and regardless of whatever we finally determine the fundamental particle and force of the universe to be, we enter the terrain of God.

The presupposition of revelation is ignorance. Of all religions, Judeo-Christianity, ancient Greek theism, and Buddhism (in its theistic forms) are particularly reflective of this. For all three ignorance is a metaphysical condition whose truth is chronically experienced. I suspect that for the majority of readers the best known mythic account of this condition is the one in Genesis that I previously interpreted. The upshot of that interpretation for our interest now is that God does not leave the man and woman completely strapped in their ignorance, a sunkenness in confusion and desperation seesawing back and forth between inquiries like, "Is this good or evil? Should I do this or not?" and so on. In this sense the whole Fall and Exile narrative has its denouement in the claim that despite unworthiness we have not been abandoned by God, but rather are the recipients of a sufficient lifting of our ignorance so as to achieve confidence about how to contour our lives. In fact, I suspect the narrative may have been placed where it is in the Bible not just to provide a framework identifying our limitations, but to offer as well, right at its very beginning, a rationale for why the rest of Scriptures was recorded: to describe the history of privileged ways God has relieved us of ignorance, or what amounts to the same thing, to give an accounting of revelation. Socrates and Gautama do something similar without such an overt use of religious myth. For Socrates ignorance is intrinsic to our nature—it is metaphysical—but so is truth. He follows this primary datum with two extraordinarily powerful doctrines: that the admission of ignorance is the defining trait of wisdom, since it is what impels us to seek the truth; and that since the truth is not external to us, needing to be bestowed, but internal, needing to be coaxed into awareness, this is done through the adroit use of successive inquiries into it, each one premised on knowledge gained from answers to previous ones. While Socrates, therefore, along with many ancient and modern soul mates, prefers to approach the resolution of ignorance as an adventure in pedagogy, the Buddha prefers a larger context. Ignorance (*avidya*) is a natural state and the basic cause of suffering. Confronting it is the principal intent of the Four Noble Truths, and ameliorating it the purpose of the Eightfold Path—which includes right thinking as a specific recommendation that is presumed in any adequate appreciation of the other seven.

We can say that the above three religious traditions capture remarkably well the three preeminent methods in all religions whereby revelation occurs. Judeo-Christianity formulates its method with a preference for history as the revelatory vehicle: for Jews above all the Exodus and the delivery of the law to Moses; for Christians the life, death, and new life of Jesus. Greek religion formulates its method with a preference for oracular vehicles, from dreams and seizures to the Socratic dialogue, as interior conversations with oneself, or exterior ones with others, foremostly one's teachers. Buddhism, finally, prefers intuition, the sudden insight into the nature of life, particularly its suffering, with the succeeding awareness that there is a way to redeem this. These descriptions are not meant to be exclusivist, since you can find all three illustrated in each of the traditions, and in fact in all religions; what I have done, rather, is briefly synopsize what I take to be the preferred method with its respective vehicle of delivery. The personalization of the divine agency in each of these methods and vehicles also differs considerably. Judeo-Christianity is the most forthrightly personal in its descriptions: it is Yahweh who is the agent, or the Father of Jesus (in Islam, the most widespread inheritor of this tradition, it is of course Allah). In Greek religion and those traditions it both reflects and influences there is usually recognition of a divine or quasi-divine partner in the revelatory dreams, seizures, or dialogues, as in Socrates' own insistence on the role of his *daimon*. Buddhism is the least personal regarding divine agency—there are many scholars who even argue that "pure" Buddhism, whatever that is, is atheistic—and aside from the very stylized polytheism it quickly engenders in common piety, Gautama himself seems to find only an inkling of this agency in the unbidden occurrence of intuitive insight. But it is a very vague and reluctantly described agency, a presence or atmosphere or awareness that is obliterated almost simultaneously with its occurrence through an intensity of experience so thorough there are no more contrasts within it, or what he calls nirvana. Again, as with the methods and vehicles, these personalizations of the divine agency are not exclusivist but preferential; they intermix to varying degrees in these three and other religions.

Whitehead writes that religion is what we do with our solitariness. This is one of many aphoristic observations in his work that gives us pause for thought. As I've mused on it over the years I've come to think that he meant something like what I described in earlier pages as obedience: the exhaustive and undistracted study and reflection that leads to a conviction about the meaning of an experience or the legitimacy of a proposal. It is in this solitude or entertainment of obedience that the conviction we call faith in God comes alive in a personal and passionate appropriation that it cannot possess as a mere inheritance from parents or teachers or as an acculturated disposition. This in turn begins to generate a personal myth of God that is variously refined or altered as one becomes a conversation partner with other myths of God. The heart of the whole process, though, is the moment of conviction, which in our current context we may now describe as a revelatory moment. In my own life so far this has attached itself indissolubly to Jesus' understanding of God as this comes through in the words and deeds of his life that are certain or so overwhelmingly probable as to be virtually certain. This is not to say that this revelatory experience of God is the only legitimate one, or even the most persuasive one beyond the scope of the subjectivity of the experience; in other words, I can say it is so only for myself and those who think similarly. Furthermore, I can affirm such judgment most successfully in the context of metaphors, particularly those of Jesus whereby he himself subjectively appropriated and expressed his own re-velatory experience of God. As a result, there is a special appeal to me in the intensification of love that he captures metaphorically in the genera-tive and life-cherishing personhood of God as father.

I must now draw a crucial and often controversial distinction. In the personalism of a relationship to God it appears to me that the use of metaphor is essential. The metaphors must be powerful enough to es-tablish a sense of individuality in the relationship, while simultaneously recognizing that God is not a proprietary possession of the individual. This was my point in recommending for the coming millennium the introduction of the *intent* of polytheism into monotheism—not to sug-gest many deities, but many relationships to the one God who is. The metaphor of parent does this superbly, in the awareness that none of us is therefore an only child, but, rather, we are siblings to one another, and more extensively, though few have made the thought their own, to ev-erything else that exists. This was a fundamental point in my remarks on childlikeness in the last chapter. Yet this use of metaphor, while essential to the liveliness of the religious consciousness and its influence over val-ues and behavior, is not sufficient in an understanding of God. Most Christian theologians have understood this, and perhaps it provides one reason why they have had ambiguous histories within believing com-munities. At some point we must attempt an understanding that is re-leased from metaphor, that depersonalizes God and seeks out the ques-tion of God's nature or being in some intellectually persuasive way that, in my judgment, will need to utilize in the coming millennium not the method but the data of science. And I note carefully the phrase, "intel-lectually *persuasive* way," since no understanding of God can be intellec-tually *compelling*—not in the sense that *everyone* must either opt for it or opt for stupidity, but only as a one-on-one effect in the peculiar work-ings of each of our minds as we follow the rigors of whatever patterns of thinking and data we are entertaining. I know that I myself have never possessed such an intellectually compelling understanding. Finally, let me note that the remarks in this paragraph seemed appropriate at this juncture, both to counterbalance the previous emphasis on metaphor as well as to give a flavor of what our concern in the next section will be. But for now I want to return to the notion of revelation.

Throughout many religious traditions we discover belief in interme-diate beings between deity and humanity, variously designated but most commonly in Western and Middle Eastern religions as angels. I do not wish to discuss here the issue of their ontological status—whether such beings actually exist or not—but will concentrate instead on the functions that get personified in them. We discover on examining the traditions that there are five of these that are almost universally acknowledged, and they all pertain to revelation as disclosure of divine will. The first one concerns the character of the revelation's authority, and the next four describe the character or intent of its contents. For Christian religion this discussion is additionally pertinent because scholarship has been indicating for some time that one of the earliest Christological views among a number of the believing communities—possibly even before claims of Jesus' messiahship developed, and certainly before the spectacular claim of his divinity—was an angel Christology: that he demonstrated in manifest ways the five functions we will describe. The Christians, of course, derived this view principally from the Old Testament's depictions of angelic activity, though some influence may also have come from Syrian-Persian sources (and originally the Old Testament depictions probably did) as well as the daimonism of Greek religion (the *daimon* being a generally benevolent spirit, sometimes capable of the malice of Judeo-Christian demons, though never on quite the scale permitted the latter). The first function is mediation.

Mediators are a commonplace in religions, and most monotheisms depict direct communication from God only at critical junctures defining the religion, as in the epiphanies to Moses on Sinai and the revelations in the Qur'an. I would suggest that there are two dominant reasons why this is so. The first is a familiar one to us by now and pertains to the issue of God's dignity when understood in a hierarchical sense: to expect God to speak directly to humans is to debase this dignity—as in ancient monarchies where the king came into contact with the common folk not because of their expectations that he do so but because of regal largesse, and then only in thoroughly stylized ways. Otherwise direct contact was to be prized as a rare and enormous boon or blessing. The second reason is more subtle and quite clever. Underlying it is the idea that between divine and human communication there is a wall that can be breached only through a mutually acknowledged mediator; in other words, there must be an interpreter of the deity's communication into a language or activity familiar to human beings. For the dignity of God requires a form of communication appropriate to deity, not to humanity, just as human communication is appropriate to itself but not to camels. The cleverness in this reason is that it provides a way out of the embarrassment of religious disputes regarding the revelation's meaning. The discrepancies and contradictions, the confusion in the revelation—or more usually, the series of revelations—derives from the mediation, most especially when cast in private or culture-bound terminologies, and not from God, whose reliability and probity are beyond dispute. Christian religion even recognizes this in the mediation between God and humanity that took place in Jesus. Disagreements about the meaning of a revelation, therefore, are not properly theological but anthropological in character: human perception and language is flawed in the reception and expression of divine communication, sometimes in the human mediator, sometimes in his or her audience, sometimes in both.

The first of the four intentions underlying the content of revelation is consolation. This is directed at the bothered mind and heart for the soothing of the source of distress. Death is often the context here, especially the painful death of the good and innocent, human and nonhuman, with the consolation attempting to formulate an effective theodicy. Defeat, failure, or frustration of any sort, communal or personal plans and pleasures gone awry, any assault on the objects of a virtuous hope, are also common contexts. The solace offered usually occurs within one or both of two contexts. In the first something beyond the individual's control has gone wrong, either unintentionally as in natural disasters, or deliberately through the malicious will of others. The varying degrees of freedom in all creation undergird these possibilities, and the disconsolate individual is to be persuaded that he or she is innocent of guilt for the manners and effects of this freedom. This is the consolation Job sought and didn't receive from his friends. The second context attempts to console through an insistence on limits. The disconsolate individual is rehearsed in the idea that there is very little we can accomplish by ourselves alone, that everywhere there arises our dependence on others to succeed at tasks and formulate workable understandings of events, that one of these dependencies is on God and the revelatory opportunities history provides for us, and finally, that we should seek the embrace of this assistance in how we think and to what or whom we turn to assuage the loneliness confusion always inflicts as its worst bite.

The second intention is healing. This is a more difficult claim for many to understand or accept. For whereas consolation pertains to spiritual or psychological restoration, and all of us have had experiences of it, healing pertains to physical restoration. The difficulty seems pertinent, however, only in more technologically advanced societies where medical science holds sway over the options people are willing to consider for themselves. The immediate conclusion drawn by many is that healing by God thus represents a more primitive confidence than they can approve or possess, almost a type of superstition that a more sophisticated knowledge has pushed aside. There isn't much that can be said to this bias, except that even a light perusal of healings in the hospitals of these medically sophisticated societies indicates a sizable number of so-called spontaneous healings whose source is unknown to the physicians, but which the patients, even those well-educated in the objective norms of science and the scrutinies of theology, attribute to divine agency. I'm not sure how willing we should be to dismiss these claims as awkward renditions of mere scientific ignorance (someday the causes of such cures will be accurately analyzed within the confines of medical science) or of psychosomatic effect (the directive power of the mind to orchestrate internal body conditions). What I do know is that the healing authority of revelatory words or deeds has been in the records of human consciousness from the start, and that in the whirl of possibilities that governs the universe at its profoundest and simplest levels, of which we too are composed, persuasions occur that alter the course of things, including human expectations. Christian religion has always been comfortable in seeing the source of this persuasion as divine, so that the whole issue likely comes down to the basic inquiry, "Can God do what physicians cannot?"

The third intention is to reprimand. In all religions I know of, a negative response to the above question would issue in an admonition based on faith's access to knowledge already revealed about God. For there is no doubt that a critical purpose in revelatory traditions is to reprimand behavior that contradicts or demeans the will of God previously mediated in a revelatory act. In fact, this reprimanding (as a new revelation) is often the sole context for interpreting the meaning of the past revelation, as happened so often in the way early Christians first reworked Old Testament prophecies in their claims about Jesus, and then interpreted the tragedies of Jewish history as God approving this reworking through punishing a nonconverted Judaism. This approach tends to be taken with a vulgar and sacrilegious pleasure by the self-righteous, whereas its purpose is more to indicate the seriousness with which the previous revelation, and what is further revealed in the reprimanding one, is to be taken. The author is using actual suffering as a coincidental assistance in establishing this seriousness, or its imagined depiction as a literary device for the same purpose. This interpretation is required by my own acknowledged bias that God only persuades toward the cherishing of life, and this in such ways as to preclude deliberate pain. Yet so appealing is violence to our own kind, so thoroughly saturated into the chemistry and psychology of what we are, that this reprimanding intention of revelation, mediated in savage terms, is for countless people also the foremost intention of religion itself: it exists primarily to rebuke us, and only secondarily—though we always hope more frequently—to console and heal. In the coming millennium Christian religion must work diligently to remove this distortion, not only because of its abuse to human psyches (through its enormous utility in a religious education toward morals), but because of its support of obscene metaphors describing God's relationship to creation, particularly the part of it we are. Any painful discipline a reprimand might involve is *ours* by choice of its appropriateness to sincere contrition.

Testing is the fourth intention. A very old and nearly universal bias in religion is coming forward here, and we've seen it before: that an untried faith, like an untried love, is worthless. This can be put somewhat differently by saying that words in and of themselves mean nothing in the demonstration of the truth or sincerity of a relationship; what matters, instead, is how the words are demonstrated in deeds. This is the likely reason why the notion of the sacredness of a person's word develops as it does in many religions, including Judeo-Christianity: the person has demonstrated repeatedly a congruity between what has been said and what has been done, and so has been proven trustworthy. This is different, then, as it must be, from a court of law, where testimony is presumed trustworthy because of an oath (though to this day the seriousness of what is occurring is usually still accompanied by some assertion of God as an unseen witness, so that perjury becomes the deeply offensive act it is not primarily because of the disruption it causes in the pursuit of justice, but because it is a blasphemy against God). One of the most widely known illustrations of this fourth intention is the garden narrative in Genesis, where it is in fact God and not the serpent who proposes the actual test by asking, "Why have you done the forbidden deed?" and revealing to the man and woman the extent to which they are unwilling to take responsibility for their actions. And there is, of course, the equally well-known story of Job, which illustrates exquisitely the additional point that faith in God, like love, is of little merit or admiration when it fits neatly into a comfortable life—a point Jesus is getting at more obliquely when he asks, "What merit is there in loving someone who loves you?" The answer is none, and thus provides us with powerful insight into the assertion that questions of merit are impertinent when applied to one's relationship with God. Within this theocentric context, in other words, revelatory testing has as its controlling motive the accrual of self-knowledge regarding how serious one's commitments are.

I have mentioned love now and then in the above analysis because each of the five characteristics of revelation is also a characteristic of love, and so extends the description of love I offered in the last chapter. In this way, all romantic sentiments about love being angelic can take on a new, more definite, and more robust meaning in place of the wispy, somewhat muddle-headed one it commonly has. It is love that mediates the relationship between lovers and impels them to console, heal, reprimand, and—to justify claims of integrity—test each other. This last is a particularly difficult intention to accept, since in many cultures love is understood more in a forensic than a revelatory sense, that is, we are expected to accept proclamations of its truthfulness as if delivered under oath, so that suspicions to the contrary are interpreted as implying a perjury. This approach has always gotten people into saddening perplexities in their relationships; already biased that love exists merely upon hearing it proclaimed, they discover that the words of love have little or no match in deeds appropriate to them. Nor, in a related context, should we be at all surprised by the parallel between functions of love and those of revelation, if, as I've argued, both are also primary categories for interpreting divine activity. To say that God is love automatically implies that God reveals.

In its function of mediation the revelatory act has as its purpose not just a disclosure of God's will but in the process a disclosure of what deity itself is like, usually in metaphoric, sometimes in metaphysical language. In Christianity this second disclosure began formulating itself very early into the concept of Trinity. This has proven a ponderous and difficult concept to employ in discussions of God, and in the specific ways it developed in the deliberations of church councils and several key theologians, it has no analogues in other religions. In the traditional approach it is, in my judgment, almost completely useless in both contemporary theology and devotional piety, in large part because of the philosophical presuppositions underlying it. But the idea of Trinity itself is perhaps still pertinent, and I would like to use it to close these remarks on revelation. I'm going to depend on the excellent recasting done by John Macquarrie—who himself depends on the works of men like Hegel and Heidegger—not just because it blends into how I myself conceive God's presence in the universe, but also because his analysis breaks the Christian exclusiveness of previous viewpoints and offers an understanding that indeed has analogues in almost all other religious traditions. Macquarrie describes the Trinity as capturing the three preeminent ways in which God is present to the universe: as creative being (in the metaphor of Father), expressive being (the Son), and unitive being (the Spirit). I want to spend some brief space on each of these.

1. **God as creative being.** This idea is found everywhere in religions, and it likely derives from the ancient yet still current conundrum as to why there is anything rather than nothing, and why it is the way it is. As we've noted before, the controlling category here became power, of a subtlety and degree not possessed by humans and so affirmed to be within the purview of something else, metaphorically personified for the sake of understanding and communication into many, often unalignable images, all of them of deity. Creativity does not of itself require creation from nothing, though this idea is held by several traditions, including the majority one of Christianity, though it does require the idea of giving form to what was formless, or better said in light of our science, of altering forms. The claim of creation out of nothing will always break upon the ancient Greek observation that only nothing can come from nothing, as well as on the way it tends to misappropriate the meaning of mystery so that the claim becomes effectively an unsolvable problem remaining unreachably beyond human cognition. There has always been a universe of one or another determination, one or another of the formats energy might take—the *tohu-wa-bohu* presumed in Genesis, the chaos of Greek natural theology—and any religion wishing to deny this for the sake of divine attributes like dignity or power will have to rework its understanding of these attributes in the coming millennium so as to prevent their out-

right denial. I suspect that what this means on the level of the whole of creation is that God as creative being will need to be understood in some sense as the source of what eternally is and the particularity of things as their response to the presence of this source. On the level of individual human lives, however, God as creative being is likely to remain caught up almost exclusively in the question of death and life after it. I will be suggesting in the next section that the classic claim of an immortal soul is no longer persuasive to resolve this question (and never was to the large majority of Jews at the time of Jesus, nor to Jesus himself), and that what is needed is something like the claim of the resurrection of Jesus from the dead found in Christianity from its very beginning.

2. **God as expressive being.** Our comments on revelation have dealt at some length with one dimension of this presence of God in the universe. They confined the understanding of revelation to the context of humanity, since as yet we have no certain ideas regarding how revelation is received by the rest of creation. If anything, the common presumption is that it *isn't* received because it isn't offered; that humanity enjoys an exclusive receptivity to God's presence in the universe because of the ways we can articulate, argue, mythologize, and abstract it—as in the very writing of this book. But this is tantamount to the "hard" version of the Anthropic Principle perpetrated by some scientific cosmologies now dressed in religious garb: that we can interpret the whole concatenation of elements that compose our species as distinct in the universe to mean that we are favored in the universe; or in a somewhat less arrogant description, that we are unique and unrepeatable in any observable way. Yet given the size of the universe, and the whirl of possibilities available among subnuclear and nuclear relationships in how things are composed, there is nothing prohibiting entities similar, very similar to us, elsewhere than on Earth. Nor can it be supported in any religion that has a doctrine of omnipresence or immanence whereby the presence of deity is thought to pervade everything that is and so prohibits any complete localization of divine influence or generosity or love, any confinement of divine providence. On the other hand, there can also be a recognition of privileged concentrations of this presence at certain times and places, in certain events and in human and nonhuman life-forms. The expressive being of God can be confined only by its own self, either through

divine choice, as in countless mythologies and metaphors, or by something thought to be intrinsic to the very being itself, as I will shortly suggest.

3. **God as unitive being.** This idea is the correlate to the previous two. Insofar as God is creative being, and as such is expressed throughout the whole of creation, God is the uniting factor of all that is—or in the terms of an earlier chapter, the single symbol of the universe. To the extent that throughout these pages I have used the terms "universe" and "creation" synonymously, the former as the more comfortably scientific term designating the whole of reality, the latter the more comfortably religious term, I have attempted to remain faithful to a rubric I set for myself in chapter 1: that religion must wed itself to science in the coming millennium if it is to remain intellectually persuasive—not so exclusively, however, as to ignore or even diminish the importance of other disciplines, but rather to borrow from the generosity of their ideas to enhance the marriage. This partnership is what I intend to honor in a thoroughgoing way when discussing God as unitive being. To some the scientific proposals I employ will appear highly speculative, backed up little by current experimental data, and they will become disenchanted, perhaps a bit lethargic in their interest, or irritated. But I myself take joy in the speculation, by its novelty and imaginative uses, and to whatever extent they exist, the linkages to hard data that shape the bases of the speculation. No theologian should ever be disenchanted by this, even when others might be, since so much of his or her own work is itself speculation, personal or borrowed from others, and meant precisely to enchant. The unitive being of God will be the leitmotif of the following, concluding section of this chapter.

Metaphors and Metaphysics

There is unique beauty in the magnitude of the universe, in the mathematics needed to describe it, and in the sight of that small fraction of it we can see in the night sky. Our imaginations are not really competent to enfold this magnitude in a single image, perhaps because of its very beauty, the kind which Francis Bacon located, as he did all beauty, in "the strangeness of the proportion." Science has closely attended to this strangeness, and some would argue that astronomy is in fact the earliest science, that is, the recording of data as observed by the senses (in this case, eyesight) and putting its pieces together in a coherent explanation. There was nothing in this branch of science that touched even remotely on human lives, not as in agriculture, say, or medicine, except as it got appropriated by the muddling analyses of astrology—many people then, after all, were like many people now: knowledge was of little or no worth unless it could be practically applied in day-to-day living. But the astronomers, like their kindred scientists everywhere, and like many theologians too, saw value in the knowledge itself, the wonder that began its search, the satisfaction of its pursuit, and the feeling of contribution upon offering explanations. Astronomy as the study of the very large, the whole breadth of the observable universe and the processes going on within it, is endlessly vibrant and fascinating in its discoveries, ones that new technologies in the coming millennium will enhance in enormous proportions, strike us one by one as strange or puzzling because unexpected, and so maintain the beauty of it all, as Bacon so profoundly understood.

It is at the other end of the spectrum, though, where this beauty is truly flattered, more in our ache to know the strangeness of the very small than in our gaze upon the awesomeness of the very large, because we know that in the very small this awesomeness has its source. Astronomy and particle physics become one at this point, and the beauty singular. This search for the very small began with Democritus and his theory of atoms: that renegade idea that our senses, particularly our vision, are not the final arbiters of just how small things can be, and that what really explains why we experience the world the way we do occurs beyond this boundary. With the advent of the optical microscope, then the electron microscope—along with pertinent theories and experimentation—the smallness of the components of matter has diminished staggeringly, so much so that one common analogy is that as our bodies are in size to the whole universe, so are these smallest components to our bodies. It is one of these small components that has gained special attention in recent years, the H boson, which some theorists argue is the ultimate particle, beyond which no further division is possible—though given the history of other claims of irreducibility in science, most proponents willingly present their arguments as powerful but quite tentative. Beyond this particle there would only be energy relics from a condition of the universe so unimaginably small and utterly simple that it is by definition impenetrable by science. As I noted in chapter 1, along with this single particle—if the hope for such an elegantly simple basis for the universe is not deluded—would be a single force combining the four now active in the observable universe: the weak and strong nuclear forces, electromagnetism, and gravity. The circumstances required to reproduce this single force, as to isolate the single particle, are currently beyond the reach of a consensus theory, let alone their duplication in any actual experiment. Some theorists even argue that such a duplication is in fact impossible except in a repetition of the primordial condition itself.

It is well known that from debates instigated in Europe during the Middle Ages and exacerbated during the Enlightenment, Christian theology has generally preferred to set its interests apart from science, and science has been more than happy to reciprocate. This still prevails in very penetrating ways today and often takes the sad form of mockery by others when theologians utilize science in their speculations, or scientists use theology. Just a few days ago I read an article in a respected magazine—the title and author don't matter; it was frustrating because it conveyed a stereotypical attitude—in which the writer ridiculed the H boson as the "God particle," telling the reader that this is what some theologians and scientists were preaching as the actual identity of the deity in all our theistic traditions. And it was published, this travesty of intelligence and honest reporting, because it is so at home in the ideology that has prevailed in the schooling of children and young adults, and in church sermons: one that has been diabolical as I described this term in chapter 1, that is, divisive in the sense of discordant, producing hostile and active antagonism or a blind, deaf, and dumb indifference. It is my own view, however, shared by a growing number of other Christian theologians, that it is exactly to the primordial particle and force that theology must look if this divisiveness with science is to be bridged. For if these ultimately constitute that from which the universe derives, then in them is encountered the foundational source of the universe's unity, as well as the primordial context for asserting the unitive being of God in creation. Mocking here is not just in poor taste, it is a foolish threat to the effective intelligence Christian religion must possess in the coming millennium. It is better for Christian religion to choose freely a partnership with science than to be forced into it, at the very least if we wish the efforts of the two to be symbolically rather than diabolically engaged among us.

At the point of the single particle and force, and the energy presumed by their existence, we can borrow terms from several religions, from philosophy, and from science itself to describe them: the Brahman of Hindu thought, for example, the Tao of Lao-tzu's vision, The Cloud or the All of Western mysticism, the *Urgrund* of philosophy, the singularity of theoretical physics, and many others—all of them designed to describe a situation of aporia, meaning the point beyond which thought cannot go. This is also what in Christian religion we more commonly designate as deity, Godhead, Being, or any other terminology seeking the nonpersonal language of metaphysics and the avoidance whenever possible of metaphor. But I want to suggest that in most of these analyses there is the implication that if through our logic or science we could push just once beyond the aporia, God would then be encountered in a directness shaded by no mediation of either intellectual or physical kinds. This is a flaw, a critically serious one, that slips us back into metaphor while metaphysics is being claimed. What I propose, then, is a clear-headedness between these two methods of analysis and language with the following consequences: first, that metaphor be reserved to designate *personal* relationships between God and human beings, and human beings and everything else, so as to assist in the formation of symbolic *affection,* the feeling of the unitive being of the universe. Secondly, I would propose that metaphysics be reserved to designate *intellectual* relationships between God and human beings, and human beings with everything else, so as to assist in the formation of symbolic *thought,* the thinking of the unitive being of the universe.

I need to attend more closely to these matters if I am to avoid the diabolic or divisive implication I may have drawn between thought and affection, thinking and feeling, or between metaphysics and metaphor. I will try to get into words an intuitive clarity I've experienced by saying that for religion the source of metaphor is in the mediations of revelation, whereas the source of metaphysics is in the mediations of science—but that they are united insofar as both are mediations of perceptions of God, and that the distinction between them is therefore not intrinsic to them (it is not fatefully diabolic) but in our choice to adopt one or the other whenever pertinent to the specific context of how *at the moment of choice* we are relating to God and how we wish to cast language to express this. A still different way of getting at the same point would be to say that when we wish to speak of God and creation where concern is self- or species-directed (how it is that things relate to us) we use metaphor; when we wish to speak of God and creation (including ourselves) where concern is universe-directed, we use metaphysics—with this one, critical proviso: that, among other sources, the metaphysics be influenced in a determinative way by science. Arguments that science changes its viewpoints too often and too much don't wash; the determinants of metaphysical analysis have always been alterable, and indeed have altered often in various schools of metaphysics. What all this leads to is a conclusion I find enormously appealing and potentially productive for the pursuit of Christian religion in the coming millennium, though I know some will be outraged. It reads: When science and religion are speaking about the unitive being that lies at the source of creation (or the universe), they are speaking of exactly the same thing—except in one the most common term is "singularity," and the whole conceptual panorama this brings with it (of gluons, baryons, bosons, etc.), whereas in the other the most common term is "God," with its own conceptual panorama (of transcendence, immanence, infinity, etc.). But the intuitive sense I described in chapter 3 tells me as it has told many others that when the proper parallels are made between the respective concepts, the data underlying them and how it is interpreted, the singularity and God will be one metaphysically, though if richness and diversity of sentiment and language is maintained beyond this paralleling, they will remain distinct metaphorically.

Certain consequences follow from the above venture into speculation. The first obviously pertains to the use of language. The metaphysical identity I am drawing between God and the singularity that originates the universe (for an infinity of space-time and an infinity of expanding and contracting rhythms) is going to be offensive to many because it dislodges comfortable distinctions between spirit and matter, eternity and time, immutability and change—comfortable, that is, in daily pieties, but not always in the history of theology—that very early in its history began to characterize Christian thought. The two points I would make in response to this are already familiar to us, but bear mentioning again. The first is simply the brief acknowledgment that a difference in terms drawn from a difference in disciplines can imply a metaphorical but not necessarily a metaphysical difference in what is being described. The second point is related and somewhat lengthier. It is that much of the debate between science and religion has come down to the issue of who is going to adapt to the other's language and conceptualities. I would recommend that just as much of Christian theology adapted itself to Platonism in the beginning centuries of its first millennium, and Aristotelianism in the beginning centuries of its second, that it do so toward the language and conceptualities of science (articulated with uncanny brilliance in the metaphysics of Whitehead) at the beginning of its third millennium. The petulant observation that this would be a "selling out" of theology knows little not just of the history but of the requirement of theology's adaptation to dominant worldviews whenever it has been successfully taught and preached not as an antagonistic elitism but as an encompassing worldview itself.

A second consequence is that if we wish to maintain the metaphor that God is a living God—and it is not possible for religion to do without this basic notion—then everything derivative from this source, which is to say, everything that is, must in some sense be alive. This is why I suggested in chapter 1 that the four common characteristics of biological life (growth, respiration, reproduction, adaptation) had to be extended to four other characteristics of everything in the universe (movement, duration, novelty, and relationship). And while metaphors and mythologies of the liveliness of God may be applied in ways that draw exclusively from those things that possess the four biological traits, the metaphysical application cannot. For this latter says that *everything*, including God, possesses the four universal traits, and so may be considered alive. This idea is very persuasive to me, first because it aligns with many other metaphors and mythologies that refuse the biological strictures describing God's liveliness, especially the refusal of all polytheisms that understand the whole of creation—from sun and moon to rivers, mountains, trees, cats, you and me—to be possessors of deity's presence. But it also appeals because of its profound implications for ecology, its insistence on the unitive being of all things that for any sensitive mind produces symbolic metaphors of sympathy, care, and loyalty—though a sadder experience knows that a harsh mind can also recognize this unitive being but instead produce diabolic metaphors of dominion, hostility, and indifference. It is the thinking premised on such diabolic metaphors directed toward the biological life-forms on our planet, including our own, and the enormous influence it exercises over our behavior, that I can now add as a further rationale for my judgment in the last chapter that we are a failed, that is, a self-destructive experiment in evolution.

Another consequence is that there is no requirement to understand the singularity as existing either outside the origination of space-time or at some exclusively and potentially identifiable point within it. The same may be asserted theologically (God as existing *outside* the universe is a common peculiarity of expression in Christian theology that has caused interminable problems by its contradictory spatiality—"outside" the universe makes no sense—as well as the metaphysical alienation it establishes between God and what is; God as existing at some exclusive and potentially *identifiable point* in the universe has never been seriously entertained in Christian tradition, except by a few vagabond understandings of what occurred in Jesus). Rather, each is understood in its respective language as an intrinsic presence in all that is, one similarly but never identically repeatable in an infinite sequence of relationships that for the scientist defines the universe and for the theologian defines creation. This seems to be one result, for example, of the suggestion by James Hartle and Stephen Hawking that the initial condition of the universe (or in the rhythmic model I prefer, the universe as derivative from the event initiating its current expansion among unlimitable others) blends space and time together in a manner that, somewhat like the surface of a sphere, excludes any point from being the only one that allows the sphere to be constructed; or in a two-dimensional image, any point on a circle as being the only one that allows the circle to be drawn. Any of an infinite number of points can function in the creation of the sphere or circle— which means there is no definitive beginning point, that is, when abstracted from our concrete images of sphere and circle, no beginning at all. Theologians have made a similar assertion for centuries when suggesting that God's creativity is better understood as a shaping and sustaining rather than an originating act.

A further consequence is that God's presence to the universe must be understood as *in* the relationships that constitute everything that is. God is not the relationships themselves, except as we might wish to use this notion metaphorically, since then this presence would be dissectable, which is metaphysically not possible—a point, I suspect, more obvious in the scientific term "singularity" than its religious equivalents, "God," "Godhead," etc. For it is *in* the relationships, in what is impenetrable about them as the singularity or as God, that there lies the actuality permitting the relationships to form, all of which are characterized by the motion, duration, novelty, and relationship itself that together produce universal life—and all of them, therefore, appearing indeed to justify speaking metaphorically of God or the singularity as cherishing life. And while the language of metaphysics again requires a usage of depersonalized categories, the parallel language of metaphor does not, thus making the latter more attuned religiously because of the affective feeling toward God it assists in human minds and hearts, while the former is attuned to interpreting the religious affection in a manner more intellectually accessible to other disciplines, especially, for our purposes now, theoretical physics. Perhaps the most useful as well as aesthetically pleasing metaphor to describe this idea that God is in the relationships is love, as when any of us recognizes that our love for another is not the relationship itself but resides within it—that the relationship expresses in myriad ways what is already there—but that what this resident might be is not fully available to our knowledge, or what I was getting at earlier in the chapter when discussing mystery.

Another consequence delineates further the expressiveness of the unitive being of God or the singularity and embellishes the meaning of the love metaphor. It is that whatever power was exercised in the universe at its initiation, it must be understood as persuasive rather than coercive. This is a critical point, since it establishes the idea that from its source freedom has characterized the universe. There is nothing in science, in other words, suggesting that the universe was compelled to exist, but rather, since it obviously does exist, that whatever the singularity was, its internal relationships were of a mutual persuasion that finally led to expressiveness in what we have, though nothing would have prohibited this expressiveness from having been different. It is this absence of prohibition, occurring because there was an absence of anything save the singularity, which denotes freedom. Only if we could penetrate the singularity could we discover if it was self-fated, so to speak, compelled to generate the universe we have. But the evidence accumulating over the past several decades, concentrating especially in the work of quantum mechanics, indicates that beneath a certain level of macroscopic entities (where all of us know that coercion can indeed exist) spontaneity increasingly becomes obvious in the behavior of things, an indeterminacy or unpredictability that exists not solely because of the limits of our observational talents, but in the universe itself as it endures from the moment the motion of the singularity persuaded from within its internal relationships—that is, from within itself—the novelty that became the universe. To the extent that what exists in the universe is in unitive being with its source, it is free, and freedom, therefore, becomes a metaphysical category; to the extent that what exists is in unitive being with anything else, it can be coerced in certain fashions and to varying degrees, and this coercion, therefore, becomes an ethical category, describing and judging the ways in which freedom has been or can be enacted. It is this coercion, for example, that shortly after the initiating event of the universe bound protons and neutrons into nuclei with a coercive force that, fortunately for us, is extremely stable, but which each particle is essentially free to break (though it can also be broken by other powerful intrusive forces) with no cause other than this freedom itself. Something of this same idea also seems to underlie contemporary chaos theory. Adherents of the theory cite the familiar example of how at a certain height a column of cigar smoke in still air will suddenly billow for no discernible reason. There is no known law of physics that demands this shift of direction; it just happens, much like sudden, similarly inexplicable alterations in weather patterns. Yet such occurrences are not *totally* random to our observation: the column of smoke does not turn to a sharp right angle or reverse itself. We may say that what allows the billowing to occur is that the components of the smoke—vis-à-vis each other and the components of the surrounding air—exercise freedom at a certain but unpredictable distance from the source of the smoke (the indeterminacy that quantum mechanics describes), while what constrains the column is the coercion of the smoke's components—again, vis-à-vis each other and the components of the surrounding air—as they relate to each other before the unpredictable distance is reached (what some physicists describe as the "strange attractor" in relationships that defines the limits of the randomness of chaos).

Most religions have been quite comfortable with the above analysis, having articulated it in their own languages for centuries, but not particularly comfortable with its applications. Ethics has been the major problem here. Throughout the metaphors of these religions we discover an almost exclusive interpretation of God's power as coercive—not constantly so (since experiences of freedom to deny God's will are everywhere abundant, and in fact form the basis establishing the need for religious ethics) but intrusively whenever God coerces the absence of this freedom (since its source is God in the prevailing metaphor, God can withdraw it) for God's own purposes, most usually punishment, reward, and the testing of faith. This is one way of interpreting the unitive being we have with God as it becomes expressive being in the actual ways it works itself out in the divine/human relationship in creation. I think this viewpoint is badly wrong because the metaphor sustaining it departs too radically from the metaphysical claim that is its source. If creation or the universe is free vis-à-vis its source in God, and if the initiating act bringing it forth originates in a persuasion within God as God is, then a better metaphor returns us to love rather than justice as the prevailing activity of God: the generative activity of God's creative being that expresses itself in the cherishing of life. To be sure, there are pains and punishments in living, just as there are joys and satisfactions. But these do not express our unitive being with God except as it is mediated in our unitive being with other things that exist, and that to varying degrees are also free. When the tectonic plates move in an earthquake and kill thousands, therefore, it is because they have the freedom to do so, as does the virus infecting your body, as does the other human being—in yet a higher degree of freedom than these first two—to put the knife at your throat. These cannot be construed as acts of God, but only as acts of freedom made possible by the very definition of God as unitive being. Or more bluntly, God cannot intrude coercively in creation because coercion contradicts the identity of God. God can only persuade, as creation itself was persuaded into expressive being in a free act. But this freedom that hence pervades creation and designates an irreversible quality of our unitive being with God is not guaranteed success as this accords with the requirements of love.

Still a further consequence, then, is that before the face of God (metaphorically) how we act makes no difference (metaphysically), and that any employment of God in punishment/reward, heaven and hell schemes in religion is an aberration, and one easily become monstrous (as occurred, for example, when a profoundly intelligent and good man like Thomas Aquinas nonetheless asserted that part of the joy of heaven is witnessing the suffering of those in hell). Yet while we will say that metaphysically it makes no difference to God how we live—or metaphorically: that while God is responsible for the freedom of creation, God neither indicts nor is indictable for its uses—it does make a difference to us.

For in any good society there are certain behavioral patterns that simply cannot be tolerated if guarantees of safety, security, adequate food, shelter, health care, etc., are to be honored. But any rewards or punishments in this context must be understood solely as anthropological requirements, never as theological ones, and all teaching and metaphors denying this, particularly in common devotional pieties, must be abandoned. We are surely capable of deliberate wickedness, and insofar as this wickedness derives from us as our freedom denies the persuasion of God toward the cherishing of life, so the healing derives from us as well. Yet to recast in our present terms an assessment from the last chapter: our freedom as we relate to our immediate place in the universe, the Earth, has often produced a distorted sense of unitive being in our metaphors that *identifies* us with God, thereby assuming to ourselves a likewise distorted claim of creative being (who will live and who will die) and expressive being (how we will behave, how we will not) that weigh not toward a healing that cherishes life in creative and expressive ways, but toward destructiveness.

A final consequence, and to me the most enchanting one, has to do with the rhythms of the universe we see all around us, and which I believe characterizes the universe as a whole (this must remain a belief until enough reliable data indicates there is sufficient mass to close the universe and give it the pulsating movement I described in chapter 1). If this belief holds—and there is every reason to think it will, with the continuing discoveries of sources of dark matter—then the universe contains an infinite whirl of possibilities as energies and particles form, unite, break apart, form and unite again in an endless cycle of birth, death, and rebirth. Here death does not mean annihilation (for if it did we would need to deny Whitehead's sagacious judgment that the living cannot come from the dead), but rather transfer from one arrangement of energies and particles to another. For this to happen, three conditions at least must prevail. first, entropy would have to be understood as a temporary or local rather than a permanent or universal phenomenon (entropy is the scientific doctrine stating that eventually all energies and particles will "even out" in the universe, with no more of the clumping needed to produce actualities beyond these primordial energies and particles; as the universe continues to expand, single protons or quanta of electrons will be indeterminable light-years apart from each other). What will be needed, in other words, are energy "glitches" or bumps or diffractions that will always prohibit a total flattening and allow gravity to maintain an attractive force powerful enough throughout the universe to over-come in localized groupings of particles the force of the expansion, and so to overcome it in the universe as a whole. The second condition is that in the contraction of the universe there is a conservation of energy such that in the moment a singularity is again reached a spontaneity of ex-pansion begins anew (as we've noted repeatedly, the singularity itself is not penetrable, as in religion the Godhead is not). The third condition, and the one wherein my enchantment finds its heart, though the one that is the most intensely speculative, is that with each new expansion there must be residues in all energies and particles—manifest at the very least when they begin to bind together in diverse arrangements—that allow some degree of identification or paralleling in what occurs anew not just in the future particularities of this universe but in all universes succeeding it forever. I would demur, in other words, from an idea now popular among many scientists and some philosophers that in an infinite number of parallel or successive universes (or in an infinite number of regions in one universe), there may well be duplicates of us. My demur-ral, however, is not over the possibility of this happening—it is an enor-mously intriguing idea—but over the fact that, even if such duplicates exist, the idea of itself does not allow us to share anything with them, certainly not degrees of awareness, and so leaves the need for *our* conti-nuity unsatisfied. Metaphysically this notion of continuity or perduring identifiability is a very difficult conceptual proposal, though I suspect its resolution will go in the direction of the unitive being embedded in the singularity, or for religion, in God. Metaphorically the closest approach I know of for application scientifically is Whitehead's notion of "feeling" as intrinsic to whatever exists at whatever point in space-time and the mutual influence of all things on each other this feeling provides (Whitehead himself, I should note, would consider this more a meta-physical than a metaphorical description). In religion, of course, the most common metaphor used to guarantee this inheritance is the memory of God; in fact, this is the metaphor Whitehead does employ in his analysis of the subjective immortality of the universe. But what I want to touch on now is something different than what might continue to exist of our-selves outside ourselves (in God's memory), or might continue to exist in such a way that the *uniqueness* of the actuality of every entity, includ-ing ourselves, gets obscured. For this I turn to the fundamental claim of my own religion.

At the heart of Christian religion is the claim that Jesus was raised from the dead; that this involves something distinctly and qualitatively different from a mere presence in preaching or an imitation of life-style; that the raised Jesus could be perceived with the senses; that it was recognizably Jesus who was alive again; that this life, while similar to the one preceding it—and hence its recognizability—was also in radical ways different from it; and finally, that the generative agent of this new life was God. In my judgment, and presuming the general persuasiveness of the remarks in the last several paragraphs, this claim has a legitimate intent to it that I find deeply susceptible to affirmation. It is not difficult for me to believe that in the whirl of possibilities in the universe it could happen that I will come alive again at some point in space-time; that this life will retain recognizability to it, increased as the binding energies and particles that move to compose me increase, yet clearly different, too, at the points of novelty where relationships among the components are not identical to previous ones; and that this process will endure infinitely, as in the past and into the future, so that my life will indeed prove itself life according to the four traits I have given all things as living, or what Christian terminology calls eternal life. And the guarantee of this will reside in God, or if you will, the singularity, and therein the creative, expressive, and above all the unitive being participated in by everything that exists from the instant the one becomes the many.

From the standpoint of physics it is not impossible theoretically that such an event occurred as rapidly as in the New Testament claim about Jesus, nor that such an event might remain unrepeated to our experience so far because of the strictures of the very small expanse of space-time our planet and our history on it provides (though similar claims have in fact been made in other traditions about other people). Nor is there a necessity that resurrection always involve a familiar repetition of *all* one's surroundings, though in an infinity of resurrections there would need to occur an endless succession of eventual and very close approximations of them. And this infinity is exactly what is required by the nature of God, or the singularity, as creative, expressive, and unitive being. For the only other option is to posit a point of *complete* annihilation, an utter nothingness somewhere within the repetitions, and this is something a contemporary science cannot do, nor any religion, even if in previous times the concept of complete nothingness appeared to make intellectual sense. This is what the great Irenaeus was already getting at in the second century when he insisted, "Neither the substance nor the essence of the creation will be annihilated . . . but the 'fashion' of the world passes away." For this reason, too, I must also disagree with any viewpoint of resurrection life—perhaps best represented nowadays in the brilliant work of J. McDaniel—that sees it only as a series of further opportunities for fulfilling needs and interests, and then ending, rather than as eternal existence. This approach would certainly bring Christianity into greater partnership with a religion like Buddhism and its doctrine of rebirth until nirvana is reached, but it neglects both the continuing existence and transformations of matter and energy, as well as, for me, the personal desire that I possess the possibility of reemerging everlastingly into identifiable lives.

Three further points, already implied, should also be brought directly forward. The first is that *everything* that was alive will come alive again, and by the encompassing characteristics I have given life, this means everything that is. This is what St. Paul perhaps had in mind when he described the whole of creation now "groaning in travail" but redeemed at the end of history (Romans 8:22) and what John Wesley definitely had in mind in his many teachings on the "general deliverance" at history's term (in both cases "history" means the current temporal phase of the world or universe ending in a quick or gradual but massive transformation initiated by God at some point in the future). In this sense, in any given universe (or more precisely, in any given phase in the infinity of space-time of the one universe that is), there is no novelty of being but only novelty of form. The second point, as against most Christian descriptions of the next format our lives will take, is that there is no guarantee of a diminution of pain, certainly not of death as the eventual breakdown of the new format—and any hope that this is not so is seeking to deny in any coming life two of the fundamentals of recognizability (suffering and death) of the only life we know. The resurrection narratives of Jesus are amenable to this view insofar as they claim only that death is not annihilation, that it is followed by a recognizable life-form, but that—though the narratives are silent on it, if not on such other recognizable experiences such as eating—the raised Jesus could also suffer and be transformed again into still other life-forms, though perhaps only recognizable to himself and others transformed similarly. This is one reason why we must be very careful before dismissing accounts of many throughout Christian history that they have seen, heard, and touched the living Jesus, since they may be right in suggesting that he is walking the Earth. And it is why at the root of the profoundest Christian spiritualities there is a recognition that Christians must also take seriously the ancient injunction to treat everyone as if that person were Christ. For it may be so. The third point is that if we affirm something like the foregoing analysis as true—that life is of itself, as of God, eternal and free in all its formats (the metaphysical affirmation), and that God seeks to persuade its freedom ever anew into transformations of love (the metaphorical affirmation)—then all behavior toward God, that is, all properly theological ethics, can have but one controlling source and one guiding maxim. The source is gratitude, thanksgiving, eucharist; the maxim is that we should live so as to make ourselves worthy of what is already ours from the past, the present, and the future.

Finally, it must be remembered that what I have said in these pages, especially in this section, is all human perception, judgment, and language by the author, shared in many of its distinct parts by others, but altogether representing only my thinking. This means that it is enormously tentative, not only for the fact that the language I would use a week, a month, a year from now would be different, but also because the future may hold for me some unpredictable experience that could alter entire groups of perceptions, the relationships between them, and the judgments subsequently made. I cannot be *coerced* into a pattern of thought even by myself, and neither can you. All I can do is be persuaded by the rightness of ideas, attend to them in the shaping of convictions, and seek to persuade and help convince others in a similar way, always hoping that what I offer will be greeted with as dexterous a field of interpretations as possible, but with all of them, *all of them* cherishing life.

Chapter six

THE AGENDA

IN THE COURSE of writing this book I thought of simply offering a theological commentary on diverse issues I judged important for Christian religion as a new millennium approached. But as the pages started accumulating I began to realize that a controlling concern was increasingly occupying my analysis; that it began to emerge with definiteness in chapter 2 and fully dominated the remarks at the close of chapter 5. I was initially quite concerned about this, thinking that I was abandoning a desire to treat each issue as an autonomous unit, relating these units to each other for purposes of further explication, and in the process offer a neatly divided chart or map of the various directions Christian religion should advance in the new millennium. But the control became embedded more and more in the writing on its own, automatically as it were, and then, at a certain point, became a deliberate choice. This control is what I have repeatedly described as the primary ideal of Christian religion, which is loving peace, and its primary expression in the cherishing of life. Had this not been present, I knew, then what I said about the universe, the earth, plants and animals, humanity, and finally God, would have been much different from what in fact I did say about them. In short, I was again provided in my life with a clear example of the meaning of bias I discussed in the last chapter.

Furthermore, I discovered that in its own turn this control issued in three additional ones that provided more specific influences over the book. They would be my provisional and very general answer to any inquiry about what I think the book's principal contributions are to an understanding of Christian religion. The first is the role of beauty. I have become convinced that it is the pursuit of beauty, more than that of goodness or truth, that drives the vital religious consciousness: that what is lovely and exalts the mind or spirit is a surer source of passion and commitment than what is true or good—or perhaps better, that what is true or good achieves its own worth precisely because it is also judged beautiful. The second is the definition of life as inclusive of all that is. I have rebelled against all tight-fisted understandings of life because they tend to create hierarchies of importance in creation that offend the sacredness or value of the whole of it. Theologically I have tried to capture this by saying that the particular formats life takes are valued by God strictly because of the life itself, and that this means everything is equally valued—on the model of the parent who values all of his or her children the same—not just those, say, more intelligent, articulate, or technologically adept than the others—even if expectations of their individual behavior may vary. If there is offense in this viewpoint, I can only take consolation in what is perhaps the oldest accusation against Christianity: that it is itself an offense. The third contribution I have tried to offer is my understanding of God. I wanted to place God as a clear presence in everything that exists without swerving into a pantheism that identifies God with the universe. I did this by drawing a distinction between metaphorical and metaphysical modes of conceptualizing God (while recognizing their mutual and intimate relationship) and suggesting the category of relationship as our key conceptual device. As the parent is in the relationships that constitute the child—at the very least in his or her genetic makeup—so God is in the relationships that constitute everything that is, including the parent and child. This is a statement of metaphysics that we then attempt to make intellectually more lovely through succeeding metaphors embellishing it. It is this presence of God that also led me to insist that everything alive remains alive, with any given death (or dissolution) being but one of an infinite succession of transformations of the format the life takes. Perhaps these three issues are not what any other reader might consider the most important or intriguing in the book; that is quite possible. But they are what come to my mind as of this writing, and in offering them I too am not just the writer but a reader of the book.

In the following section the agenda promised in the subtitle of the book is offered. Before examining it, however, I ask the reader to keep the following points in mind, in fairness both to his or her own expectations as well as to my intention in constructing the material the way I have. The first point is that it is an *agenda,* and this means that it will abdicate details in describing its successive items; it provides neither arguments for these items nor always the relationships between them, except as they all fall under the general concern listed in each chapter's title. Secondly, these lacks in the agenda are absolved in the respective section of the previous five chapters that the items are intentionally capturing in only very brief statements; in the chapters themselves are the details, argumentation, and relationships. Thirdly, the analyses in the chapters are nonetheless themselves limited from considerations of time, space, and talent on the author's part, and are meant primarily to provide prior discussion indicating the direction I would like to see further discussion of the items take. Fourthly, I could have put the agenda at the beginning of the book (a table of contents is basically an agenda), but this would have been a quite lengthy document I judged awkward as an introduction. More importantly, though, is that I wanted the agenda to be more a refreshment than a lengthy anticipation of the material in the five chapters. Also—and perhaps due to my many years of department and committee meetings at a university—I wanted an agenda whose content and presentation was not an unanticipated "surprise," but one for which preliminary discussions had already occurred. Fifthly, the agenda can be reworked to combine its various items in a whole variety of relationships, including the addition of pertinent new items or a shift of emphasis on ones already indicated, as a given reader sees fit for reflection, discussion, or further study. Also: the discussion of an issue listed in a particular section of a chapter is not necessarily confined to that section. Finally, the agenda as populated and composed by me is therefore unequivocally tentative: the very same point I made about all the preceding chapters at the end of the last one. This means that while what I've offered throughout is not fated to either success or failure, they both nonetheless remain possibilities, as they do in all things in all the universe. A smile is needed here, one that comes deep from within and is born from humility, that there is some hope that some success has been achieved. The agenda is as follows.

I. The Universe

Introductory Comments; The Beginning of the Universe

1. The distinction between the symbolic as what unites and the diabolic as what sunders or alienates; their importance in the determination of patterns of thinking and behavior.

2. The partnership between science and religion as a symbolic act; overcoming religion's suspicion or indifference to science as a pathway to knowledge, and its embarrassment over the successes of science.
3. The need to blend the theoretical, but especially the hard-data claims of science with the claims of religion; the acknowledgment of differing but congenial vocabularies and concepts between the two.
4. Theology's obligation to reanimate the conviction of many centuries that the final intent of science is to give honor to God.
5. The willingness of Christian religion to receive as its own and to encourage the conviction of science that thinking is fundamentally a game of discovery, or a pursuit of insight.
6. The obligation of Christian religion to recognize that the *application* of the discoveries of science merits considerations of approval or disapproval according to a discernment of the teachings of Jesus.
7. To delight in science's search for knowledge about the beginning of the universe—the specific concern of the section—since knowledge of origins is critical to the adequate appreciation of anything.
8. To acknowledge that the above search regards an ultimacy that Christian religion must absorb into its understanding of the creative activity of God.
9. Christian religion's anthropological and pastoral interest (almost always more intense than that of science) in how our knowledge of what is, how it came to be (as in number 7 above), and what it is becoming can assist a knowledge of ourselves.

The End of the Universe

1. To appreciate that creation properly understood describes that activity that gives identifiable form to what had none, or changes previous forms into new ones.
2. The abandonment of the awkward notion of creation out of nothingness, and its frequent correlate of a return to nothingness.
3. The affirmation that novelty is at the very root of things; the consolation of hope.
4. The assertion that creation as divine activity is continuous.
5. The requirement that the universe be closed, and that it pulses or oscillates in rhythms of expansion and contraction that are infinite in space-time.

6. While novelty must be respected in these rhythms, a degree of identifiability must also remain throughout; future-shock.

7. Applied to Christian religion, the above item provides a guarantee of the fidelity and familiarity of divine activity while simultaneously acknowledging that it can provide something new or unexpected, as in the renewed life of Jesus as involving more than a mere resurrection into the memory or life-style of his followers.

8. The obligation of Christian religion to defeat both despair and sybaritism over the end of things, and to maintain devotion to the future as the context not just for divine but for human creativity.

9. Assessing the future and the past for determining the strength of our vision of the present and its requirements upon us.

10. The perishing of an unprotected earth as inevitable, if for no other reason than the sun's evolution.

11. The obligation of religion to encourage science to find ways to avoid our demise at this juncture (the far-distant view) or at any that might occur preceding it—as, for example, in the development of weapons or unbridled biochemical research (the near-distant view). This encouragement also applies to nonhuman life-forms.

13. The controlling bias for interpreting the demise of anything is premised on the following principle: *Once a possibility becomes an actuality, the actuality from that point on remains a possibility.*

Life Elsewhere in the Universe

1. Religion is the most ancient passion that takes us beyond ourselves into worlds and times that are not our own.

2. The curiosity of religion and the impetus toward shaping an attitude regarding the possibility of life, particularly intelligent life, elsewhere in the universe.

3. The above item must be coupled to Christian religion's specific insistence on the limitless abundance of the divine generosity in persuading life into being.

4. Xenophobia—all attempts to insist that what is strange or novel must fit the contours of our values and expectations—is reprehensible.

5. The idea of other life in the universe as deflating too great an attentiveness on ourselves, encouraging a broader compass of interest and what we could call an ecology of the mind.

6. As a prelude to the above development, an applied ecology centered on the earth would demonstrate an initial respect for linkages that bind us to an immediate environment, one that life elsewhere would expand and enrich.

7. An ecology of the mind could generate moral reform as perhaps the most important goal of the coming millennium, in a permanent spirit of repentance toward all proclivities or enactments of a suspicious or arrogant species-centrism.

8. Refusal of such an ecology indicates a contempt or indifference toward creation that Christian religion must clearly define and confront as sin.

II. *The Earth*

Introductory Comments; The Land

1. Rejuvenating the ancient organic understanding of the earth on the model of the earth as mother-provider of safety and security.

2. It has been difficult for Christian religion to respect the earth. There are three dominant reasons: it never deified the planet; it never developed the idea of care for the earth as integral to its historical self-understanding; it interpreted Scripture, especially Genesis, as providing the right to use the earth however we see fit.

3. The above attitude needs to change, as most Christian theologians now agree, and chemical and biological science confirm. The motive for the change must be more profound than just the security provided by healthy land, water, and air; it must be the motive of healing what is already damaged, and then cherishing it.

4. The above motive must also be anchored in fidelity to the image of ourselves as caretakers and caregivers to what surrounds us, rather than its master; it must be supplemented by gratitude and religious humility.

5. Christian religion must seek without compromise to guide science and technology in the direction of this healing and cherishing, gratitude and humility: for the purposes of this section, especially regarding the land.

6. We must reinvigorate and extend to the whole planet the biblical notion of a promised land, assisted by the growing intimacy that our

travel and communication technologies, as well as our knowledge of the intricacies of ecological networks, have provided toward the image of the earth as a global village.

7. In the above situation efforts toward establishing a single religion or religious vision, a religious *oikumene,* become more feasible, one allowing pluralism within communion, neither an utter relativism nor a tyrannizing ideology.

The Water

1. A primary healing activity must be directed toward a cleansing of the pollution we have released into the land, water, and air of the planet. Our specific concern in this section was with water.

2. Christian religion must abdicate its complicity in this defilement through the practice of ascesis: the multifaceted discipline, imposed or willingly engaged, needed to secure success at a task.

3. The primary emphasis in the above ascesis must be on the biblical notion of the *mitzvah,* or good deed, that replaces in relevant and proportionate ways an evil done. An overreliance on God to secure this redemption conduces toward the moral flaw of presumption.

4. The pollution has resulted largely from an overconfidence in technological developments, a profligacy in their use, and an ambiguity or indifference toward the destructive or evil consequences of this use.

5. In the task of confronting this situation, as in all similar ones, an appreciation of two maxims drawn from the finest strands of Greek and Hebrew spirituality must be acknowledged and honored. The first is captured best by Socrates and reads, "The unexamined life is not worth living"; the second is captured best by the Hebrew prophets and reads, "The uncommitted life is not worth examining."

6. Among his teachings, Jesus' parable of the talents provides a particularly worthy impetus toward the redemption required: We must leave the earth better, not worse, or even the same, than we found it.

The Air

1. Overcoming the "distant land" neurosis (if it is not happening in our immediate environment, it is only remotely, not urgently important.)

2. The deterioration of the ozone layer in Antarctica is an example of item 1. Yet questions of the quality of our breathable atmosphere—the concern of this section—emerge not just in a far place, but in every large urban area in the world.

3. Conflicting scientific reports on air quality give an example of the confusion science can create, and should initiate healthy inquiries into both the reliability and honesty of scientists.

4. Attentiveness to the land, water, and air of the planet impels Christian religion to reinvigorate traditional interests of natural theology, refusing to consign these interests solely to the investigation and reflection of scientists.

5. Natural theology may be described as drawing contemplation on God from contemplation on the earth, its geological, atmospheric, and biological phenomena, and more extensively from contemplation on the universe.

6. It is God's *beauty* more than any other attribute that is the central concern of a revitalized natural theology: the desire to describe and extol this beauty and its manifestations in the universe.

III. ANIMALS AND PLANTS

Introductory Comments; Hope and the Cherishing of Life

1. The proposal that there are four traits in the definition of life: movement, duration, novelty, and relationship. These underlie four other traits specific to *biological* life: metabolism, growth, reproduction, and adaptation to a particular environment. My proposal of the first four traits implies that everything is alive.

2. The proposal that it is life, not its particular format, biological or otherwise, that is of fundamental concern to Christian religion.

3. Defining biblical tragedy: all the choices confronting you are evil, and you must choose; appraising the ethical maxim: the end justifies the means.

4. The specific defining characteristics of a particular format of life determine its destiny and freedom (what is controllable) and its fate and finitude (what is not controllable).

5. In Christian religion hope is the preeminent context for assessing the relationship between fate and destiny, finitude and freedom. There are three general approaches to this hope: hopelessness, escape, and mission. The last is the one most in accord with the teachings of Jesus.

6. Dangerous memories.

7. The role of computer simulations in assisting the cherishing of life.

8. The concept of world loyalty as breaking the self-or species-centricity of psychological, political, and religious ideologies.

9. Peace, under the rubric of cherishing of life, as the primary ideal guiding Christian behavior. The morally obliged freedom of scientists to refuse work on wicked or morally ambiguous projects when judged in the context of the cherishing of life.

Educating One's Conscience

1. The obligation of Christian religion to teach and manifest its primary ideal of cherishing life in critical and analytic ways. This may regularly place it in conflict with science, as in the examples of genetic and weapons research and application.

2. Conscience as an irksomeness in the mind that propels us toward our right and responsibility to become involved in all issues pertaining to the cherishing of life.

3. The relationship between the notion of genetic disposition (or genetic memory) and the classic Christian doctrine on prevenient grace as what inclines the individual in certain behavioral directions.

4. The old tradition that Jesus was ransomed for our sins, while theologically repugnant, has a positive analogue in the idea that plants and animals are always being ransomed to our well-being. The proper response is a eucharistic (thanksgiving) ethics.

5. Animal abuse.

6. As a companion to chapter 2, "The Air," number 6 above, beauty as the context for judging nonhuman life-forms, now specified in the pursuit of ideals. An ideal as anything we judge beautiful whose beauty is a controlling ingredient in our behavior, our decisions and deeds.

7. To assist in establishing the ecology of the mind recommended in this and the previous chapter, the metaphysical vision of Alfred North

Whitehead provides a basis for Christian thought in the coming Christian millennium, such as Platonism provided in the first millennium and Aristotelianism in the second.

Values and Violence

1. Anthropomorphism as a method for achieving sensitive consciousness of the communion of all life.
2. An aesthetic reformation that refuses to continue using artistic or metaphorical portraits of animals as evil.
3. The effective and grateful use of plants and animals for psychological/spiritual therapy.
4. Cooperation more than competition as an evolutionary-adaptive requirement for survival.
5. The character of intuition and the role of the intuitive sense in understanding non-human life; intuitive wariness toward genetic research and application.

IV. *HUMANITY*

Introductory Comments; The Doctrine on Childlikeness

1. Mutual cooperation and the survival of our species; humans as genetically determined ethicizing beings.
2. The ability to abstract and theorize, inductive and deductive reasoning, memory: contributors to directedness in life and the formulation of ethics.
3. The definition of spirituality as encompassing the whole of life; the refusal of its equation with devotional piety.
4. The turn toward Jesus in describing a Christian spirituality, its Christocentrism.
5. The doctrine on childlikeness as involving wonder, responsiveness, righteous anger, and persistence.

The Messianic Traits

1. The doctrine on messianic servanthood as involving obedience, generosity, mercy, humility, and poverty.

The Doctrine on Love

1. Adaptation for survival.
2. The doctrine on love; the traits of *agape* and *eros*.
3. The fundamental theological inquiry for evaluating an experience or proposal: "What does it require me to say about God?"; eliciting what to say about God from the doctrine on love.
4. Eros directed toward Jesus; the continuing study of his place in first-century Palestinian Judaism; the encouragement of this historical awareness for purposes of contemporary application.
5. Lack of confidence in humanity.

A Failed Experiment

1. Humanity as a failed experiment in evolution.
2. The issue of the "weight" of our behavior; spectacular and banal evil.
3. The imaginative "as if" and the renewed role of ideals. The proposals of behavior in the book asking that we act as if we will survive as a species.
4. Ideals can never be fully gained; the striving for them, not their achievement, as possessing worth. The challenge this provides a culture, and particularly a science, that is success oriented.
5. Acting as if we will survive as fidelity to the saints who have gone before us.

V. GOD

Introductory Comments; The Pursuit of Natural Theology

1. Religion comes alive not because of an historical record but because deity is experienced in what we are.
2. Reaffirming the need to return to a natural theology; recognizing that this must also include the needs of the human heart.
3. Theodicy and the issue of God's coercive or persuasive power; God as responsible but not indictable for the uses of freedom.
4. All of creation as free; the varying degrees of freedom.
5. The return to polytheism and paganism; "pagan" as defining country folk, those whose lives are most closely attached to land, water, air, plants, and animals.

6. Natural theology as needing to be both ecological and psychological.
7. The defeat of all forms of religious tribalism.
8. The three dominant ways of understanding God: monarch, unmoved mover, moral agent, and Whitehead's definition of love.

Conceptual Tools

1. Some conceptual tools for approaching Christian scripture: bias (with six types discussed), myth, objective and subjective history, problem and mystery, literary approaches (literalism, creedalism, existentialism), inspiration, revelation.

Revelation

1. The intent of Christian polytheism as the assertion not of many deities but of many relationships to the God who is; the pertinence here of Jesus' metaphor of God as parent of *all* that is.
2. Christian theology as needing to use the data but not necessarily the methods of science.
3. There always has been and will be a universe of one determination or another.
4. No understanding of God can be intellectually compelling, but only persuasive.
5. The character of God's revelation in Christian religion; the angelic traits of mediation, consolation, healing, reprimanding, and testing.

Metaphors and Metaphysics

1. The creative, expressive, and unitive being of God.
2. Freedom as a metaphysical category, coercion as an ethical one; the two as coexisting.
3. Relationship as a universal reality.
4. The identity between what Christian religion calls God and science calls the singularity; the origin as present in and influencing the relationships of all that follows.
5. The marriage of metaphysics and metaphor in constructing statements about God.
6. The resurrection of all things and the final cherishing of life.

Final Words

A spirit of melancholy prevails in me. It has for years. It is not because of death, since I know death occurs only to begin anew a process of releasing me into the universe for a time when I will come alive once more, and that this is also true for everything else that is. There is no permanent death: this is the final and finest statement of the cherishing of life. No—my melancholy is the child of the life I am living now, and the contempt or indifference toward life I see like a dark halo around our species, or like a massive, weighty tumor growing more intransigent within us, and unhealable—a killing malignancy in how we think and feel toward our own life-form and others. So for the writing of this book, as for every other task I now join because I judge it important, I write again what I wrote to soothe my mind at the close of the chapter on our own humankind: I did it as if it mattered.

Bibliography

Alexander, Richard D. *The Biology of Moral Systems.* Hawthorne, N.Y.: De Gruyter, 1987.

Barbour, Ian. *Issues in Science and Religion.* New York: Harper and Row, 1971.

———, ed. *Earth Might Be Fair: Reflections on Ethics, Religion and Ecology.* Englewood Cliffs, N.J.: Prentice-Hall, 1972.

Bateson, Gregory. *Steps to an Ecology of Mind.* Northvale, N.J.: Avonson, 1987.

Becker, Ernest. *The Denial of Death.* New York: Macmillan, 1973.

Berry, Thomas, and Thomas Clarke. *Befriending the Earth.* Mystic, Conn.: Twenty-Third Publications, 1991.

Bohm, David. *Wholeness and the Implicate Order.* London: Routledge and Kegan Paul, 1980.

Bonhoeffer, Dietrich. *The Cost of Discipleship.* Translated by R. H. Fuller. New York: Macmillan, 1963.

Borg, Marcus. *Jesus in Contemporary Scholarship.* Valley Forge, Pa.: Trinity Press International, 1994.

Boslough, John. *Masters of Time.* New York: Addison-Wesley, 1992.

Bowman, Douglas. *Beyond the Modern Mind.* Cleveland: The Pilgrim Press, 1990.

Brooke, John Hedley. *Science and Religion.* Cambridge: Cambridge University Press, 1991.

Brueggemann, Walter. *The Prophetic Imagination.* Philadelphia: Fortress Press, 1978.

Buber, Martin. *Good and Evil.* New York: Scribner's, 1953.

Capra, Fritjof, and David Steidl-Rast. *Belonging to the Universe.* San Francisco: HarperCollins, 1991.

Carson, Rachel. *Silent Spring.* New York: Fawcett, 1970.

Choron, Jacques. *Death and Western Thought.* New York: Collier Books, 1963.

Cobb, John B., Jr. *A Christian Natural Theology*. Philadelphia: Westminster Press, 1965.

————. *God and the World*. Philadelphia: Westminster Press, 1969.

————. *Christ in a Pluralistic Age*. Philadelphia: Westminster Press, 1975.

Cobb, John B., Jr., and David R. Griffin. *Process Theology: An Introductory Exposition*. Philadelphia: Westminster Press, 1976.

Collingwood, R.G. *The Idea of Nature*. Oxford: Oxford University Press, 1945.

Commoner, Barry. *Making Peace with the Planet*. New York: Pantheon, 1990.

Crossan, John Dominic. *Jesus*. San Francisco: HarperCollins, 1994.

Davies, Paul. *The Mind of God*. New York: Simon and Schuster, 1992.

Davies, Paul, and John Gribbin. *The Matter Myth*. New York: Simon and Schuster, 1992.

deRougemont, Denis. *Love in the Western World*. Translated by M. Belgion. New York: Pantheon Books, 1956.

Dyson, Freeman. *Infinite in All Directions*. New York: Harper and Row, 1988.

Ebeling, Gerhard. *The Nature of Faith*. Translated by R. G. Smith. Philadelphia: Fortress Press, 1967.

Ford, Lewis. *The Lure of God*. Philadelphia: Fortress Press, 1978.

Frei, Hans. *The Identity of Jesus Christ*. Philadelphia: Fortress Press, 1975.

Fritzsch, Harald. *The Creation of Matter*. Translated by J. Steinberg. New York: Basic Books, 1984.

Fromm, Erich. *The Anatomy of Human Destructiveness*. Greenwich, Conn.: Fawcett Publications, 1973.

Fuller, Robert. *Ecology of Care*. Louisville, Ky.: Westminster John Knox Press, 1992.

Gilkey, Langdon. *Nature, Reality and the Sacred*. Minneapolis: Fortress Press, 1993.

Gustafson, James. *A Sense of the Divine*. Cleveland: The Pilgrim Press, 1994.

Haught, John. *The Cosmic Adventure*. New York: Paulist Press, 1984.

Hawking, Stephen. *A Brief History of Time*. New York: Bantam Books, 1988.

————. *Black Holes and Baby Universes*. New York: Bantam Books, 1994.

Heffner, Philip. *The Human Factor*. Minneapolis: Fortress, 1993.

Heisenberg, Werner. *Physics and Beyond*. New York; Harper and Row, 1971.

Hendry, George. *Theology of Nature*. Philadelphia: Westminster Press, 1980.

Hoffman, Frederick. *The Mortal No: Death and the Modern Imagination*. Princeton, N.J.: Princeton University Press, 1964.

Hosinski, Thomas. *Stubborn Fact and Creative Advance: An Introduction to the Metaphysics of Alfred North Whitehead*. Lanham, Md.: Rowman and Littlefield, 1993.

Jantzen, Grace. *God's World, God's Body*. Philadelphia: Westminster Press, 1984.

Jones, C., G. Wainwright, and E. Yarnold (eds.). *The Study of Spirituality.* New York: Oxford University Press, 1986.

Kaspar, Walter. *Jesus the Christ.* Translated by V. Green. New York: Paulist Press, 1977.

Kierkegaard, Soren. *Works of Love.* Translated by Howard and Edna Hong. New York: Harper and Row, 1962.

Krishnamurti, J., and David Bohm. *The Ending of Time.* New York: Harper and Row, 1985.

Leopold, Aldo. *A Sand County Almanac.* New York: Oxford University Press, 1949.

Lepp, Ignace. *The Psychology of Loving.* New York: New American Library, 1965.

Lewis, C. S. *The Allegory of Love.* New York: Oxford University Press, 1958.

Lightman, Alan, and Roberta Brawer. *Origins: The Lives and Worlds of Modern Cosmologists.* Cambridge: Harvard University Press, 1990.

Linzey, Andrew. *Christianity and the Rights of Animals.* New York: Crossroad, 1987.

MacIntyre, Alasdair. *After Virtue.* Notre Dame, Ind.: University of Notre Dame Press, 1984.

Macquarrie, John. *Principles of Christian Theology.* 2d ed. New York: Charles Scribner's Sons, 1977.

Marcuse, Herbert. *Eros and Civilization.* New York: Knopf, 1961.

May, Rollo. *Love and Will.* New York: Dell, 1969.

McDaniel, Jay. *Of God and Pelicans.* Louisville, Ky.: Westminster John Knox Press, 1989.

————. *Earth, Sky, Gods, and Mortals.* Mystic, Conn.: Twenty-Third Publications, 1990.

McFague, Sallie. *Models of God: Theology for an Ecological Nuclear Age.* Philadelphia: Fortress Press, 1987.

————. *The Body of God.* Minneapolis: Fortress Press, 1993.

McKibben, Bill. *The End of Nature.* New York: Doubleday, 1989.

McLaren, Robert. *Christian Ethics: Foundations and Practice.* Englewood Cliffs, N.J.: Prentice-Hall, 1994.

Menninger, Karl. *Whatever Became of Sin?* New York: Hawthorn Books, 1973.

Moltmann, Jürgen. *Theology of Hope.* Translated by J. Leitch. New York: Harper and Row, 1967.

————. *Hope and Planning.* Translated by M. Clarkson. New York: Harper and Row, 1971.

————. *The Crucified God.* Translated by R. A. Wilson and J. Bowden. London: SCM Press, 1974.

Munitz, Milton. *Cosmic Understanding*. Princeton, N.J.: Princeton University Press, 1986.

Murray, John Courtney. *The Problem of God*. New Haven, Conn.: Yale University Press, 1964.

Nygren, Anders. *Agape and Eros*. Translated by P. Watson. Philadelphia: Westminster Press, 1953.

Panikkar, Raimon. *The Cosmotheandric Experience*. Maryknoll, N.Y.: Orbis Books, 1993.

Pannenberg, Wolfhart. *Jesus—God and Man*. Translated by L. Wilkins and D. Priebe. Philadelphia: Westminster Press, 1968.

———, ed. *Revelation as History*. Translated by D. Granskou. New York: Macmillan, 1968.

———. *Toward a Theology of Nature: Essays on Science and Faith*. Louisville: Westminster John Knox Press, 1993.

Peacocke, Arthur. *Theology for a Scientific Age*. Minneapolis: Fortress Press, 1993.

Pelikan, Jaroslav. *The Christian Tradition*. 5 vols. Chicago: University of Chicago Press, 1971–.

———. *Jesus Through the Centuries: His Place in the History of Culture*. New Haven, Conn.: Yale University Press, 1985.

Polanyi, Michael. *Science, Faith, and Society*. Oxford: Oxford University Press, 1946.

Polkinghorne, John. *The Faith of a Physicist*. Princeton, N.J.: Princeton University Press, 1994.

Prigogine, Ilya, and Isabelle Stengers. *Order out of Chaos: Man's New Dialogue with Nature*. New York: Bantam Books, 1984.

Ricoeur, Paul. *Fallible Man*. Translated by C. Kelbley. Chicago: Regnery, 1967.

———. *The Symbolism of Evil*. Translated by E. Buchanan. Boston: Beacon Press, 1969.

Rolston, Holmes. *Science and Religion*. New York: Random House, 1987.

Santayana, George. *The Sense of Beauty*. New York: Dover, 1955.

Santmire, Paul. *The Travail of Nature*. Philadelphia: Fortress Press, 1985.

Schell, Jonathan. *The Fate of the Earth*. New York: Knopf, 1982.

———. *The Abolition*. New York: Knopf, 1984.

Schweitzer, Albert. *Reverence for Life*. Translated by R. Fuller. New York: Harper and Row, 1969.

Sloyan, Gerald. *Jesus in Focus*. Mystic, Conn.: Twenty-Third Publications, 1984.

Sobosan, Jeffrey. *The Ascent to God*. Chicago: Thomas More Press, 1981.

———. *Christian Commitment and Prophetic Living*. Mystic, Conn.: Twenty-Third Publications, 1986.

————. *Bless the Beasts*. New York: Crossroad, 1991.

Sölle, Dorothee. *To Work and to Love*. Philadelphia: Fortress Press, 1984.

Sorokin, Pitirim. *The Ways and Power of Love*. Chicago: Regnery, 1967.

Suedes, Lewis. *Love Within Limits: A Realist's View of 1 Corinthians 13*. Grand Rapids, Mich.: Eerdmans, 1978.

Tillich, Paul. *Theology of Culture*. Edited by R. C. Kimball. London: Oxford University Press, 1959.

Tipler, Frank. *The Physics of Immortality*. New York: Doubleday, 1994.

Toulmin, Stephen. *The Return to Cosmology*. Berkeley, Cal.: University of California Press, 1982.

Trefil, James. *The Moment of Creation*. New York: Macmillan, 1983.

Via, Dan Otto, Jr. *The Parables*. Philadelphia: Fortress Press, 1967.

Weinberg, Steven. *The First Three Minutes*. New York: Basic Books, 1977.

————. *Dreams of a Final Theory*. New York: Vintage Books, 1993.

Whitehead, Alfred North. *Religion in the Making*. Cleveland: Meridian Books, 1960.

————. *Science and the Modern World*. New York: Macmillan, 1926.

————. *Process and Reality: An Essay in Cosmology*. Corrected edition by David R. Griffin and Donald W. Sherburne. New York: Free Press, 1978.

————. *Adventures of Ideas*. New York: Macmillan, 1933.

Wilber, Ken, et al. *The Holographic Paradigm and Other Paradoxes*. Boulder, Colo.: Shambhala Publications, 1982.

Wildiers, N. Max. *The Theologian and His Universe*. New York: Seabury, 1982.

World Commission on Environment and Development. *Our Common Future*. New York: Oxford University Press, 1987.

INDEX